"Reading *My Native Land is Memory: Stories of a Cuban Childhood*, through my own memories of my teacher, allowed me to discover a new story, something different from the person I knew as a teenager and her student, but fascinating and enriching at the same time. This book helped me discover the brave nakedness of her soul. It made me understand again that each human being can be a source of enlightenment for others if that person is able to write down dreams, losses, weaknesses and triumph. In reading this book I discovered my own life anew, the life I left behind when I left Cuba and I understand."

Virginia Aponte
Theater Director and Professor Emerita |
Universidad Católica | Andrés Bello, Caracas, Venezuela

"Right from the beginning, *My Native Land* is a raw, compelling journey to a Cuba about to be changed forever. Oliva Espín's unique perspective and powerful writing emotionally captures an immigrant's story that resonates across countries and is relevant today."

Ronnie Ramos
Executive Editor - *The Daily Memphian*

"Oliva Espín gives us a personal and moving view of her life as a girl looking for her identity and independence in those difficult days in Cuba. Beautifully written."

Teresita Yániz de Arias
Movimiento de Mujeres | Secretaria Nacional del Plan Alimentario Nutricional
Diputada de la República 1999-04. 2004-09 | Panama

My Native Land is Memory

Stories of a Cuban Childhood

My Native Land is Memory
Stories of a Cuban Childhood

Oliva M. Espín

San Diego State University Press
2020

My Native Land is Memory: Stories of a Cuban Childhood
by Oliva M. Espín is published by San Diego State University Press.

San Diego State University Press publications may be purchased at discount
for educational, business, or sales promotional use.

For information write:

SDSU Press Next Generation Publishing Initiative (NGPI)
San Diego, California, 92182-6020

Cover and Book Design by Emily Buckley

sdsupress.sdsu.edu
hype.sdsu.edu
amatlcomix.sdsu.edu

FIRST EDITION

Printed in the United States of America

ISBN-13: 978-0-916304-19-5

La patria es el recuerdo... Pedazos de la vida
envueltos en jirones de amor o de dolor;
la palma rumorosa, la música sabida,
el huerto ya sin flores, sin hojas, sin verdor.

Our native land is memory… Pieces of life
wrapped in shreds of love or sorrow;
the rustling palm, the well-known music,
the orchard stripped of flowers, leaves or
greenery.

La patria son los viejos senderos retorcidos
que el pie desde la infancia sin tregua recorrió,
en donde son los árboles antiguos conocidos
que al alma le conversan de un tiempo que pasó.

Our native land is the old winding trails
that from childhood my feet walked without
pause,
where ancient familiar trees are old friends
that talk to our souls about a time long past.

....

Quizás nunca supiera que te quería tanto
si el hado no dispone que atravesara el mar.

Perhaps I would have never known I loved
you so much
if fate had not decreed that I would cross the
sea.
....

Oh, patria tan pequeña que cabes toda entera
debajo de la sombra de nuestro pabellón,
quizás fuiste tan chica para que yo pudiera
llevarte por doquiera dentro del corazón.

Oh, native land so tiny that you fit whole
beneath the shadow of our flag,
perhaps you were that small so I could
carry you everywhere within my heart.

Patria (fragment), Ricardo Miró (1893-1940)

Contents

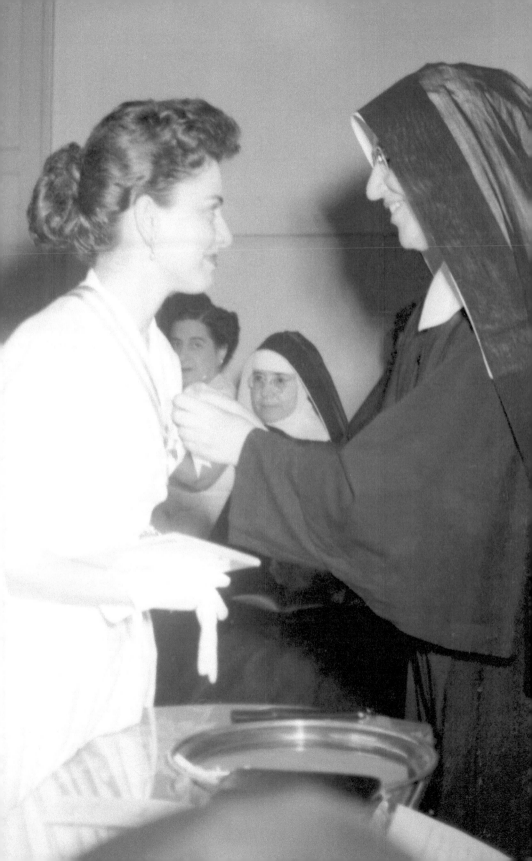

Acknowledgements

No other person has been as significant in my life as my sister Nery. This story is also, in many ways, her story because it is the story of our shared childhood. Therefore, I want to acknowledge and thank her for the blessing of her sisterly love and her constant presence during the decades of our parallel lives. Her absence, after her death last summer, has left an enormous void. Years ago, when I began writing this book, she read the manuscript and told me in no uncertain terms that some parts were boring and others inaccurate. I heeded her advice and re-wrote some sections. After all, she had been there, witnessing my life, more than anyone else. I don't know if she would have approved of this final version, but I want to dedicate it to her to express my gratitude for her love and support and for the beauty of her soul that will always stay with me.

My youngest brother Mario, who also died this past summer, was an avid reader of my writing because it told him stories about a time and place he barely remembered. His questions helped me clarify points and events.

Others have read this text and given me feedback through the years of its development. The women of my writers' group—Anne Marie Welsh, Lillian Faderman, Janice Steinberg, Abbie Padgett, Sheryl Tempchin, and Carolyn Marsden—have been a source of inspiration and validation, cheering me up every step of the way. They have enriched this memoir with their careful reading, comments, and encouragement. Anne Marie, Lillian, and I read each other's work in greater detail for a longer period. Our conversations strengthened my writing and helped me refine the story. Later, both Anne Marie and Janice read and commented on the latest version, honing some last details. For all their dedication, wise advice, and support I am grateful to these friends.

Krizia Puig read an early version of my story and urged me to make it appealing to many people not just those who belong to my generation.

Other friends have offered individual feedback at different times in this process. Carol Goodenow, Andrea Dottolo, Matt Kueffler, and Al and Mary O'Brien read earlier versions of the manuscript and gave me many valuable comments. Natalie Porter and Ellyn Kaschak also read earlier versions. We spent long hours discussing our writing and writing quietly at Ellyn's home. Last year a small group of friends—Marie Thomas, Sharon Foster, Pam Rood, Kim Price and Staci Beavers—read one of the recent versions of the manuscript and gathered at my place for several hours to give me comments and editing suggestions.

The input of all these friends who generously gave me their time is present all over in this rendering of the story. I am deeply thankful to all of them.

Finally, I am thankful to Bill Nericcio and the Board of San Diego State University Press for publishing this book. San Diego State University has been my academic home for thirty years, even after I retired from active teaching. I am delighted that this book is coming out under their auspices. Literally and figuratively, I have put my life in their hands. I am grateful to Bill for taking it under his wing.

Needleless to say, this book is closer to my heart than anything I have written before. As such, I am bound to be more emotionally invested in it than in any other book I have published. Errors and inaccuracies are mine alone. I have sought to describe the Cuba of my childhood and adolescence to the best of my capacity. I trust that this book is faithful to my experience and to a world that now exists only in memory.

Prologue in Three Parts

Al Partir/As I leave

"La pecera"
Havana, Cuba. July 7, 1961

My father had left five days earlier. On July 2, after his documents had been checked, he was directed to *la pecera*— "the fish bowl," where those leaving Cuba were held for several hours until the moment of departure.

My parents embraced for a long time before he entered the enclosed space. This was to be their first long-term separation in the almost quarter century of their marriage. On the other side of the thick glass wall, my mother gestured and mouthed her farewell and "I love you" and "I hope to join you soon." They put their hands on each side of the transparent wall, as if willing the glass to melt under the heat of their feelings.

Neither of my parents could imagine life without the other. A few days before leaving, they had their picture taken together. I still have one of the two copies they made of this photograph, on which my father's neat handwriting had inscribed *"Our bodies and our souls remain united despite the distance. Until we see each other again."*

Those inside *la pecera*, moved about restlessly or were glued to the glass wall pantomiming last goodbyes. My father waited with them for the call to walk onto the tarmac and climb the metal stairs to the plane that would carry him across the Florida Strait away from Cuba.

He was going to Miami because he had a visa to enter the United States that had been granted several years before. His forty-five minutes Havana-Miami flight cost about forty dollars. My mother and I did not have U.S. visas. By then Cuba and the United States did not have diplomatic relations. Instead, we could get visas for Spain, so we were going to the other side of the Atlantic, to Madrid, rather than one hour away to the United States. I used up my savings—eight-hundred dollars—to pay for our two one-way tickets to Spain.

Even though not everyone who wanted to could leave and, despite the government's increasing controls on travel, the Havana International Airport was so crowded and the procedures were so slow, that people were allowed to come to the airport twenty-four hours before their scheduled departure to check their *gusanos*.

Gusanos–worms—were the slim, tubular suitcases most of us used, nicknamed after the government's disparaging label for people leaving the country. These suitcases definitely looked like giant *gusanos* or sausages. Our worm-like bags were not made of the material used now for soft-sided luggage, but rather of vinyl that tore easily. Despite their flimsiness, *gusanos* provided maximum capacity without exceeding the forty-four-pound limit allowed. Our three cylindrical *gusanos* competed for ugliness. My father's was dirty brown, my mother's brick red, mine an intricate green print.

Twice that week we went to the airport to check our suitcases and returned home to wait for the next-day departure—once for my father and then for my mother and me. The madness at the airport was nerve wracking. Lines were extraordinarily long. Luggage was piled up on curbs or at the feet of travelers standing in line. The jumble of suitcases made passengers stumble whenever the line advanced a bit. People pushed and shoved and yelled instructions to each other. Cubans have never been known for speaking in low voices. The angst of the moment, the fear of imminent separation and an unpredictable future, the apprehension created by the possible loss of the few treasured possessions in the *gusanos*, raised the decibels to deafening levels. Porters were nowhere to be seen. To help these distressed *gusanos* who were abandoning the country was not patriotic; they deserved as much of a hard time as possible. And, of course, the sultry days of the Cuban summer did not make things any easier. Yet, mysteriously, despite the chaos at the crowded airport, luggage was not lost.

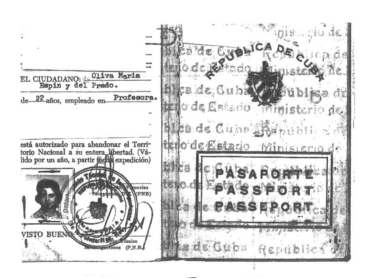

My exit permit, 1961

And so, my time came to enter *la pecera*. My mother and I went through the process: checking *gusanos* the day before, presenting documents, entering *la pecera* to wait for our flight to be called while those who had come to say goodbye stayed outside the glass enclosure. Before going in, we kissed and hugged my mother's sister Marina and my two best friends. My aunt Marina and my friends mouthed good wishes through the glass while my mother and I waited anxiously on the inside. My mother looked sadly at my aunt who was weeping on the other side of the glass. It was the last time I saw Marina; she died before I returned to visit Cuba.

The document checking, baggage search, bureaucratic procedures and whatever else was going on before our departure seemed to last an eternity. Some relatives endured the long wait until planes left. Most returned home after several hours of silent vigil outside *la pecera*. Marina and my friends left after five hours standing by the glass wall. They were exhausted, and so were we. When they left, Mami and I sat together in silence. We were both fidgety. There was nothing to do but wait…and wait we did while thoughts that could not be voiced in that enclosure raced through our minds.

We were not allowed to take any money with us. So, I had resorted to smuggling some minuscule resources. I glued quarters to the false bottom I created with a carefully cut piece of cardboard that fit the bottom panel of a round talcum powder box. Never mind that I never used talcum powder. Even though not many quarters fit flat at the bottom of the round box, they provided a few dollars, so it was worth using some space in my *gusano* for this otherwise useless item. I bought a box of expensive Cuban cigars, one of the items that could be taken out of the country without restrictions, to sell in Madrid. I eventually got twenty-four dollars from the sale of the cigars, a fortune in our precarious financial circumstances. Thanks to these schemes, I was taking with me a little over thirty dollars; we had no other money. The rest of what my mother and I needed would have to be provided by my friends in Madrid until I found a job.

After the long, unnerving wait, we had to go through the final *registro*–the last search before leaving the country. We were called individually to a tent-like structure where each one of us stood in front of our *gusano*—checked a day earlier, but efficiently traced to its owner—while a Cuban officer in uniform went through our belongings to make sure we were not carrying with us anything we were not allowed to take out of the country. When my turn came, I felt relatively calm, but uneasy, not sure of what to anticipate.

The officer looking through my suitcase was of medium height, thin, with blondish graying hair and a big smile. He looked handsome in his olive-green army uniform and his shiny epaulettes; he had the agile energy of those who are happy to do what they do. Chatting pleasantly, he carefully moved his hand around inside my *gusano*. Meticulously, he took things out, looked at them, and replaced them inside the suitcase. He inspected everything closely: my few blouses and skirts and dresses, my two pairs of shoes, my underwear and pajamas and linens—sheets and towels that we would not have money to buy in Madrid. Squeezing pieces of clothing down, checking for hidden lumps, he said something inane meant no doubt to put me at ease, "I like the colors of your clothes."

"Let's see what we have here," he said pulling out the talcum powder box. My heart skipped. I looked on, nervous about what could happen if he found my coins but said nothing as he poked inside the box to explore the talcum with a pen. Satisfied that there was nothing amiss, he put the box back in the suitcase.

And then he asked, "Why are you leaving?"

I answered what we had rehearsed many times, the same justification given to the officers who decided on our exit visa, "My mother is sick," I said.

I explained that she had a very serious skin rash–which was true—and added that we were going to Spain to visit some relatives to see if the different climate healed her skin.

"I see..." he mumbled, clearly not believing a word of what I had said.

My parents last photograph together in Cuba, 1961

In May, I had told my parents I wanted to leave. It may seem odd, but my parents and I left Cuba when I, a twenty-two-year-old, decided we should leave. They had wanted to leave for several months, but they had been waiting for my signal. My two younger brothers, Orlando and Mario, had been sent to the U.S. a few months earlier through the Peter Pan Program—*Operación Pedro Pan*—organized by the CIA and the Catholic Church. That program airlifted 14,000 unaccompanied Cuban children to the United States in the early 1960s. Parents felt they were ensuring safety for their children by sending them out of the country. The memory of Jewish children's fate during World War II and of Basque children at the end of the Spanish Civil War was still fresh.

My sister Nery, like my father, had a U.S. visa. She had left for Miami in early March to join a boyfriend, who eventually participated in the Bay of Pigs invasion, without telling my parents that he was waiting for her there.

Until that disastrous invasion in April, I was adamant that we should stay to support the few good programs the revolutionary government was implementing and to protect those who were actively protesting the negative or arbitrary policies. I was in my early twenties. Unrealistic idealism motivated most of my decisions.

Nevertheless, after the failed Bay of Pigs invasion and the government's "nationalization" of all schools, I faced a dilemma. If I wanted to keep my job in the—until then—private Catholic girls' school where I had been teaching, I was required to go to a summer school for educators to learn how and what to teach my students, following government dictates. The nuns were now gone. The school was run by a government designated official. We had been ordered to inventory every piece of furniture, every book, every teaching tool on the premises. As we went about this task, "informal" conversations made it clear that, in order to continue working there, all teachers must learn to conform to the official ideologies and to teach accordingly.

Financially, I did not have the luxury of leaving my job. But I felt I could not come back in September to teach adolescent girls to believe in the greatness of the Soviet Union, the virtues of the yet to be declared, but looming Cuban Socialism, or the new, punishing laws I strongly opposed. I could not use my influence and authority to bend young minds in favor of those political ideologies, just so I could keep my job. If I had had a position involving only adults, I probably would have stayed. But changing jobs at that point would have raised suspicions about my ideological alliances. The government was by then the only employer. There was no way of dodging risky explanations for why I wanted to leave teaching.

Our preparations began as soon as I told my parents I was ready to leave: making plane reservations, securing the exit permits, inquiring about visas for my mother and me. At that time, more than a year before the Cuban Missile Crisis of October 1962—when most commercial flights out of Cuba eventually stopped—it was still possible to make your own plane reservations. Leaving Cuba was not forbidden then, as it would be after 1962. Those wanting to depart just had to undergo bothersome and long-winded bureaucratic procedures to be granted an exit visa. Most people were allowed to leave if they could get a seat on a plane and pay for it. Thousands were scrambling to get out. Flights were booked to capacity for several months ahead. We were fortunate to get those seats, compared to other people who did not have this opportunity no matter how much they wanted to get away.

After what seemed like an eternity, the officer searching through my belongings finished replacing my clothes back inside the *gusano* without detecting my grandmother Fefita's diamond ring that I had sewn inside the hem of a dress. I did not intend to sell this ring despite its monetary value; I just wanted to keep it with me as the treasured heirloom it was.

Then, the officer took out my little jewelry box. I had put in it some plastic and rhinestone costume jewelry of no real value. Mixed with them was a small gold bracelet, engraved with my name. Tío, my father's brother, and my godfather, had given me the bracelet for my fifteenth birthday. The officer looked at it intently and turned it. There was no mistaking what was written on the back: *18kt*. With so many details to be aware of, I had not thought carefully enough when I left the little bracelet inside the jewelry box.

"This is gold," he said as pleasantly as he had said everything else. "You know it is forbidden to take gold out of the country."

"I didn't know it was gold," I mumbled. "It is just a little bracelet I got from my uncle." "Well, there is no doubt that this is gold. Can't you see the eighteen-karat imprint?"

I stayed silent and looked at him. I was not going to risk my chance of leaving by arguing.

"I have to requisition this bracelet, but you can claim it when you come back to Cuba at the end of your summer in Spain, once your mother is healed."

A little smirk on his face told me he knew I would never see this bracelet again. But he filled out a lengthy multicolored form with three carbon copies. He had me sign it and signed it himself.

"There you go," he said, handing me the yellow copy. "Make sure you bring this back with you when you return."

Satisfied he had found something that could be taken away and kept by the government as punishment for my refusal to be faithful to the Revolution, he zipped my *gusano*, gave me back the little padlock to close the end of the zipper, and cheerfully said, "Have a great trip! I hope to see you back in a few months."

I was nervous when I came back to join the other passengers in *la pecera*. I whispered to my mother what had happened. She nodded and drew out from the cleavage in her breast the paper tissue she kept there to blot the sweat on her face. We both knew that wrapped inside the crumpled tissue was a platinum ring with tiny diamonds and sapphires my father had given her when they got married. It had survived the search of her *gusano*. Even if she had been selected at random for a strip search, no one would have paid much attention to a wrinkled, sweaty tissue. I regretted not having done something clever with my bracelet as I had done with my grandmother's ring, or my mother had done with hers, but at least, both rings had cleared the search. The sadness of losing the bracelet was overshadowed by the anxiety I still felt and the relief that now we were both cleared for leaving.

During those last moments on Cuban soil, the verses of Gertrudis Gómez de Avellaneda's poem, "¡Al Partir!"— "As I leave!"—kept crossing my mind.

> ¡Perla del mar! ¡Estrella de Occidente!
> Hermosa Cuba, tu brillante cielo
> la noche cubre con su opaco velo
> como cubre el dolor mi triste frente.
>
> (Pearl of the sea! Star of the West!
> Beautiful Cuba, your brightly luminous sky
> night covers with its opaque veil
> just as grief and pain cover my sad brow.)

Avellaneda wrote this poem in 1836, when she was fourteen, as she was leaving Cuba, also for Spain. Children learned this poem in school when we also learned that she was the first woman to be proposed for induction into the Spanish Royal Academy of Language, an honor she was denied because she was a woman. At that moment, sitting in *la pecera*, her words touched feelings that were barely below the surface. "*Voy a partir*—I am leaving—*La chusma diligente/ para arrancarme del nativo suelo/ las velas iza...*" And although there was no "diligent rabble unfurling sails" in the Havana airport as they had been at the port in Avellaneda's poem, I was painfully aware that all these procedures were also "tearing me from my native land."

I did not know then that this was a permanent departure. And yet, Avellaneda's words recalled at that critical moment gave voice to my pent-up grief. Teary-eyed, I began to dimly realize the truth of what was happening and didn't want to believe yet. I felt Avellaneda's feelings as mine and could barely contain them inside my tangle of confused thoughts.

Finally, passengers were called to board.

We walked briskly single file from the gate, across the tarmac, up the metal steps to the propeller plane that would take us across the Atlantic. The sun was beginning to set. Our shadows danced in front of us as we walked, as if mocking our contained feelings. The Cubana de Aviación plane in which we were leaving was Cuban territory. Passengers exchanged knowing smiles, nothing more. The silence was overwhelming.

In the months and years since, I did not give much thought to my bracelet, and Avellaneda's poem faded from my mind. But I know now what I did not know then standing inside *la pecera* on July 7, 1961: That little bracelet, brusquely taken away from me, was a tiny symbol of all the losses to come.

My picture for the U.S. green card, Madrid 1961

"Los toros son ángeles que llevan cuernos"
Picasso in Madrid. Summer 1961

The twenty-two-hour flight across the Atlantic felt interminable. The propeller plane reverberated with the anxious silence of the passengers and the incessant whirling of motors.

After the long and tense flight, it was a relief to embrace my friend Tory. She picked us up at Madrid Barajas Airport. Her big eyes and warm hugs reassured me that I could relax now; she was taking command of the situation with her usual efficiency. When we arrived at the apartment she had arranged for us, she led us up the staircase to the third floor of a rather plain building.

I had met Tory during my first trip to Europe in 1958 when she was almost fifty and I was nineteen. She was closer to my mother's age, but an unlikely friendship developed between the two of us. Tory was single, as were many women who had been young during the years of the Spanish Civil War. She relished caring for me. I felt our unusual friendship was a gift. When we met, she was impressed by what she saw as my courage travelling through Europe by myself at such a young age. I was fascinated by her vivid stories about the Spanish Civil War, narrated with fire and enthusiasm, her spicy and irreverent use of language, her strong opinions and her frequent jokes. When my mother and I left Cuba, Tory made it her mission to alleviate our precarious situation. She offered us this free apartment and made sure we went home well fed several times a week.

Tory opened the door of the flat and walked us through the apartment, while pointing and commenting at rooms and their content.

I put down my green *gusano* and took in my new surroundings.

The owner of this apartment and his wife, who was Tory's niece, were overseas. He was a professor, a minor but recognizable name in Spanish literature. The walls of the living room were lined with floor-to-ceiling bookcases, holding thousands of volumes of Spanish and Latin American literature. "Obviously he reads a lot; sometimes things no one should read if you ask me," Tory said, making a wide arch with her right arm as if to stress the large area occupied by the books. She didn't like the professor much because he was not a devoted follower of Franco, as she was.

Still chatting, she led us from the living room to the bedroom. The twin beds with carved wood headboards looked inviting just then. Jet lag combined with the tension of leaving and the lengthy flight had been draining. I longed to lie down and close my eyes. Tory led us from the bedroom to the bathroom and kitchen, across from each other on the narrow hallway.

Finally, we stepped into the last room, a narrow office with a desk and chair. Above the desk, a sheet of paper with the outline of a bull's head in black ink caught my eye. The phrase, *"Los toros son ángeles que llevan cuernos"*— "Bulls are angels with horns," and Picasso's familiar signature jumped at me. An original Picasso drawing was attached with a thumbtack to a wall in our new dwelling, dangling there as if it were a stray bit of crayon doodle by a child! We did not have a penny for rent. It felt ridiculous to live with an original Picasso in our borrowed space.

Tory pointed at the drawing and again expressed her disapproval of her niece's husband. "I don't know how he got this. I suppose Picasso painted it impromptu for him during one of José's visits to Paris. And I suppose he is proud of that. I know they are friends. All these 'pinkish' people run together anyway," she added acidly, alluding to the communist leanings she attributed to her niece's husband and Picasso and anyone who did not love Franco.

I had had my fill of political commentary in the last few years. And, although at that time I did not know better and still believed Franco had saved Spain from danger, I did not want to ponder the political leanings of our absent host. All I wanted was to go to bed.

The tour of our temporary home completed, Tory handed us two sets of keys and said good night. My mother and I unpacked sheets and towels and pajamas we had brought in our *gusanos* and went to sleep immediately.

Reading had been my refuge and my delight from an early age. But, ironically, cocooned in the reader's paradise that was this Madrid apartment, in the summer of 1961, I could not finish a book. I could not concentrate; my mind was absorbed by the dawning realization of the magnitude of the loss and the desperate efforts to capture some threads of hope. I carried one or another of those books as I went about my daily life, trying to read in the metro and on buses, but I kept forgetting what I had just read. My usual escape into books failed me. Unable to read—and with no television, radio, or other distraction—I sat in front of Picasso's drawing and stared.

The apartment was located in Barrio de la Concepción, a barely developed working-class neighborhood on the outskirts of Madrid. Barrio de la Concepción was as dismal as my life felt at that time. The identical box-like, four-story buildings had no architectural details.

The streets of the Barrio were barren dust roads, with no bushes or trees, and a few sidewalks under construction. Every street was named after some appellation of the Virgin Mary: Virgen del Rosario, Virgen de los Dolores, Virgen del Pilar, Virgen de la Candelaria. I had never seen so many designations for Mary in one place. Our apartment was on Virgen de la Consolación. But regardless of the name of the street where we lived, my mother and I were inconsolable.

It was understood that I would be the provider. By then, I had helped support my family in Cuba for several years. And my mother, who was forty-nine years old, had never worked outside the home, and neither she nor I could imagine her finding a job. My mother's only skills were as a homemaker. A married woman from a "good family" in Cuba or Spain was not supposed to work outside the home at a menial job. Later, in the U.S., my mother would work as a maid, cleaning private homes and hotel rooms. She would also work as a nanny and as a "finisher" in a showroom in the garment district of New York. Shame was not associated with these jobs in the U.S., and she had always been a hard worker. But in Madrid, it would not have been possible for her to find acceptable employment.

My skills, on the other hand, were marketable. And, indeed, I found a job a few weeks after our arrival. I supported us by working as a Spanish-English bilingual secretary in the plush offices of Esso Standard Española, with its tall windows overlooking El Retiro Park. I hated the job, I hated being stuck in Barrio de la Concepción, so far from Cuba and so removed from the beautiful center of Madrid that I had loved and enjoyed in the summer of 1958, and now could only glimpse on my way to work.

My job entailed monotonous tasks, made more difficult by inconsiderate bosses. Work days were a succession of taking dictation from one or another of them, sitting at a typewriter transcribing my shorthand squiggles, bringing the typed documents to the men for revisions or signature. In this pre-computer world, my immediate boss, Señor Vílpido, a short fiftyish man with a thin moustache, a perpetual smile, and a striped three-piece suit, once made me retype a letter several pages long just so the date—*Madrid, 27 de agosto de 1961*—was placed one line below where I had originally typed it.

While I was at work, my mother cooked and tended to the apartment, lamenting every day and every mile that separated her from my father. She ventured out each morning to the neighborhood shops to buy small amounts of the cheapest foods she could find—potatoes, green leafy vegetables, white beans, perhaps a piece of cheese, *chorizo*, *morcilla* or ham—being careful not to exceed our measly food budget.

These apartments, as most homes in Spain at the time, had no refrigerators, but they had a wide kitchen windowsill that stayed cool despite the intense summer heat. This was called *la fresquera*, "the cooling spot." Cheeses, bread, and vegetables were kept there, but they still had to be eaten quickly, before they went bad.

One day, someone gave us a decapitated, ready-to-cook rabbit. Neither my mother nor I knew what to do with it, and the poor headless, skinless creature looked as pitiful as we felt. Mami did her best to cook it in some sauce she invented. It was not too bad, but I will forever associate the taste of rabbit meat with sorrow and loneliness. I have never again eaten rabbit.

In that summer of 1961, when President Kennedy was still alive and the Cuban missile crisis had not happened yet, the front page of newspapers carried worrisome reports about a wall going up in Berlin, separating East from West. Public transportation, cafes, and other locations in Madrid were full of nervous conversations about what this could mean. The news of the building of a wall in Berlin that August was another foreboding of the world divisions that would forever mark my life. But I could not recognize yet the irreversibility of what I had lost.

One morning at work, while I was drowning in the usual tedium, taking dictation for another uninteresting piece of correspondence, one of the men I worked for, Señor Barranco, who was not yet forty and had a head of dark curls and a sour face with thin lips, mumbled dryly and quite unexpectedly,

"You will never go back to Cuba."

I felt my insides contort in pain. Although secretaries were instructed to never contradict the bosses, I could not contain myself and answered with passion. "Oh, I know I will go back, if nothing else because there will be a Third World War that will destroy communism."

He sneered and continued to dictate impatiently.

I am horrified now that I hoped for another World War to save me from a life in exile. The magnitude of my internal laceration, of the pain and dread of perpetually being far from all that had been my life up to then, was revealed in that extreme, destructive wish. But sitting in that office in Madrid with pen and notepad in my hand, nothing seemed worse or more apocalyptic to me than the possibility of never returning to Cuba.

I had left, as so many other Cubans did then, believing that the absence would be brief; eight or nine months, a year at most. The shattering of the hope of return felt unbearable. Living day to day far from Cuba was hard enough that summer; a lifetime of exile was unfathomable. Yes, my life in Cuba had not been perfect. But it was mine. Now, each day felt like a page borrowed from someone else's life.

My life was all the more dreary because I had to deal not only with my sadness but also with my even sadder mother. Unremitting memories of Cuba filled us. In the middle of our mostly silent dinners, one of us would mention Marina, left behind and alone in our Havana apartment. Or we talked about my father and Nery, making ends meet in an airless studio apartment in Miami subsidized by the U.S. Government Cuban Refugee Program. Or about my two brothers, living in an orphanage in Ohio until my parents could be reunited and claim them. And, inevitably, we both started crying, separated by the kitchen table and our different feelings of sorrow.

Crying together in our shared pain did not improve my relationship with my mother. I felt trapped, stuck with her in Madrid for these long months, envying my sister her good fortune of being with my father in Miami even though he was also in a very gloomy mood because of my mother's absence. I had always adored my father; I wished I were with him rather than my mother. Later, I learned from Nery that all he did was cry, calling out my mother's name and praying for their reunion as my mother was doing in Madrid.

While my mother's only thought was reuniting with my father in Miami as soon as possible, I was unhappy with the idea of going to the United States. I wanted to live in Europe, where, in 1958, I had tasted independence for the first time in my life. I felt restless, reluctant to leave Madrid—a city I knew was full of possibilities if I could give myself a chance to explore what it offered me—for a place that had never appealed to me. As an adolescent, while my peers swooned over American actors and talked about wanting to go to Miami to shop, I instead admired women actors in Spanish films and memorized the songs in those films. Now that I was here, I did not want to leave. I imagined and schemed ways in which I could stay in Spain, even though I knew my parents expected me to join them in the U.S.

A friend of my father's, who had an account in a Spanish bank, had offered to pay for our two tickets to the U.S. once we got visas at the Embassy in Madrid. Otherwise, we would have had to stay in Spain for an indeterminate amount of time. His generosity suited my parents' plans but hindered my dreams of living in Spain that had been truncated once already a few years earlier.

Finally, on one of those teary evenings while we shared our dinner in silence, I said hesitantly and fretfully, "Mami… I do not want to go to the United States… I prefer… I want to stay in Spain… Here, it will be easier and cheaper to return to University…"

Before I was even finished, her forceful answer came in the same firm tone of voice she used in Cuba, "I don't care where you want to live. You can earn more money than your father. We need you to support the family in the States."

It was the first time she had said this in so many words. Although this was a pressure I had grown accustomed to in Cuba, somehow it became more evident. At that moment of emotional vulnerability, and despite my usual feistiness, I kept my mouth shut and, once again, resigned myself to the inevitable.

The following week, sitting in front of the Picasso, I filled out our applications for green cards that would allow my mother and me to become legal residents in the United States. As I looked distractedly at Picasso's bull, while filling out the applications, I resented the superficiality of the little drawing, and yet was amazed to be living with a Picasso. Some of the questions in the application seemed absurd, "Do you intend to engage in prostitution upon arrival in the United States?" "Do you intend to conspire to kill the president?" I carefully answered all questions, submitted the forms to the Embassy, and then waited for what seemed to my mother like a very long time to receive the coveted green cards that would make us "legal aliens." As soon as my mother's green card application cleared, she booked a flight to Miami with the money borrowed from my father's friend.

I, however, I still hoped I could find a way to stay in Spain or wished the wings of Picasso's angel-bull could transport me to Cuba and back to my old life.

Decades later, when I discovered this Picasso etching had been reproduced and sold at auctions, the swirl of feelings of those days in Madrid came back in full force. And I wondered if I had, in fact, lived with an original Picasso, regardless of what Tory had said and I thought I had seen. But, in a way, I was not surprised; so many things I had firmly believed to be true in those days turned out not to be.

"La patria es el recuerdo"
My native land is memory

T wenty-three years, five countries, and many life events later, I returned to Cuba for the first time for a two-week visit.

On Thanksgiving weekend, 1983, I woke up to a chilly, gray morning in Boston. A perfect day to stay in pajamas, reading. In the previous weeks I had been busy writing a draft of what would be my first book. This weekend, I felt I deserved to read a novel and relax, slowly drinking my morning coffee and dozing off if I felt like it.

And then, the phone rang. My mother's voice. "Marina died yesterday," she said without preamble when I picked up the phone. "Cerebral hemorrhage."

I was speechless. My aunt Marina had lived with us in Havana since I was eight years old. When we left, she eventually returned to the family house in Santiago to live with her sisters. My mother had gone back to that house in 1981, to see her siblings for a last time. Returning to Cuba for family visits had just become possible. The Cuban government had begun allowing those who had left twenty years earlier to return, beginning with those airlifted as children in the early 1960s through Operation Peter Pan. My aunt Celia had died of breast cancer shortly after my mother's visit. But Marina's death was unexpected.

She had told my mother then that she still had the adolescent diaries I entrusted to her when I left. She had kept them, unopened, for two decades. My mother offered to bring my journals back, but Marina said that she had promised to keep them until I returned. She would only give them to me. *Now, she would not be able to. And I have not fulfilled my promise to her that I would return,* I thought with tears in my eyes.

Ironically, the book I was reading on that chilly Thanksgiving weekend was Christa Wolf's *Patterns of Childhood*, an autobiographical novel in which she narrates her return visit to the German town of her childhood, now in Polish territory. Wolf's description of her experience of return was making me wonder idly what it would be like to go back to the places of my childhood and adolescence. But I had never considered the possibility of going back.

After several months in Spain, I had arrived in the U.S. in December 1961, and, within a few months, went to live in Panama and later in Costa Rica. For the following nine years, I had come to visit my parents where they lived—in Florida or New York—for Christmas and the New Year. In 1970, after I had finally finished a BA in Psychology from the University of Costa Rica, I had moved to Belgium with a fellowship to do graduate work. I returned to the U.S. for a brief time to complete my doctorate and then took a job as a professor in Montreal. Finally, in late 1975, I had taken a faculty position at a university in Boston.

Oliva 1970s

Oliva 1980s

During those years when I lived in several different countries, I had studiously avoided most things Cuban. Partly because it was deeply painful, partly because it was exhausting to be involved in useless conversations that ended up in comments like "Next Christmas in Havana." I had already abandoned all hope of return. It was clear that Fidel Castro's government was there to stay. As that reality sank in, I focused on my personal life and education, developed important relationships and friendships, and learned a lot about who I was. Cuba was not constantly in my mind. Here and there I was confronted with my uprootedness, but after the initial severe distress of those months in Madrid, I had adjusted to my life. My absence from Cuba was not an unremitting or acute pain.

Through the years, I had had my share of unpleasantness from the left-wing ideologues who populate academic hallways and speak about Revolutionary Cuba as if it were a dream come true. No matter how many times I repeated that I had not even owned the amount of Cuban "land" that fits in a flower pot, many of my colleagues continued to believe that I was a privileged rich girl who could not accept the wonders worked by the Revolution because they must have taken my privileges away.

And then, there were those Cubans in the U.S. who had included my name on lists of Castro sympathizers in their weekly rags. Some students had heard me say that there was social and economic injustice in Cuba before the Revolution; that change was needed in a country with such economic disparities; that some things had become better for poor Cubans in the early years of the Revolution. Even though I followed these comments by saying that the kind of change imposed by Castro had ended up being more destructive than beneficial, my statements violated the myth, so cherished by most Cubans in Miami, that everything was wonderful in Cuba before 1959 and had become terrible since. Moreover, I had dared to organize an academic conference in Boston in the late 1970s about Cuban women in and out of Cuba, and I had written some articles on women in Cuba. My mother by then lived in Miami and had been subjected to phone calls from "friends" telling her I must have communist leanings since I was interested in the topic of women in Cuba. Never mind that my research focused on the psychology and gender roles of women from Latin American countries; including Cuban women in my work was almost a given. The phone calls and the comments about me on conservative Cuban radio stations in Miami had made my mother's life unpleasant. Those same people, no doubt, would interpret a return trip as proof of my supposed leanings.

I had persuaded myself that I could gain nothing by going to Cuba. In fact, now it probably made less sense than ever. *Marina is dead. It would not make any difference. No sense in expressing my love for her with a return she would not witness.*

But whatever my logical reasoning, as the weekend progressed, a sense of urgency and restlessness persisted no matter how hard I tried to shake away the thought. Marina's death made me feel that returning to Cuba was necessary.

I was not sure how it would feel to be there, but it now felt as if I could not *not* do it. And I knew I had to do it alone. Without friends. Without people who had never been to Cuba before. Without people who had also been born in Cuba and thus had their own feelings about being there. This would be my own emotional journey.

Finally, in late October 1984, I set out to re-encounter the first half of my life.

The journey did not start with the actual trip. For weeks before I went, I had sudden flashbacks of familiar scenes, places, events that I had forgotten or at least not remembered for those twenty-three years. I would suddenly feel as if I were standing at the corner of Galiano and San Rafael in Havana, next to the old Woolworth's across from El Encanto department store, or walking with my father in Old Havana, or reading quietly in the two rooms behind my father's school, or reciting poetry under the direction of my teachers. Or in Santiago, playing under the *mamoncillo* tree in my grandparent's house or in Parque Céspedes, watching a Carnaval parade from the balcony of Hotel Casa Granda. Bits of Cuban songs kept floating into my consciousness, making the memories even more vivid by the power of music to evoke forgotten moments. These flashbacks were stunning. They absorbed me and distracted me from the activity of the moment. They had an almost hallucinatory quality as if I was suffering from post-traumatic stress. I guess I was. This was something I had not experienced before.

On the actual day of the trip, endless hours of waiting at the airport in Miami increased my anxiety. U.S. officials looked carefully and insistently at all travelers' papers. Several customs and immigration officers looked at my U.S. passport as well as the Cuban passport and entry permit required of all visiting émigrés. During my stay in Cuba I would be just another Cuban citizen subject to the laws of the country. My U.S. passport would be used only to re-enter. Officers asked several times over, "When did you leave Cuba?" "What's the purpose of this trip?" "How long will you stay there?" "Do you have relatives in Cuba?" "Where do they live?" And also, "Where do you live in the U.S.?" "Where do you work?"

In the early dawn, as if concealing the fact that we were visiting Cuba on a flight departing from U.S. territory despite the official embargo, we finally boarded the plane.

After a forty-five-minute flight from Miami, I arrived in Havana around 5:00 a.m. The transition was quick and dramatically abrupt. From my plane window, I could see the lights of Key West and the lights of Havana simultaneously, with just a dark narrow strip of water between them. The lights of Havana brought tears to my eyes. They had been so close and so far from my touch for so many years!

My actual arrival at the airport in Havana is a blur. Except for one incident. Two science professors from the university at which I taught in Boston had asked me to bring a draft of a book manuscript for a Cuban zoologist. About a year earlier they had conducted a study of Cuban bat species in collaboration with this scientist and wanted him to see what they had written and intended to publish. But this thick stack of typed pages in English seemed suspicious to the Cuban custom officers. What if this was something having to do with *"diversionismo ideológico"*— "ideological diversionism"—that could contaminate Cuban scientific minds? Or worse, what if this manuscript was not about bats at all but about some CIA secret plan to invade Cuba? After flipping through the pages, the officer who was checking the contents of my suitcase called his supervisor and showed him the document. Without reading anything (*could he read English?*), the supervisor informed me that they had to keep the manuscript. They would give me a receipt for the scientist to whom it was addressed, and he could come to the Customs Office at the airport to pick it up himself.

This entire process, complete with pieces of official paper forms, was a reminder of the moment two decades earlier when another Cuban officer had taken away my gold bracelet. But the airport looked rather different in 1984 than in 1961. *La pecera* was not there any longer. There was more concern about those who were coming back than about those departing. The balance had tipped.

It was still dark when I walked outside. The weather was seasonably cool. Late October in Havana is breezy. Just past the exit door, several men were lifting a taxicab from the ground while one of them struggled to change a back tire. The vehicle swung back and forth slightly as they struggled with the weight of the car. The lack of a jack was an instantaneous demonstration of the prevalent scarcity of so many things in Cuba and of the resourcefulness that scarcity produces. I walked by them as I fast as I could, carrying my suitcase. I didn't want to witness the crushing of a limb and was eager to get to the hotel after a sleepless night.

After a short wait, I found a taxi that I could share with an American couple. Driving into the city, from the taxi windows I looked avidly at buildings and streets, still dark before sunrise. It was hard to believe this was actual reality rather than another flight of memory and imagination. All I could think was, *I can't believe that I am really here! I am here, I am here, I AM HERE! My God! I am in Havana!*

I was brought out of my trance by the taxi driver asking his three passengers, "Is this your first trip to Cuba?"

"No," I said without missing a beat, "I was born here."

He looked at me in the rearview mirror with surprise and so did the American couple. "How long have you been away?" The three of them asked almost simultaneously.

"Twenty-three years," I said, still looking at the dark streets of Havana that were rolling by.

"*¡Oiga pa' ahí!* That was before I was born!" The young driver looked at me again through his mirror, in awe.

I had not heard this Cuban expression of surprise in two decades. I smiled faintly, already comforted.

As he dropped me at the hotel, he pulled my suitcase from the trunk of the taxi while saying, "*Que la pase bien*"— "Have a good time," the expression of amazement still on his face. Returning Cubans were not a common sight in Havana yet. He probably went home with a big tale about our encounter.

By 7:00 a.m. I had checked into the hotel, taken a shower, had breakfast and cried because for the first time in twenty-three years my coffee was sweetened with Cuban sugar. Cuban sugar had been out of my reach like so many other once familiar things during those two decades of absence. Sugar was Cuba and Cuba was sugar. Cuban identity and economy had been linked to the cultivation of cane and the production of sugar since the late eighteenth century. "*Sin azúcar no hay país*"— "There is no country without sugar" as an old slogan used to say. First Spain, then the U.S. and, more recently, the Soviet Union determined the price of Cuban sugar. And because the world can live without sugar, life became bitter in Cuba after the dismembering of the Soviet block and its directed economies in the 1990s.

The moment I stepped out of the hotel I knew exactly where I was, what corners to turn, what buildings would be waiting for me on the next block, and which one of the buses going by would take me to which place in the city. In a few hours, I had walked through my old neighborhoods, I had gone by my school, I had walked familiar streets and had come back to the hotel without ever having the slightest confusion about where I was or worry about getting lost.

For me, the distance between Cuba and the United States had not been ninety miles, but a quarter of a century and a dense wall of memory. The long months of preparation for the trip and the two-week visit to Cuba set off a flood of memories. Emotions dormant for two decades were awakened. "Boxes" closed for decades opened up. A torrent of remembrances jostled for my attention.

This trip to Cuba put flesh on the bones of the psychological theories I had studied and taught: Historical events and individual lives intersect to create autobiographical memory. When powerful dislocations occur in life, memory provides the only sense of continuity. Places and people change, so the only way of knowing who you are—that you are—is to remember. Although autobiographical memory is important for everyone, for those of us who have lived in many places throughout our lives, memory binds the array of shifting experiences into a sense of personal identity and subjectivity, a sense of continuity that can be encapsulated as "who I am." I am aware that memory is the one and only witness to my life. It is my way to *re-member* all the scattered pieces that constitute my personal history. It gives me a sense of continuity despite the many breaks and dislocations that have characterized my life.

My return to Cuba made me realize that my memories had a geography. That what I remembered had actually happened in a definite physical space that continues to exist in reality and not only in my memory. Cuba, in fact, exists beyond what I think or feel or remember about her. This realization, which may seem all too obvious, was powerful because before my return, I never knew that I felt Cuba had no real existence beyond my memory. For the most part, I remembered the events of my first twenty-two years as events and memories of *my* individual life. But the return visit made me oddly aware that my life had happened in a specific place, in a specific time—in a context that shaped my life story.

My native land is alive in my memory as I age. This writing is an exercise in understanding the building blocks of my life, the cultural context in which I grew up and the entanglements of Cuban history that are knitted into the fabric of my life and the person I have become. As I write about these emotionally charged memories of childhood and adolescence, I am aware that, like all autobiographical memory, mine undoubtedly contains distortions. Now that I have lived most of my life, I know there is much that is genuine in my memories; some of these are etched in stone.

I have returned to visit Cuba several times after this first one. Each one of those visits has been emotionally charged. I have encountered memories and reinforced and contrasted them with reality every time I have returned to Cuba. Like all memories, mine are imperfect and subjective, kept in some internal inaccessible vault until those moments of encounter; the real geography of the place superimposed to that of my memory. I now remember better how streets connect with each other, where parks are located, the patterns of the floor tiles in my grandparents' house. Memories are refreshed, clarified, reinforced and challenged; they are evoked and retrieved from places inside my brain where I did not know they had been dormant for decades.

And here they are, those memories of my childhood and adolescence, coalescing in front of my mind's eye and shaping these words and pag

I

Havana Childhood

"La Nené"

I would not exist if it were not for my parents' chance encounter at a *quinceañera* party—a coming-of-age dance for a fifteen-year-old girl—in Santiago de Cuba, at the eastern end of the island.

They were both too old for *quinceañera* parties. My mother, who was already twenty-five, went to accompany her sisters. My father went with another young man, almost as a joke. He had just turned thirty. He had recently become a lawyer in the Cuban navy, a position he had earned after days of written examinations. Armed with his shiny white uniform and newly acquired credentials, the freshly appointed Lieutenant had set out to find a wife, but never thought he would find one at a *quinceañera* party. Being the good Catholic he was, he had prayed to St. Anthony for a bride. On this June 13th, St. Anthony's feast day, he met my mother. They were married six months later, on December 11, 1937.

As a child, I looked at photographs of their wedding with unending fascination. Three photos in particular, attracted my attention. In one, my mother advances alone down the aisle of the cathedral of Santiago, preceded by two girls and two boys, smiling, a big bouquet of white carnations and roses in her joined hands. She did not want to be "given away," and her father had no objection. My mother's choice to walk by herself proclaimed her character: a firm will and a tenacity that came to my father's rescue many times during their marriage and wove themselves into my own sense of self.

Another photograph, taken in the middle of the ceremony, shows my parents' young and serious faces—she in her white satin dress and long veil, he in his gala uniform with golden epaulettes—standing in front of the imposing Monsignor Zubizarreta, Archbishop of Santiago, who sits on his throne dressed in full regalia: a tall miter on his head, an embroidered cape, a staff in his hand. My mother's father, Abuelo Cándido, stands next to my mother; my father's mother María Luisa next to my father.

My parents' wedding-My mother entering the church

My parents' wedding-During the ceremony

The Archbishop did not marry just anybody. But Abuelo Cándido had plenty of money to validate his hard-won social standing; he decided it was worth giving a big donation to the cathedral to persuade the Archbishop to perform the wedding ceremony for the first of his daughters to get married.

My mother arrived at the cathedral at eleven o'clock at night. The Archbishop had been ready since nine, the scheduled time for the ceremony. He waited impatiently for my mother's arrival, irritated with the delay. I have heard that, although it was fashionable for brides to be late, her lateness was too much for the Archbishop, who grumbled and fidgeted while he waited.

When I look at this photograph I wonder if my grandmother Abuela Boqui was thinking about her own wedding. She had been married at the church of St. Francis Xavier in New York in 1896, while in exile from Cuba, which was then still under the Spanish Crown. At the time of my parents' wedding, grandfather José Manuel had been dead for twenty years but Abuela Boqui still dressed as a widow—black dress and hat with a veil that covered her face. I wonder if she thought about the irony: her youngest son was marrying the daughter of Spaniards who had opposed Cuban independence while her husband, her brother, and other men in her family had risked their lives to fight against the Spanish colonial powers in Cuba. But her face under the thin veil, is inscrutable, as are the faces of all the other people standing at the altar.

My parents' wedding-
The arch of swords

3

The third photograph, the one that impressed me the most, shows my parents, already married and smiling broadly, walking under a canopy of crossed sabers—*la bóveda de acero,* the arch of swords—raised by my father's military colleagues. The two lines of officers opposite each other, their drawn steel touching at their tips, create a tunnel for the newlyweds to walk under. In the photograph, as they emerge from the tunnel of swords, they both look joyful, young and in love, happy to begin their life together, despite the rumblings of approaching war in distant Europe.

I was born one year later, on December 12. I was named after my mother, but with a middle name to distinguish us from each other. My birth was a family event. I was the first child, the first granddaughter, and the first niece on both sides of my family. My aunts called me *la nené,* the baby. The cherished child.

Three months old, in my mother's arms

In my father's arms

Oliva about one-year-old

My sister Nery was born thirteen months later. One of my father's sisters had given birth to a boy two months before. Nery was just another baby; her birth was not an event as mine had been.

Nery and I were both born at home with the help of a midwife, as was common then. A *manejadora*, a maid who specialized in taking care of children, helped my mother with her two little daughters. Another maid cooked and another one cleaned the house and did the laundry by hand and ironed each item meticulously, including sheets and pillowcases. My parents were not rich, but they were solidly middle class. My father was securely employed, and therefore, like others in their same social situation, they were able to afford and were expected to keep several servants.

Oliva: two years old, sitting at the fountain's edge

We lived half a block away from my mother's family in Santiago, in a house with a central courtyard full of leafy trees ringing a gurgling fountain. I was placed in a big tin bowl that served as my boat as I floated round and round that fountain under the watchful eyes of the *manejadora*. In a picture of myself, two years old, perhaps, I am sitting very properly at the fountain's edge, my ankles crossed and my hands clasped together, a big smile on my face. I am dressed in a short white cotton dress, white ankle socks with little lace ruffles and black patent leather shoes with tiny buckles, a bow on top of my head.

Then, in December 1941, everything changed.

And no, it was not because of Pearl Harbor. It was Fulgencio Batista.

He had been elected president for the first time in 1940 after several years of lurking in the corridors of power and acting as strong man in Cuban politics through the 1930s with the encouragement of U.S. ambassador Sumner Welles. Welles had been sent to Cuba by President Franklin D. Roosevelt to "mediate" political conflict between opposition leaders and President Machado. When Machado was forced to resign in 1932, Welles tried to install his chosen president, and, when that did not work, he turned to Sergeant Batista who had already demonstrated his thirst for power.

Batista was a mixed-race man of humble, rural origins who worked as stenographer for the Army. He was both physically attractive and cunning. He had risen quickly up the ranks taking advantage of the chaos left after Machado was deposed.

Shortly after his election as president, Batista set out to "reorganize" the Cuban Armed Forces to insure the loyalty of the military. And that was the end of our idyllic middle-class life.

Batista fired my father and all other officers who were not his enthusiastic supporters. He knew the Cuban upper classes tolerated but despised him. The slightest disaffection in the military compromised his base of support. He could not afford unsympathetic officers.

My father, regardless of what he may have thought, had not actively done anything against Batista. He was not one to initiate or participate in rebellions. But it was known that the officers who were my father's closest friends and mentors were leery of the new president and his ruthless ways. In a sweeping blow, Batista fired all of them, my father included. He was left without a job and with a young wife and two daughters to feed—in Santiago, a city where the chances of finding work were grim because of the chronic underemployment in Cuban society.

Lawyers, unless they were employed by an institution, did not earn much in 1940s Cuba, and, in any case, my father was not adept at making money. He knew that working as a private attorney was not his best alternative. In the first court case he had worked on, right after receiving his law degree, before joining the Navy, he had defended a young man who was accused of stealing a hen. My father was unsuccessful in his defense; the man was convicted and fined. Embarrassed and contrite, my father apologized to his client who nonchalantly answered him, "Don't worry, *señor abogado*, after all, I did steal the hen!" This was a story my father used to tell tongue-in-cheek, without dwelling on his failure but rather on the client's lack of respect for the law. Regardless of his intent, the story told a lot about his lawyerly abilities.

Havana

Barely six months after Batista's "reorganization," we moved from Santiago to Havana to a flat above a paint store in a commercial district. The patio of our Santiago home with its trees and its fountain disappeared from my life, and I found myself in a cramped space amid the bustling traffic of Havana.

In addition to his law degree, my father had teaching credentials from before joining the military and, with more hope than understanding, he decided to start his own elementary day school that doubled as an evening adult business school.

The display window on the façade of the paint supplies store at street level below my father's school showed a tilted can dropping red paint on the globe and a sign that read "Sherwin Williams covers the world." A narrow iron gate on one side of the display window opened into an equally narrow staircase that led to the upper floor where the school was located. In front of this gate a diamond-shaped white and green sign read *Colegio-Academia Oscar Espín.*

Whoever heard of a school located above a paint store in the middle of a commercial district? Just the street address and location advertised how little business sense my father had and forecast that his school was doomed to failure.

The flat on Calzada de Reina where my father's school was; we lived there in two back rooms for 10 years (2011)

Calzada de Reina—or *Simón Bolívar*, the official name of the street where my father launched his school—was a major thoroughfare in the center of Havana. The typical houses on this street were two-story buildings sharing walls with each other. Usually, family homes were on the top floor, businesses on the ground floor. Along Calzada de Reina, two-foot wide balconies with wrought iron balustrades perched on top of wide covered sidewalks. Colonnades and arches separated the sidewalks from the street. Buses, trucks, and cars went up and down incessantly tooting their horns. Trolleys clanged their bells, people talked loudly as they went by. Vendors peddled their goods on the shadowed sidewalks—fresh oyster shoots, fried foods, trinkets, lottery tickets. People walked hurriedly or waited for buses or trolleys at corners, protecting themselves from the sun or the rain under the arches.

Nery and I, around the time we moved to Havana

The school occupied the five front rooms of the rented upstairs flat and we—my parents, my sister Nery and I—shared the two bedrooms in the back. A room on the roof over the kitchen was occupied by two maids: the *manejadora* and Teresa. A small loft above the family bathroom, off a stamp-size inner courtyard, later became my aunt Marina's bedroom.

On the street level, next to the paint store, fabric and sewing notions were sold by a family of European Jews—Polish, I think—who were refugees from the war that was raging in Europe. Cuba had been a safe haven for Jews trying to escape Hitler's Europe, the shameful episode of the St. Louis notwithstanding. Some of them used it as springboard to the U.S. but others settled in Cuba permanently. My neighbors seemed to have chosen the second course. Long tables held bolts of material in multiple colors and prints. A shabbily dressed, teary woman and her equally shabby husband walked intermittently among them. Their two children, Reglita and Enriquito, played in the narrow spaces between tables. Their "cubanized" names probably reflected the sounds of their original Hebrew names or perhaps the Polish versions of those names. Reglita was about my age and spoke Spanish as well as any other Cuban child, but we never played together. In fact, in that hectic and scary neighborhood, I never played with other children.

Nery and I, 3-4 years old

The flat adjacent to ours, above the fabric store, was rented by a Cuban-Lebanese family whose son was in Europe fighting with the few hundred Cubans who had enlisted. The tower of a Jesuit church loomed several blocks up the street. This was the church of the Sacred Heart of Jesus, but everyone called it *la iglesia de Reina*—the church on Reina. The sound of its bells marked the passing of hours and could be heard above the din of truck, bus and car motors, horns, and vendors' shouts.

At night, when street noise subsided, there was something menacing about hearing alley cats on the surrounding roofs. Nery and I awoke crying in the middle of the night frightened by the incessant "¡Arrrauuu! ¡Arrraauuu!" of cats' cries. My mother came to our bedroom to calm us and said something like, "The cats are just calling Raúl, thinking that he is visiting from Santiago; can't you hear they are saying 'A Raúl, A Raúl'?" Eventually, we went back to sleep wanting to believe that the cats were calling one of her brothers. But her tale did not completely assuage our fears about the danger of cats that felt like one more menacing something in our loud and frantic Havana neighborhood.

I was frequently awakened by scary dreams. Mami had taught Nery and me some little prayers so we were not scared at night and went to sleep promptly. Whatever her opinion about religion, she probably thought it was a good idea to take the edge off our night fears by invoking heavenly protectors. So, every night before going to bed she helped us dutifully repeat these prayers:

> *Angel de la Guarda, dulce compañía,*
> *no me desampares ni de noche ni de día.*
> (Guardian Angel, sweet companion,
> do not forsake me day or night.)

> *Cuatro pilares tiene mi cama, cuatro angelitos que me*
> *acompañan,*
> *Juan, Lucas, Marcos y Mateo. Duérmete Oliva María y no*
> *tengas miedo.*
> (Four pillars has my bed, four little angels who keep
> me company,
> John, Luke, Mark and Matthew. Go to sleep Oliva
> María and don't be afraid.)

But the little prayers did not fully do the trick. I knew I needed to stay vigilant. Monsters could be lurking under our beds and scary dreams could happen unexpectedly. And when that happened, Mami would come to our room, looking rather drowsy and told us to ask Baby Jesus to make us sleep— *"Niñito Jesús, duérmeme."* I suppose she was eager to ask for Baby Jesus' help if that made it possible for her to go back to bed.

Our fear of cats never fully disappeared. Once, on an early Saturday morning, Nery and I saw a stray cat walking toward us from the balcony of the Lebanese family next door and ran terrified as fast as we could, stumbling over students' desks. Nery could get to the kitchen at the back of the flat. I fell among the toppled desks and screamed in terror until my mother came to rescue me from the fearsome beast that, by then, had probably darted away from the balcony scared by the commotion.

In those early years in Havana, when my parents believed that their difficult financial situation was only temporary, there was still a bit of money to pay for a *manejadora* who could relieve my mother from the constant care of her two daughters. Mami was still smiling, hoping for her husband's future success. And there was also Teresa, the maid who did the daily shopping, washed dishes after meals, and helped my mother with other chores. Mami was not yet thirty. Even though her household tasks had increased considerably, life was still full of possibilities. She played frequently with Nery and me. We often played the same game: both of us sitting on her lap, she pretended to bite us furiously while the three of us laughed out loud with delight. We felt her sweaty skin next to ours, her thin frame full of energy, her joy at playing with us, and our joy at being so close to her body. She seemed to glitter then when she was playful.

Nery and I with my mother

13

But gradually, her mood darkened, and she stopped playing with us. Her increasing housework load did not leave much time for play. The *manejadora* was dismissed because there was no money to pay even her small salary. The man who had come to clean the school classrooms daily was let go. Only Teresa was left. My mother picked up the slack.

She cooked meals on the coal stove in the kitchen. Gas stoves were not available. Electric ones were unheard of. Coal fires are labor intensive, dirty, and hot. A coal stove cannot be turned on and off as a gas or electric one can be. Tending the coals required constant attention so the fire was not extinguished. She started the fire early in the morning, a process that took a while, and kept it going all day until she smothered it at night before going to sleep.

No washing machines were available. All clothes had to be washed by hand, including sheets and towels. Washing clothes took the best part of two days each week. Teresa and my mother took turns scrubbing, rinsing, wringing and hanging clothes, sheets, and towels on the building roof to dry. Most laundry had to be ironed, which took one or two more days. Irons were not electrical either, they had to be heated on the stove and carefully cleaned so coal smudges did not stain the clothes. My father's shirts had to be ironed and starched; the starch was produced by hand on the stove. And on the same stove, my mother softened and cooked the splinters and chips of leftover soap to make more soap with which to wash clothes and linens while Teresa scouted for whatever limited food might be available in the nearby *bodegas*. These were the darkest days of World War II. Material goods were scarce and rationed.

Daily, Mami and Teresa swept the school rooms and the students' bathroom, washed the floor tiles, dusted the students' and teachers' desks and cleaned the blackboards with a wet rag to take away any traces of chalk. On Saturdays, they cleaned all the classrooms more in depth and they also cleaned our two bedrooms and bathroom—the only private space we had in that flat. There was no vacuum cleaner. Brooms, dustpans, and mops were the cleaning tools. I don't know if fancy household appliances and conveniences were available to wealthy families then in Cuba—or even in the U.S.—but, even if they were, we would not have been able to afford them.

My aunt Marina in the early 1940s

A few years later, when my aunt Marina came to live with us, she played with my baby brothers and helped Nery and me with our schoolwork while my mother cooked and took care of other housework. Marina and Teresa lightened my mother's load. But the responsibility of making sure the school rooms looked proper and all of us were clean and fed was my mother's.

Neither Nery nor I had any specific chores except caring for our baby brothers. Their births and Marina's move to Havana further reduced our space.

I spent my childhood surrounded by desks and blackboards. We ate lunch and dinner under pressure because our dining room had to be turned into a classroom for the afternoon and evening classes and back from classroom to dining room twice daily. My activities were limited by our cramped living quarters. I invented games that did not involve making noise or require physical space. We all learned to stay as quiet as possible behind closed doors so that my father's classes wouldn't be disrupted by our presence.

A tiny incident illustrates the difficulties of the limited and limiting space in which I spent my childhood. It was time to go to bed, but I urgently needed to go to the bathroom before putting my pajamas on. My mother was tired after another long day, and she was no doubt looking forward to putting Nery and me to bed, so she could rest for a while. She whispered a peremptory command, "Oliva María, come to your bedroom; time to go to sleep!" I quietly said, "I am coming…" and continued to do my business. I knew Mami's impatience would increase with each minute that passed. I knew that if I did not respond to her call I would be in trouble. After her third call, the menace in her voice was seriously scaring me. I saw no alternative but to respond to her in as low a voice as I could manage, "¡Estoy haciendo caca!" My pronouncement was followed by roaring laughter from the adult evening students and their teachers who could not help hearing me in those close quarters. I was embarrassed, red-faced, on the verge of tears. Mami came swiftly into the bathroom and shook me, "What do you think you are doing?" Her whispered fury now multiplied exponentially because she, too, was embarrassed and the easiest outlet for the awkwardness was to scold me for making her uncomfortable. Now, this little episode seems hilarious but then it felt scary and dramatic.

"Mi mamá me ama..."

Apparently, I learned so well to entertain myself quietly and alone in that restricted space that my parents became concerned. I would sit for hours looking at picture books or playing with paper dolls, dressing and undressing them in their printed clothes, while mumbling their imaginary dialogue. After some failed attempts at making me play with other children, my mother took me to a pediatrician to consult him about my worrisome isolation. Perhaps he could find a way of making me more sociable.

On a mid-August afternoon, when I was about four years old, after the daily torrential rains had passed as quickly as they had come, Mami and I took a trolley to El Vedado, the nice neighborhood where the pediatrician's office was located. He lived in a stucco one-story house with his office on the side. Doctor Tres Palacios wore a striped suit and a dark blue tie; his straight dark hair, graying at the temples, was parted carefully on the left side. Doctor Tres Palacios listened to my mother's concerns and then, he turned to me. He had a thin moustache, and his hazel eyes twinkled gently when he looked at me. With a wide, kind smile he started asking questions that I thought were rather silly for such a big man.

"What games do you like?"

Games? What did he mean by games? Were the stories I constructed in my mind a game? I didn't think so. This was not the answer to his question. I shrugged and sat further back in the big chair that a moment earlier had made me feel like a grown-up person, my feet dangling in the air in front of me.

"Do you have friends no one else could see?"

Now, that was a strange question! No, I didn't. What business was that of his, anyway? Rather than answer his questions, I remained silent and pondered his strange name, *Why is he called Doctor Tres Palacios? Does he own three palaces? If he does, why does he live in this house?*

After some more conversation with Mami, Doctor Tres Palacios sent me home with some tonic; I had to take a spoonful each morning at breakfast. *What was this mysterious tonic that was supposed to make me want to play with other children? Why did I have to play with other children? What other children, anyway? I did play with Nery and with my cousins... a bit.* Did the tonic make any difference? I am not sure. Perhaps I became slightly more active and more talkative, but I continued to feel most content playing by myself.

Fantasies derived from my reading fed my good and bad dreams. Reading was my favorite pastime even before I started first grade.

My mother, in one of the few moments she was relaxed, had taught me to read one rainy afternoon when I was not yet five years old.

My father's elementary school students had left for the day. The adult evening students would not arrive for a few more hours. Mami sat on a teacher's chair in one of the classrooms, placed a little booklet called a *cartilla* on the desk facing her, and asked me, "Do you want to learn to read?"

I nodded, not quite sure what the task would entail. I stood next to her chair while Mami read the letters of the alphabet from the *cartilla*.

"A" she said, pointing to the first letter.

"A," I repeated, looking at the two shapes of the letter: A, a.

"Be" she went on, pointing at the second letter.

"Be," I said, my little finger next to hers, pointing to B and b.

After we went through the names and sounds of all the letters, she started pointing at the letter combinations provided by the *cartilla* while making the sounds that corresponded to those combinations,

"*Eme* A: Ma; *Eme* E: Me. *Eme* I: Mi" After a few tries, I could read the first full sentence included in the *cartilla*: "Mi mamá me ama." I was startled and excited.

"¡Mi mamá me ama!" I screamed with delight, "It says, MI MAMA ME AMA!!!! I can read! I CAN READ!"

Mami smiled. "Yes, it says 'mi mamá me ama.' Now, let's go to the next page."

In a few more hours I had read all fifteen pages of the *cartilla*. My excitement mounted with every page as the previously mysterious squiggles started acquiring meaning in front of my eyes. Later that afternoon, right before dinner, I demonstrated my newly acquired skill for my father. From the corner of my eye, I could see my parents exchanging meaningful looks. Not quite sure what their expressions meant, I knew enough to know that I had just done something they really found enchanting.

As I became comfortable with the written word, I read anything I could get my hands and eyes on. Children's books, fairy tales, lives of saints. I created fantasies around the stories I read. Forests, palaces, and beautiful dresses materialized in my imagination. Challenging adventures emerged and transformed into long hours of daydreaming. My uncle, my aunts, and my father started giving me books as presents.

At first, I read what they gave me. Later, I started asking for specific books I wanted to read. I devoured those books and sank into them during vacations and weekends, getting up from my chair only to go to the bathroom or when I was called for lunch or dinner. I read and read. Madame de Ségur's *Las Niñas Modelo*—a story of two French sisters, Camille and Madeleine, their close friend Marguerite, and their cousin Sophie. Fairy tales with beautiful heroines who had fairy godmothers. Stories of saints, Robin Hood, The Three Musketeers, and other historical tales enthralled me. Once, when I was about ten, I read all of *Uncle Tom's Cabin* on the same day I received it as a gift from my uncle. The gratification I got from reading, daydreaming, and fantasizing, compensated for the lack of physical space or friendships with other children.

Mami y Papi

As the years progressed, my mother became more impatient and angry; the corners of her mouth perpetually turned down. She was then in her early thirties, struggling with a life of penury and drudgery she had not anticipated. She was always busy, always annoyed, always scolding. Her company was not pleasant; instead of speaking or asking, she complained or commanded.

"Pick up the book you left on that chair!"

"Your brother is crying! Stop reading and go play with him!"

"Set the table. Move. Don't do it so slowly! We have to rush!"

"Comb your hair! It looks like a rat's nest!"

And then, there were her eyes, which commanded without a word. If she looked at you in a certain way, you knew you would get in serious trouble if you did not do what you were supposed to.

"Housework makes you stupid!" she repeated frequently—her rebellion against her daily duties. Since I do not like housework much myself, I can now empathize with her irritation, but when I was a child, her relentless misery and bad mood made me dislike her.

But, even with her constant frown, she was a beautiful woman. Her thin body, chestnut hair, expressive brown eyes and almost transparent freckled skin, all contributed to her elegant demeanor.

My mother in her early 30s

Papi's gentle disposition and easy smile contrasted vividly with my mother's impatience. Because his work at the school was a few feet away, when he took breaks, he walked to the back of the apartment, into the kitchen or wherever my mother was, and they exchanged little kisses and gestures that only the two of them understood. And no matter how upset or overwhelmed or sweaty from standing at the hot coal stove she may have been a few minutes before, the moment he walked in she focused on him as a flower turns toward the sun. He touched her disheveled hair, put the loose strands behind her ears, smiled at her. I yearned for the attention he got from her, for that loving woman he could find inside my angry mother. How did he manage so easily to make her look lovingly at him? My mother, who was always demanding and exasperated, who made no bones about how the children added work to her days and little pleasure to her life, focused on my father's needs and desires easily. This father I so loved absorbed all her positive emotional energy because he made her feel loved and special. Seeing the effect he had on her, and lacking any other form of understanding, I concluded that he was, indeed, the sun.

We all loved Papi. He celebrated our successes in school, attended to our personal little troubles and triumphs, found books for me. He looked at us playfully, with a mischievous twinkle in his eyes. Whenever my siblings or I were ill with something—a cold or a feverish reaction to some vaccine—he sat by our beds for hours telling stories that provided distraction from whatever was ailing us. In my mind's eye, I can still see the shaft of bright sunlight that came through the bedroom door, revealing specks of dust that did not seem to exist except inside that beam of light, while I listened to my father's stories or his little rhymes or songs. He was loving, tender, caring, charming. He "mothered" us to perfection while my mother complained that by getting sick, we were increasing her load.

Except for him, no one could do anything right in my mother's eyes. But, whatever he did or said enchanted her. Her voice softened when she talked to him. He, in turn, seemed oblivious to her grouchiness and nagging. Perhaps because it was never directed at him. His loving kindness obviously made an impact on my mother when they met; I am sure he represented a big contrast to her own mother's harshness.

My mother's mother, Fefita, was proud of her cruelty to her own children. As Fefita described it, relishing every detail, she made a circle every morning in the middle of the living room with all the chairs in the household and ordered her children—their ages ranging from twelve years to a few months—inside this circle. They were to stay in the enclosure as she went about her household tasks. She carried a leather strap around her neck and shoulders. Should any of the children venture outside of the circle of chairs before she allowed them to do so, she belted them back inside, until finally none of them dared risk the punishment. At the end of the day she gave them permission to move out of the makeshift enclosure and marched them to bed. If any of the children disobeyed her orders in any other way, she belted them. Even as a child, listening to Abuela Fefita's idea of what constituted effective ways of disciplining children, I understood, in an imprecise way, that my mother's habit of constantly finding fault with her children's behavior was, in fact, a vast improvement on her mother.

More or less dimly, I was aware that my mother would gladly have performed her daily tasks just to please my father had there not been any children. This, of course, remained unsaid. All I felt was that her reactions to him were diametrically opposed to her reactions to us.

I suppose she would have been happy enough with just Nery and me. But my father wanted boys. He did not impose his will; he never did. Most probably he just asked. And she could never say no to him. I think my two brothers, Orlando and Mario, born in 1947 and 1950, respectively, were her gift to my father. I didn't have real awareness of these adult issues then, but I remember overhearing her say to someone, "I could have stopped after the two girls, but Oscar wanted boys."

Four children did not constitute a large family then. I don't know what sort of birth control was available. But they clearly used something between us girls and the two boys who were born considerably later when Nery and I were already attending elementary school. Perhaps they used the Church approved "rhythm method," perhaps my mother took it upon herself to use something else. After the boys were born—Orlando when I was eight years old, Mario when I was almost twelve—it became even more evident that children were a burden, not a source of enjoyment for her. But, despite her bad temper, she dutifully fulfilled her motherly duties. Orlandito was often sick or getting himself into accidents. She took him to doctors and spent days in the hospital with him. She always took care of us, made sure our clothes and school uniforms were clean and well-ironed and our shoes shiny. Food was always at the table on time.

Did she ever resent her husband for his failure to provide the economic comforts she had been used to at her parents' home? I don't think so. As an adult, I came to understand why she was so attached to a man who generously gave her his deep love, even though he couldn't give her the financial security she had expected. Marrying my father, she was fulfilling her dream of increasing her social status from daughter of a self-made rich immigrant to wife of a professional man from a patrician family. But her actual life had turned out to be smaller than her dreams. However, he made her feel cherished in ways she had never been. This awkward and shy man loved her with a tenderness no one had ever shown her before. She was the queen of his heart. Financial troubles were tolerable, in exchange for his unwavering deep love. And, in turn, my father seemed to marvel that this beautiful woman accepted his weaknesses and respected him despite his ineffectiveness. Grateful for her love, he constantly found little ways of showing his devotion to her. She had a difficult temper, but he knew she loved him like she loved no one else. She was as strong and energetic as he was insecure and apprehensive. Were it not for her constant encouragement, my father would have collapsed. He needed her reassurance of his worth despite his inability to be a successful breadwinner. Sustaining his self-esteem, she felt valued.

Furthermore, they both understood our tight financial circumstances as something beyond their control. She knew the penury that burdened her with the housework tasks she hated and "made her stupid" was the product of Cuba's political upheavals and economic situation. Most Cubans lived in financially precarious conditions. Cuban incomes fluctuated with the world market for sugar. But profiting from increased sugar prices was limited to those at the top. The bleak and unstable environment was a reality in the lives of many Cubans even as the Cuban economy emerged and flourished at the end of the war and the political instability lessened in the 1940s.

My parents were young then, battered by events they didn't have power over, confronting those events with their idiosyncratic strengths and weaknesses. Had the political and economic conditions been different, they were sure they would not have been trapped in these circumstances. My mother knew my father was as much a victim as she was. He was not to blame. He just had bad luck, as she was fond of saying. Had the roles been reversed, she might have succeeded as a provider. But in that cultural context at that time, that was not a choice. It was completely out of the question that my mother would work outside the home. She had an eighth-grade education, and her skills at cooking, embroidering and lace-making were not marketable. No brief training could have provided her with a decent job. My father's already diminished prestige could not be tainted any further. Middle class women did not seek employment, unless they were professionals with a university degree or wanted to advertise that they were poor.

When my aunt Marina began working as a clinic administrator in Havana, my grandmother Fefita forbade Nery and me to mention it to anyone in Santiago lest someone assume that the family had lost its money, why else would Marina take a job?

There was only one disagreement between my parents: my mother's refusal to go to church. She had learned from her parents to despise priests, the Church, and anything connected to religion. Despite her love for my very Catholic father, her hostility toward religion did not abate.

One day when I was in first grade, she was braiding my hair while I was repeating some prayers I needed to memorize for school, "… *a mi me pesa de todo corazón haberos ofendido…*" – "I regret with all my heart that I have offended Thee…" a somewhat complicated wording for a seven-year-old. She corrected something I had said wrong. My father looked up quickly from whatever he was doing and smiled at her with a somewhat puzzled look. She smiled back, "I do remember those words, you know," she said softly, "I'm just not interested in them…" They gave each other one of their loving looks. My mother kept braiding my hair while I finished learning the prayer. I pondered what had just gone on between them. I think this was the first time I became consciously aware of what was a given: my father went alone to church on Sundays and sometimes on weekdays while my mother stayed home.

This was rather unusual. Cuban men did not go to church much unless there was a wedding or a funeral or the First Communion of one of their children. And, on those occasions, they definitely did not go to communion. My father had been raised without religion by my atheistic grandfather with no apparent objection from my grandmother. But after my grandfather's death, when my father was already an adolescent, Abuela Boqui sent her children to Catholic schools for the first time. There, the Jesuits taught my father to believe in God, and religion became central in his life.

My mother's negative response to church and religion had no importance in the Cuban social context. Cuba was never a very religious country, even though most Cubans were nominally Catholic. Many people didn't go to church; no one paid attention to others' Church attendance. Their disagreement about religion did not seem to matter much for my parents. Perhaps this was the best measure of how much they loved each other, because my church-going father tacitly accepted my mother's refusal to attend Mass on Sunday.

El Salón de los Pasos Perdidos/
The Hall of the Lost Footsteps

Thanks to my father, music and history surrounded my childhood.

Cuba was then, and still is, a music paradise. From the days of the Spanish colony to its role in world politics in the twentieth century, Cuba has also been at the heart of historical events. It was in Cuba that Spain finally lost what for centuries had been a vast empire. It was Cuba, before and after Castro's Revolution that challenged the U.S. hegemony over Latin America.

Papi loved Cuba and he loved music and his love for both was contagious.

He had grown up surrounded by music. Piano playing and *bel canto* singing were a common pastime when we visited my grandmother Abuela Boqui at her house in the Havana suburb of Almendares on Sunday. Papi and his siblings all played the piano. His sister Loly had a beautiful voice. I remember her singing in languages I did not understand. She also sang Cuban operettas such as Gonzalo Roig's "Cecilia Valdés." I can still "hear" her singing the opening song of the title character, *"Cecilia Valdés me llaman, me enamora un bachiller..."*

Despite our limited financial resources, my father bought an upright piano, hoping that Nery and I would learn to play, but neither of us showed the slightest inclination to do so. He had to be satisfied with playing it himself, which he did frequently. While he played, we sat around him on chairs or on the floor. He played Chopin nocturnes and polonaises, Strauss waltzes, and the music of Cuban composers Ernesto Lecuona, Eduardo Sánchez de Fuentes, José White, Ignacio Cervantes, Gonzalo Roig.

As much as he loved playing, Papi was conscious that he was no concert pianist, and he appreciated when he could hear others play. While his siblings attended concerts regularly, Papi had to be contented with listening to music on the radio because he had no money to pay for tickets to live performances.

I listened to the music on the radio programs he enjoyed from my dark and silent bedroom, when I should have been sleeping. Intrigued by what I heard, without acknowledging what had awakened my curiosity, the next day I would ask him "What is this or that music called? Who is so and so?" One weekend evening, after he finished listening to an opera on the radio, I asked, "Who was singing?"

"Enrico Caruso," he answered.

"Why does he sing in English?"

With an amused smile, Papi told me it was not English but Italian. I was puzzled. *Italian? What is Italian? Why Italian or English or whatever, instead of Spanish?* I also concluded right then that my father must be terribly smart to know what Italian was and to understand Caruso's singing. Eventually, in my teens, I sang while he played traditional Italian songs such as *"Torna a Sorrento," "O Sole mio"* or *"Santa Lucia,"* even though I still did not understand the meaning of the Italian words.

On Saturday mornings, while Teresa, my mother, and my aunt Marina cleaned the school rooms and the rest of our flat, Papi took Nery and me through Havana's neighborhoods and parks. The three of us walked for hours on the streets of Old Havana, ostensibly accompanying Papi while he ran errands.

It was great to be away from my crying baby brothers and from demands to do this or that to help Mami, Marina, or Teresa. Unlike Nery, I had no inclination to domesticity and thought babies were a nuisance. I was happy to be out with Papi who was such a great storyteller and who was never grouchy like Mami.

La India

Our Saturday excursions took us frequently to *Parque de la Fraternidad* and to a traffic island next to it dominated by *La India*, an imposing marble statue of a stern woman sitting on a throne surrounded by four dolphins spewing water. Walking around it, I asked questions about the statue, the cornucopia of Cuban fruit in her hand, the leaves in her crown. *La India* had been sculpted in 1837, more than a century before I was born. She represents the indigenous women of Latin America, none of whom survived in Cuba, decimated by the conquering Spaniards through disease, slavery, and despair-induced suicides.

Most Saturdays, after looking at La India, we would walk over to the Parque Central. "The statue in the center is of José Martí, the hero of Cuban independence. Before independence, the statue on this pedestal was of Queen Isabel II of Spain," Papi would repeat, even though we already knew that because he had told us many times before.

Statue of Jose Marti in Central Park, Havana

As we walked, Papi named the cobblestoned, narrow streets and the wide paved ones, "This is calle Obispo, this is calle O'Reilly..." and pointed out features of the colonial structures of the Old City, "This is the place of the Spanish Governors, this is the palace of the Aldama family...". He urged us to look at the façades of buildings and their decorative statues and cornices. The imposing eighteenth century palaces that had been previously owned by the richest Cuban families were now public buildings. They had central patios where wide leaves and intricate climbing vines encircled the perimeter; green grew in every stone interstice.

At the Palace of the Spanish Colonial Governors, Havana 2011

One of the many colonial buildings I visited with my father in Old Havana

Havana Cathedral

Sometimes the Saturday walks took us to Havana's cathedral, a building considered the best exemplar of "Cuban baroque," a unique architectural style developed in the island during the eighteenth century. The elaborate façade is covered with columns, niches, and convoluted details, and flanked by towers. The buildings surrounding the cathedral contribute to the elegance of its small square. Every time I see a photograph of Havana's cathedral, I can hear my father's voice describing its architectural features.

In the late twentieth century, Old Havana was declared Patrimony of Humanity by UNESCO because of the beauty of the colonial architecture that witnesses to Cuba's prominent role among the Spanish colonies. No matter how many times we saw them or how many explanations Papi had already given about the buildings, streets, statues, and parks, there were always new details to discover.

I was a little machine spewing questions; our Saturday excursions gave me an opportunity to exercise my endless curiosity. Papi always made a point of letting me know that he thought my questions were intelligent. "Who made this?" "What is it made of?" "Who put it there?" "How long has it been here?" On and on... I only kept silent while twirling my tongue around an ice cream cone, usually mango, my favorite flavor.

Every so often we went to the Sears building in Old Havana that boasted an *escalera rodante*, the only escalator in all of Cuba. I could not stop looking at it in amazement and asked Papi, "How does it move?" "Who makes it move?" "Why doesn't it stop?" Every visit to Sears involved several trips up and down the magical contraption for Nery and me while my father waited patiently at the bottom, smiling and reminding us to hold the handrail when we got too excited and started jumping in place on one of the steps while descending toward him.

My father's blue eyes, behind rimless glasses on which a faint light might flicker, his dark wavy hair and white *guayabera* shirt made me think he was very good-looking, although in reality, he was rather plain. He had a stocky build, was not tall, and had a slight "nerdy" look about him. As self-assured as he was about details in Cuban history or about musical compositions, he seemed to be painfully uncertain about himself, aware of his own inadequacies. He was not like other girls' fathers or like other Cuban men I knew. He didn't go out drinking; he was not interested in sports; he did not look lasciviously at women or make comments to them as they went by. When he graduated from the University of Havana, his classmates had teased him, writing on the yearbook that he was ambitious about accumulating degrees, but also kind, reserved, and taciturn. All that was still true during my childhood: still studious and intellectual, still quiet, still preoccupied with the needs of others. And still insecure.

While we walked around, Papi told us what seemed like fantastic stories about his father's family, "They left Cuba when your Abuelo José Manuel was three years old. His family settled in Jamaica and, eventually, he studied medicine in the U.S." It was surprising to find out that even though Abuelo José Manuel grew up speaking Spanish at home, he was always more fluent in English since he had been immersed in it most of his life.

Abuela Boqui and
Abuelo José Manuel
New York, 1896

José Manuel, who had just graduated from medical school, met his fifteen-year-old cousin María Luisa in New York while she was at the Sacred Heart boarding school for girls and fell in love with her. My grandmother's parents had sent her and her brother Ramón to boarding school in New York, away from the war for independence from Spain roaring in Cuba. But her brother, who was seventeen years old, had run away from his school and returned to Cuba surreptitiously to join the forces fighting against Spain. Young María Luisa felt alone in New York. Her cousin's visits became her consolation and, eventually, a year later, she left school to marry him. Their wedding certificate from St. Francis Xavier church in New York, dated 1896, contains a note saying they had received a special dispensation to marry because they were first cousins.

Papi continued, telling us about his parents return to Cuba in 1898 during the American occupation. Abuelo José Manuel worked in public health. He was actively involved in the campaign to eradicate dangerous mosquitoes.

Before we studied it in school, I had learned from Papi that Carlos Finlay, a Cuban doctor, had postulated for years that mosquito bites transmitted yellow fever and varieties of malaria. But the Spanish government was not about to pay attention to the theories of some Cuban. During the U.S. occupation, Finlay's theory was tested and confirmed. The discovery in Cuba that mosquitoes were the agents of transmission of yellow fever made possible the construction of the Panama Canal. When the American occupation ended in May 1902, Abuelo José Manuel continued working for the newly established Cuban Ministry of Health. In 1904 he went to Baltimore to specialize in tropical medicine at Johns Hopkins. Upon returning to Cuba a year later, he focused his writings and work on the eradication of mosquito-borne diseases. One of the articles he wrote at the time includes a funny caricature of a mosquito drawn by Abuelo. In it he argues that Cuba is in "danger of losing its independence to a mosquito" because unless the murderous insects are eradicated, Cuba was in constant peril of American intervention under pretext of health concerns.

Ironically, Abuelo José Manuel died of *paludismo*, another deadly fever produced by mosquito bites, in 1919, when my father was twelve. My father, who was afflicted with *paludismo* at the same time, survived the illness. When he recovered consciousness after the high fever, his father was dead.

My grandmother María Luisa—Abuela Boqui—was thirty-six when he died. A young widow with six children, she was completely disoriented and unprepared to make practical decisions. Papi always added at this point in the story that the experience of his mother had convinced him that his daughters should have decision-making skills and be self-reliant rather than depend on husbands or male relatives to solve their problems. I know his comments about his mother's helplessness made me think I didn't want to be like that.

El Capitolio, Havana

Our Saturday walks took us to the *Capitolio Nacional*, an imposing building that in its design and name recalls the United States Capitol. My school bus drove in front of the *Capitolio* every day. From the school bus windows, I looked at its cupola, at the stone steps that led to the entrance and at the large bronze statues that flanked the portico on either side. But, used to seeing it every day, I didn't think there was anything extraordinary about this building.

The first time Papi took us there, as we walked down the narrow staircase that led from our flat to the street, he told us, "Today we are going to see something very special. It will be a surprise." Although I asked many times what the surprise was as we walked toward the center of Old Havana, my father simply smiled playfully and said, "You will see when we get there."

The tall *escalinata*, steep steps of limestone and granite leading to the main entrance, was a challenge for the short legs of eight- and nine-year-olds to mount. Nery and I made ourselves dizzy looking up constantly as we ascended. By then, Nery was already several inches taller than me, so she was slightly faster. The *escalinata* led up to the central portico. Beyond the portico, three large bronze doors with bas-reliefs allowed access to the largest room I had ever seen. We entered the huge hall slowly, almost reverently. The immensity of the place dwarfed adults and children alike. As we walked in, almost whispering, my father said, "This is *El Salón de los Pasos Perdidos*—The Hall of the Lost Footsteps." Entranced by the marble-laden floors and the magnificence of the vast space that did not look like anything I had ever seen, I whispered, "Whose footsteps? Why are they lost?" My father answered also in a low voice, "Because the vastness of the space makes it impossible to hear the steps or the voices of people as they walk the length of it." I noticed then that although others were walking and talking at both ends of the Hall I could not hear footsteps or words. The room was almost silent.

Continuing in a soft voice, Papi launched into one of his usual explanations. "*El Capitolio* was inaugurated on 20 May 1929, by President Gerardo Machado the day I turned twenty-two." Even then I knew that Machado was a very bad President who had built important things but had also killed many people. The Capitolio and the Central Highway—*la Carretera Central*—that linked the main cities in the island were Machado's most cherished projects.

Nery and I knew that my father had been born on May twentieth on the fifth anniversary of Cuba's independence from Spain and from U.S. occupation. He had told us many times that as a child he thought the flags were out all over Havana on that day because it was his birthday, which made us giggle and tease him about how silly he was, since we were old enough to know that flags were flown for national holidays not for any person's birthday.

Cuban flag

"This is the tallest building in Havana," my father's sentence trailed off. In front of me was a gigantic woman, *la Estatua de la República* — the Statue of the Republic, covered in gold. I craned my neck to look at her face. The *República*, dominated the inside of the main hall under the cupola. She looked like a Greek goddess in a book I had recently read.

To the left and right of the *República, el Salón de los Pasos Perdidos* extended in what seemed like an endless expanse. Bronze lamps ran along the walls. Despite the bright sun outside, the light in the Hall was subdued, apparently to match the solemn atmosphere of the place. And then Papi pointed down to the floor in front of the statue. Embedded in the floor in the center of the hall was a diamond, surrounded by a symmetrical marble design. To me, the diamond looked like an irregular transparent lemon.

I was sure that the Hall of the Lost Footsteps, with its inlaid marble floors and gilded lamps, the statue of the Republic and the diamond, was the most beautiful place I had seen. Nery and I held hands and turned in circles, looking in all directions. Wearing our matching outfits, we looked like twins, the same astonished look on our faces.

Those Saturday morning excursions among the buildings, tree-lined streets, and parks of Havana retained their thrill for some years. They competed with the adventures of Tarzan and the stories of saints I read. As I was learning about history and music and family stories, I was also learning who my father was and what he could have been. Summers took Nery and me to the freedom of my grandparents' big house in Santiago, but during the school year going up and down the escalator at Sears, or looking at *La India*, or the Cathedral, or the Capitolio, asking my endless questions, were my best pastime.

In 1984, on the second week of my first return visit to Cuba I took a bus from my hotel in El Vedado to the Capitol building in the center of Havana. I was going to the Capitolio to hand the unknown Cuban scientist the receipt for the bats' manuscript that had been confiscated by the authorities at the airport when I arrived. I was mildly irritated that the zoologist had not had the courtesy to come to my hotel to pick up his piece of paper—after all, I was doing him a favor.

The Capitolio became home to the Cuban Academy of Sciences and the headquarters of the Ministry of Science in the 1960s, after Congress was dissolved. It had served as the seat of the Cuban legislature until the beginning of the Revolution in 1959. In the intervening years, I had learned that the National Capitol of Cuba is considered one of the six most important palatial buildings in the world. Its 300 feet high Italian Renaissance cupola is one of the highest of this style, and *la República* is the world's third largest indoor statue. At least, I thought during the bus ride, it would be nice to look at the building up close. The Capitolio was closed to the public; no visitors were allowed.

The young scientist met me at the back of the Capitolio by the door he had directed me to when we spoke on the phone. When I arrived on that breezy November afternoon, he took the receipt from me and said, "Let's go this way." I vaguely remember we took an elevator. The next memory I have is of finding myself at one end of *El Salón de los Pasos Perdidos*! Stunned, I started to deliberately walk the length of the magnificent Hall I still remembered from my childhood. Taking pleasure in the marble designs on the floor, appreciating the bronze lamps, enjoying the quiet serenity of the empty Hall and the soft light of dusk that came through the windows, I took it all in and prolonged the moment as much as I could. The zoologist walked a few paces ahead of me, glancing back and smiling softly. He was aware of how moved I was. I was thankful that he did not disturb our unhurried amble and my reveries by saying anything. I stopped for a few minutes in front of the statue of the Republic, looked down at the diamond on the floor, and continued walking slowly to the other end of the Hall. The visit of long ago was alive and present as was my father's voice, even though he had been dead for ten years.

When we had walked the length of the Hall, my host said gently, "I figured you would want the opportunity to see the Salon." I looked at him, still with tears in my eyes and simply said, "Thank you," touched that he would express his gratitude in such a sensitive way. I was slightly embarrassed that I had thought he should have come to my hotel to pick up the receipt and felt deeply appreciative that he had chosen to give me this intangible gift.

We shook hands as he let me out of the building and I stepped into the bright Havana streets, still in tears. I was grateful to have had *el Salón de los Pasos Perdidos* all to myself for those few minutes. It felt as if my steps were not all lost; they belonged there in that building, in that land of my birth regardless of how many years I had been away and how many steps I had taken in other places.

Teresa/*"Ocho Años"*

Another adult was important for me in my early years. Teresa was an important part of my Havana childhood. She had started working as a maid in my maternal grandparents' house in Santiago when she was fifteen and my mother was eleven. Fifteen years later, soon after my parents' marriage, Teresa moved in and later moved with us to Havana from Santiago. For most of her life, she knew no other family, and for most of my childhood, I did not know life without Teresa.

Having a maid living at home was not the exclusive prerogative of the privileged. Despite our limited economic means, it was not unusual that someone like Teresa would be there. Her salary was meager; room and board were part of her payment.

Every evening after dinner, I went to the kitchen in the back of our flat, to sit with Teresa. I wanted to hear her tell what she had done that day. Mostly, she had waited in line at different stores looking for this or that. In the years of World War II and immediately after, food, soap, and other basics were hard to come by in Havana. Her shopping took long hours because of the scarcity and our limited budget.

While my mother stayed home tending the coals, cooking our meals, and performing other household chores, Teresa stood in line in several of the small grocery stores in the area to get rice, beans, cans of condensed milk, perhaps potatoes or plantains, and, if she was lucky, some thin beef. Pork and chicken were unaffordable luxuries, even if she found them in a store.

As soon as I started to read, even before I went to school, I made it my mission to teach Teresa my newly acquired skills. Although illiterate, she had managed to survive fairly well. She could recognize some words, particularly when they were brand names on store bulletin boards or signs, but she could not even write her name. She saw no point in learning to decipher squiggles and even less point in trying to produce them herself. Still, she humored me.

On a typical evening, I'd trace some letters on a notebook and ask her to copy them in her own handwriting. "Look, Teresa, this says *leche*, this is how you write *carne*, and this is *carbón*." I thought these everyday words would be easy for her to copy and learn. Every evening she did her best to copy what I assigned her to do. She held the pencil very intently as she applied it to the page trying to reproduce my models, but after several unsuccessful attempts she gave up. Whenever she forgot a letter yet one more time, she laughed her bell-like, sonorous laughter, showing her big, white teeth and pink gums. I was not sure why my wonderful Teresa had so much difficulty seeing the letters and reproducing them; the kitchen lighting was good enough. And, in any case, she used every opportunity to distract me from my teaching pursuits by telling me stories about her day. Whatever she invented to make me laugh made me forget easily what I wanted to teach her.

"Hey, look!" she would say imitating the crooked face of the shopkeeper at the corner of Campanario Street, "He is this thin," she finished, pointing up with the little finger of her left hand. Her apt imitation drew peals of laughter from me; she really looked like the shopkeeper when she made those faces! At other times she demonstrated for me her efforts to be the first in line by play-acting how to skip ahead, fooling unwary people standing in the same line. Frequently, she made me play the role of the person in front of her, distracting me with conversation while moving ahead without being noticed. She role-played her behavior and made me play with her until I got the knack of it. And, eventually, both of us were laughing out loud at her success advancing in the line.

I don't know if she was embarrassed by her repeated failures to read and write but I think she understood my childish efforts at teaching her as a demonstration of love. I don't know if Teresa ever learned anything from me, but from her, without being fully cognizant of this, I learned to respect people who are "street smart" even if they are not "book smart."

Teresa nicknamed me *"Ocho Años,"* — "Eight Years"—when I was four or so, because of all the self-important little ways in which I spoke and how "know-it-all" I acted despite my tiny size. With all her imitations and jokes, she encouraged me to be less serious and more playful. She perceived that I was too grown up for my years and she probably saw my loneliness even though I was not aware of it.

My daily visits to Teresa's kitchen before bedtime provided some needed distraction from the physical constraints of our quarters. Although Teresa stayed out of my battles with food that developed later at the family table, when I visited her in the evenings, she frequently said with a serious expression, but pretending to just tease me, "You need to grow your body, not just your brain." A little girl had to eat to be healthy. Repeatedly, she would tell me she had stood in line for three hours to get these thin sheets of beef or whatever, so I had better eat my share no matter how much I hated it.

Teresa was in her late thirties then. But despite her lack of education and mental shortcomings, my mother, indeed my whole family, would not have been able to survive those challenging times without her. My father, who never really understood how important she was to all of us, fired Teresa one day for I don't know what reason. I know she had doused one of her legs with alcohol after it was burned with hot cooking oil, making the burn even worse. Perhaps Papi was afraid that she could do something similar to some of the children because of her limited mental capacity. I don't know if my mother protested but, whatever the case may have been, Teresa was gone. By then, I was already in school and had long ago given up my efforts to "cure" Teresa's illiteracy. Nonetheless, her absence left a hole.

There were other maids after her but there was never anyone like her. The best proof of her incomparability was how little time those others lasted.

One of the "maids" who came after Teresa was Luis, a young man from a rural area who wept loudly every night in his room repeating incessantly, *"¡Mi pueblo! ¡Mi pueblo!"* – "My village! My village!" Several others— Dora, Catalina, Adelfa—came recommended by nuns who specialized in protecting girls from rural areas who were in the city looking for domestic work by placing them with "good" families. Bella came also from a rural area. Her family was Seventh Day Adventist and every so often her father or one of her brothers came to check up on her to make sure she was not seeing any man who was not part of "the mission." Despite their vigilance, she managed to see as many men as she could whenever she had free time from her job with us. Guillermina, a thin, nervous, middle-aged woman, yelled at my mother about something having to do with a broom and was quickly fired.

All of them were white. It was not until years after Teresa when Luisa, another Black maid, came. She left of her own volition because she had fallen in love with a handsome stevedore. Angela, a quiet, cinnamon-colored young woman, was my favorite among the other maids who worked for my family, but none could ever truly compete with Teresa for my affection. In between them, there were long stretches of time when not even a maid's meager salary was affordable, and my mother and Marina did all the house work, including cleaning the school rooms.

Through the years, after Teresa was no longer working for us, when one or another of my mother's sisters came to Havana from Santiago, we always went to visit her wherever she was working as a maid. And when she saw me, she hugged me and laughed and still called me "Ocho Años" even though I was already older than eight.

When I returned to Cuba in the 1980s, going to see Teresa was at the top of my agenda. We had not said goodbye to her when we left Cuba because her niece's husband was in the revolutionary militia and we were afraid that any indiscretion on her part could have endangered our departure. She was now living with this niece and the husband. I got the niece's phone number from Lilia, my mother's cousin, and I invited myself to come for a visit.

As I came in, across the room from the front door I could see Teresa sitting in the balcony on a flimsy rocking chair, looking toward the street below. I got closer to where she was sitting and realized she was mumbling the names of my mother and my aunts as if having a conversation with them. By then some form of dementia had taken away the brain cells that made her a clever person, capable of getting the scarce cans of condensed milk, the few plantains or bars of soap available or the last bag of cooking coal before anyone else on the line during the war shortages. However, she still remembered my mother, my aunts, my grandmother Fefita… the women who had been the only family she ever truly knew and loved.

But she did not remember or recognize me. It was impossible for her to see "Ocho Años," the little girl who had tried to teach her to read and write, in the middle-aged woman standing in front of her and saying her name. She looked at me blankly. I do not physically resemble my mother or any of her sisters. Therefore, I was not a member of her family. For this eighty-year-old Teresa, I, as an adult, did not exist.

Tarzan on Saturdays
Trolleys on Sundays

On Saturday afternoons, after the walks with Papi loaded with his informal history lessons, Mami got us ready for a different kind of fun: a visit to her aunt, Tía Matilde.

These visits were Mami's chance to get out of her everyday house-wife's garb and dress in nice clothes. She wore short-sleeved blouses and flowing skirts or cotton printed dresses, put make up on, and carefully combed her dark auburn hair. A girdle held her stockings in place. Pantyhose did not exist yet. She carefully checked that the seam at the back of her nylon stockings was completely straight as she balanced herself on her high heels. No crooked seams or other careless-ness fit her style.

Nery and I wore softly colored frilly dresses, fancier than our morning outfits. We skipped around with anticipation as Mami helped us with our white socks and patent leather Mary Janes and tied big bows on top of our heads. It was important that we looked like "nice" girls should. For us, this was another chance to escape the constraining space in which we lived; it was an early lesson from my mother on how to dress well with little money to impress others and feel good about ourselves. Even as a child I knew these weekly dressing up was Mami's effort at recapturing something of her life before the abrupt financial downturn that had deprived her of the niceties she so loved.

After Mami made sure the three of us looked right, we walked down the stairs and turned left, away from the Jesuit church, leisurely walking toward the commercial center of Havana. On the way, we walked along side streets and passed small houses built right at the edge of the narrow sidewalks. The folding panes of wooden shutters in the floor to ceiling windows were usually open to let the breeze come in. The inhabitants of these houses sat by their windows fanning themselves in the afternoon heat; they looked at us idly as we passed. I always noticed an overweight double amputee man with olive skin and big eyes, who sat by his window looking vacantly at the street. Wrought iron bars, also floor to ceiling, gave the illusion of separation. We were at arm's length. We could see these people looking at us, and we looked back at them without a word as if they were pasted images rather than living, breathing individuals. Acknowledging each other's presence would have been an invasion of privacy. I guess we were part of their Saturday afternoons' entertaining parade. Besides, my mother thought that most people in this neighborhood were *"gentuza"*—low class people who were not like us. We had to live near them because of our momentary hardship, but we did not need to interact with them.

Indeed, this neighborhood we walked through was not the best in Havana. These gray streets were uninteresting. There was no vegetation. The small houses along our way were in various degrees of disrepair. Chipped paint, damp patches, and dark blotches coated the walls. Missing pieces of plaster showed older layers of color. The elegant balconies, terraces, arches and high galleries that characterize Havana architecture in other parts of the city were non-existent in this area. From the inside of the dwellings wafted smells difficult to identify.

Each city has a unique smell that evokes its memory. Havana is a city built by the sea; it is a city of water. It looks at water from the length of the Malecón. Even in areas where you cannot see the water, you sense its presence in the ceaseless breeze that softens the tropical heat. Being close to water felt as essential as breathing, even though hurricanes threatened the whole island every so often with furious winds and waves that pummeled buildings erected too close to the cliffs of the Malecón. The salty smell of the Havana of my childhood that was ever present in other areas of the city was absent here. In this neighborhood, the sea and the wind did not exist. The turquoise colored sea and the bright blue light of the sky were also absent. This neighborhood appeared to turn its back to the sea and to the river that bisects the city, not wanting to acknowledge their liquid presence. The wind that might appear suddenly, instead of bringing the salty smell of the nearby sea, stirred up the accumulated dust and left-over trash on the street corners we crossed on our way to Tia Matilde's home.

Nery (right) and I (left) with Abuela Fefita and Tia Matilde
(She went with us to Santiago that summer)

42

Tía Matilde lived in a fourth-floor walk-up flat on Neptuno Street near El Encanto, the fanciest department store in Havana at the corner of Galiano and San Rafael, where Tío Luis, her husband, worked. We climbed the granite steps of the *escalera de caracol*—the spiral staircase that led to her high flat. I hated the difficult climb. Tía Matilde, who climbed these steps every day thinking nothing of it, stood at her door cheering us on from the top of the stairs.

In addition to Tía Matilde and Tío Luis, their daughter Lilia, a blonde blue-eyed beauty, and their nervous skinny son Carlos, also lived there. When we finally got to the top floor, Lilia and Tía Matilde welcomed the three of us with multiple hugs and kisses. Then, Tía Matilde turned to Nery and me to ask us what we wanted for our *merienda*. "Do you want Coca-Cola with condensed milk?" she asked. The answer was always an excited "Yes!" Nery and I loved the cold, thick, sweet drink with its tiny bubbles that lightly tickled the tongue and the top of the mouth. My mother usually had coffee with Lilia and Tía Matilde.

Lilia, my mother and my aunt Marina in the 1930s

Lilia worked as an administrator in one of the cooperative medical clinics in Havana. I thought she was so accomplished. A middle-class woman who worked was a rarity then. When Lilia was about to get married, the Saturday visits included a display of her frilly nighties that were carefully kept wrapped in tissue paper. The one I found most beautiful was made of black lace with tiny pink ribbons. I did not understand why anyone needed so much sleepwear just because they were getting married. I must have asked something about that because I remember Tía Matilde saying something that had to do with *gozar*— enjoyment, which puzzled me even more.

Tía Matilde usually handed me the comics section of the Saturday paper, together with an icy glass full to the top with the bubbly concoction of Coke and condensed milk. And, with my cold drink in hand, I sat at the dining room table and pored over the adventures of Tarzan that filled half of the front page of the comics section, in full color. Tarzan kept me entertained; no need to constantly ask one question or another, interrupting the adult conversation, which I would undoubtedly have done otherwise.

On the radio program of Tarzan's adventures, which I listened to every day at noon, I heard the splash of water, the trumpeting of Tantor, Tarzan's elephant, when he responded to a summons, the shrieks of the apes, and Tarzan's voice—enacted by famous actor Enrique Santiesteban. There was no television yet. The comic strips complemented the radio sounds and made the dense jungle, gorgeous flowers, thick undergrowth, and animal trails come to life.

I am not sure where my fascination with Tarzan came from. I suppose I was attracted to his selflessness and heroism, the same qualities that attracted me later to the figure of Joan of Arc and other women saints. All I know is that I was one of his fans, along with Jane Goodall, who once described the Tarzan stories as having a major influence on her childhood.

Every Saturday we returned to our flat on Calzada de Reina when the sun was beginning to set. Nery and I skipped part of the way a few steps ahead of my mother. In the growing darkness, the inhabitants of the houses we passed as we walked back home could not see us well, but now I could unabashedly peek inside those dwellings; my curiosity about this *gentuza* was ever present despite Mami's disdain for these people.

The weekly visits to Tía Matilde stopped without an explanation in 1946. My brother Orlandito was born some time after that. I assume the big climb up the stairs at Tía Matilde's flat plus the long walk to and from her place, wearing high heels, was not good for my mother's pregnancy. But, of course, I did not know she was pregnant. All I knew was that I could not read Tarzan's adventures every week, which frustrated me.

Our Sundays were not as interesting. Every Sunday in mid-morning, after my father came back from church, we went to his family house in Almendares, about thirty minutes away from the city center, on the other side of the Almendares river, to spend the day with his mother, his siblings, and my cousins.

We started our journey by taking a trolley that stopped in front of my father's school. The trolley looked like those now in use on the F line in San Francisco. They were not "historic" then, they were just the means of public transportation that everyone used in most cities in the Western world. In the early 1950s, Havana's trolleys were retired, their railings dug from the pavement, their routes taken over by buses with the same number designations and itineraries. It was common knowledge at the time that gasoline vehicles were more modern and faster than electrical ones.

A few minutes after we got on the trolley, we passed in front of the imposing *escalinata* of the University of Havana. A dark bronze statue sat halfway up the tall, wide staircase with her arms open as if ready to embrace those who approached. "That is the *Alma Mater*," my father said almost every time we went by and he saw my eyes fastened on her. I yearned to be embraced by the *Alma Mater*; to be a student at the centuries' old University of Havana where Papi, Tío, and their older sister Mamie had received their degrees. Violence against rebellious students had happened at that exact place before I was born. Universities all over Latin America had been centers of protest against political injustice for several decades as they later became in the U.S. in the 1960s. During Batista's second stint in power in the 1950s, the *escalinata* and the curved hill that the trolleys had passed ever so slowly on my childhood Sundays, were again the site of police assaults against students.

The University of Havana

A short while after passing by the University, we had to change trolleys at the corner of 12th and 23rd Streets. Taking advantage of that interval, we walked a block to the monumental entrance of Colón Cemetery, one the great cemeteries of the world. Colón Cemetery is filled with mausoleums in white marble, black granite, bronze or stones of several colors, white sculpted angels or mythical figures and gold inscriptions naming those who inhabit this silent place. Here Cuba's rich families paid tribute to their departed and the country honored its heroes with columns, wrought iron gates, stained glass windows, and art nouveau decorations. Plaques that imitated open books showed inscriptions with the names and dates of birth and death of those buried inside smaller graves.

Many years later, at the Staglieno Cemetery in Genoa, a tour guide told me that the Colón Cemetery was considered the fourth in the world for the beauty of its mausoleums. Having seen other cemeteries in the intervening years, I have to agree that Havana's contains striking funerary sculptures.

Entrance to Colón Cemetery

However grand, Colón Cemetery was not my favorite place. The miniature alleys of this city of the dead with its stone expressions of grief and sorrow felt sad.

Abuelo José Manuel was buried there but not in one of those mausoleums. Instead, he was buried in a grave typical of middle-class tombs, less fancy than the chapels of the rich. His grave looked like a single bed in white marble with bronze handles on its four corners. Every Sunday we left some flowers on Abuelo José Manuel's grave before continuing on to Abuela Boqui's house.

Espín family grave in Colón Cemetery

Late on Sunday afternoons on our way back from Almendares, we transferred trolleys at the corner of 23rd and L streets. A different attraction waited for me at that corner. On an empty lot where the Habana Hilton—the Habana Libre, as it is called now—was built in the late 1950s, several men and ponies waited to offer rides to children in exchange for a few coins. The ride on *"los caballitos"*—the little horses—was the highlight of Sundays. A man guided the ponies around the perimeter of the vacant lot as we held on to the saddle. After the ride, Nery and I climbed another trolley with Mami and Papi that would take us again by the University on our way home. It was already getting dark, so the *Alma Mater* and the quad behind it were dim. We were ready to have some black bean soup and go to bed.

"Pin-Pin, cayó Berlín. Pon-Pon, cayó Japón"

One Saturday, returning from our visit to Tía Matilde, we heard that the war in Europe had ended. On our walk back home, firecrackers—forbidden during the war—were going off all over Havana, their glow competing with the remnants of light in the approaching dusk. Distant voices could be heard chanting *"Pin-pin, cayó Berlín, Pon-pon cayó Japón"* ("Pin-pin, Berlin has fallen, Pon-pon, Japan has fallen") a song set to Cuban rhythms that had become popular as the war's end drew near. But the celebratory mood on that May Saturday was deceiving. This was not the end of the war. Berlin had indeed fallen, but Tokyo had not. The actual end of war was yet to come.

I had been born a few months before the Nazis invaded Poland. War was in the news for as long as I had any memory; print media and radio discussed it incessantly. Cubans followed the events of the war with fervor. As the end of the war approached, I heard daily talk on the radio about the advancing of a mysterious entity called "the Allies." I enacted what I imagined to be the Allies' movements, jumping from chair to chair in Abuela Boqui's porch. I did not know who the Allies were, but I did know they were good. War was bad. Hitler was *very* bad because kind Abuela Boqui wished him dead instead of Roosevelt. I had no idea who Roosevelt or Hitler were, but what my grandmother and other adults said gave me a feeling of impending danger from this Hitler who was obviously much worse than any bad person I knew of, including Batista, whose term as president had thankfully come to an end.

Cuba had declared war on Germany and Japan in December 1941, making it one of the first Latin American countries to enter the conflict. Although Cuba's involvement in the War was modest, it was significant. Several hundred Cuban men enlisted voluntarily to serve in Europe; among them was the son of our Lebanese neighbors. Cuba's strategic location at the entry to the Gulf of Mexico gave it a vital position patrolling the waters of the Caribbean that were infested with German submarines and spy craft. The Cuban Navy escorted hundreds of Allied ships through hostile waters and rescued U-boat victims, saving them from drowning. Between 1942 and 1944, seven Cuban ships were sunk by German U-Boats and more than eighty Cubans were killed in these operations. The efficiency of the Cuban Navy was praised by the U.S. Congress, particularly after they sunk a German submarine off Cuba's Northern coast. Ironically, Papi's dismissal from the Navy was now a good thing—he was not in danger during the War.

Then, a month before I started first grade, the atomic bombs were dropped on Hiroshima and Nagasaki. One of my most vivid childhood memories is the voice of the President on the radio on a sweltering August day, announcing the end of the War. I was sick in bed with a summer cold and, oddly, my mother was not giving her usual tirade about the annoyance of sick children. She and my father were silent when the President's voice came through on the little white radio that every day at noon brought me the adventures of Tarzan. The President's voice was joyful. He almost sounded as if he were singing one of the playful victory songs that had been carried over the radio waves for weeks and heard incessantly in the streets as the sense of approaching victory grew.

Before the President spoke on that August day, the national anthem played and flags were displayed all over the city... But, of course, the President spoke in Spanish, and the anthem played was Cuba's national anthem and the flag was the Cuban flag. The President was Ramón Grau San Martín. He had defeated Batista a year before, on June 1, 1944, in one of the few fair presidential elections in Cuba's troubled history.

Grau was a professor of medicine at the University of Havana. He had been one of the leaders of the rebellion against Machado in the 1930s. During his earlier brief presidency—from which he was removed by Batista and his cronies—he had succeeded in abolishing the Platt Amendment to the 1901 Cuban constitution that authorized the U.S. to intervene at will in Cuban affairs. The U.S. government, advised by Ambassador Sumner Wells, mistrusted Grau. Although Welles had refused to recommend U.S. recognition of Grau's government in the 1930s, he recognized Carlos Mendieta, within five days of his installation by Batista, who was now a Colonel. But even after being deposed, Grau was instrumental in the development of the progressive 1940 Cuban Constitution.

When he won the 1944 presidential election, Grau had been Batista's antagonist for more than a decade. During Batista's four years as President between 1940 and 1944, the Cuban Treasury had been ransacked. Cubans were delighted with Grau as their new President.

On his Election Day, in June 1944, cars, buses, and trucks loaded with young men had gone by for hours under the balcony of my father's school, chanting and cheering Grau's victory. "¡Viva Grau! ¡Viva Grau!" they shouted as throngs of them kept coming, banging the sides of their buses and trucks as improvised drums.

A year after Grau's election, at the end of the war, young men again chanted noisily all over Havana. This time they repeated "Pin-pin, cayó

Berlín, Pon-pon cayó Japón" for hours and days. Although I still did not fully understand what was going on I knew it was very good. Happiness was in the air. The streets of Havana, kept dark during evenings for as long as I could remember, were now full of lights. Our Cuban-Lebanese neighbors' son and the other Cubans who had gone to the war in Europe would be coming back home very soon. The word *paz* was now on everyone's lips.

Soon after the end of the War, the nine o'clock cannon shot—*el cañonazo de las nueve*—began again. For several centuries, during Colonial times, a cannon had been fired every evening from La Cabaña fortress on the other side of Havana Bay to signal that the heavy doors of the wall that surrounded the city were about to close. After those walls were torn down in the nineteenth century, *el cañonazo de las nueve* was preserved as a quaint custom; a tradition kept beyond its original raison d'être. During the years of World War II, the practice had been discontinued to avoid disturbing the inhabitants of Havana who, though far from the European and Asian battlefields, were painfully aware of the war and knew that German U-boats were marauding in the nearby waters. I had never heard *el cañonazo* until it was reinstituted after the War. But then it became part of my and everyone else's daily life. We set clocks and watches to the timing of *el cañonazo*. The cannon shot is now performed as historical pageantry and it has become a tourist attraction, but when I was growing up it was just a distant sound from the other side of the Bay, another daily feature of life in Havana.

Fake cannon ceremony done for tourists at 9 pm nowadays in La Cabaña

The nine o'clock *cañonazo* was a reminder of Cuba's historical importance for the Spanish Empire. The walls of Havana had been constructed in the late seventeenth century, when Spain believed that walls and cannons were the best tools to protect its wealth and defend it from enemies. The walls that surrounded Havana were built at a time when all the wealth of the Empire converged in Havana. Following repeated pirate attacks on unprotected vessels that conveyed the wealth of the colonies to Europe, the Spanish authorities decided to transport those goods across the Atlantic in protected fleets. Ships on their way to Spain loaded with gold, silver, and other precious metals, stones and woods from Mexico, Peru, Chile and even the Philippines congregated in Havana Bay. They were loaded with riches from the Americas or from across the Pacific Ocean transported by land through Central America. When all the vessels were assembled, they left together to cross the Atlantic Ocean surrounded by heavily armed galleons. The large fleets protected by war ships usually arrived in Seville unharmed.

The gathering of the fleets brought wealth to the city and to an island that could not boast to be a source of material goods as other places in the Empire. But the assemblage of all those vessels loaded with treasures waiting for each other before crossing the Atlantic transformed Havana itself into a target for pirates. Hence the construction of the heavy walls with its attendant cañonazo that struck every evening warning when the doors were about to close.

Havana was then the Paris of the Antilles, and the British coveted it because of its key geographical position and its accumulated wealth. Finally, after more than a century of failed attempts, the British captured Havana in 1762 during the Seven Years War between England and France to which Spain was allied. Cubans, however, were loyal to Spain and saw the British as their enemies despite the positive economic measures they instituted during the year of occupation. In 1763, Spain exchanged Florida—a vast swampy peninsula on the continent, near the North American British Colonies—for Havana. Movements for independence from Spain did not stir in Cuba for another half century.

Centuries later, the remnants of the walls in some spots of the city, the cannon shot, and the palatial colonial buildings in Old Havana made me aware that we lived surrounded by our history. I was aware that growing up in Cuba was never just about our individual lives. History, politics, and world affairs were always present.

Tío

Grandparents, aunts, uncles, and cousins were actively involved in our lives. They were family, not just "relatives." Our days were intermingled.

My father's older brother, José Manuel, was a bachelor and my godfather. We called our aunts and uncles by their first names, but he was only and always *Tío*—uncle. He lived with Abuela Boqui, his three sisters and the two children of one of my aunts in the Almendares house and he visited us frequently in our flat in the center of Havana.

A professor and a poet, Tío taught literature in an institute of public education. Although not the equivalent to a college professor, this position was well respected. Instructors in these institutes were called "professors" and were given a higher status than a high school teacher in the U.S. Since not many Cubans received a secondary education, students who attended these institutions were seen as privileged, and so were their instructors.

Tío also had a degree in pharmacy from the University of Havana. He supplemented his teaching income supervising several private clinics' pharmacies. By Cuban standards, he had a substantial income that allowed him to enjoy life and be generous with the children of his less successful brother and his divorced sister.

He went to the center of Havana every evening, elegantly dressed in a starched white *guayabera*. In the 1940s *guayaberas* were worn by Cuban men to dress up while avoiding wearing a coat and tie in the island's heat. *Guayaberas* are made of cotton or linen in pale hues, embroidered with tiny designs in the same color, with buttons down the front and very narrow pleats running the length of the shirt, uninterrupted over their front pockets. They are worn outside trousers, not tucked in. Tío wore expensive, well-tailored, long-sleeved *guayaberas*. He was not tall or slender, but he looked distinguished and self-possessed. His hair had turned gray when he was in his thirties and white soon after. When I think of him, I picture his white hair and his white *guayabera*.

I knew nothing about his private life, but I imagined he spent his time talking about poetry late into the night in Havana's literary cafés. I thought all his friends were *"bohemios"*—a term used in Cuba to describe artists. If he did anything else in his sleepless nights, I never knew. It would not have occurred to me to question what else might be going on in his life.

Because he went to bed several hours after midnight, he never woke up before noon. Luckily, all his classes were in the afternoon or evening. After he awoke, he ate unusual things for breakfast or lunch. My cousins who lived in the Almendares house and Nery and I, when we visited, watched him, fascinated, as he wrapped lettuce leaves around white sugar or dipped carrots in honey or poured salt on slices of pineapple. I tried each of the exotic combinations at least once, and pretended to like the strange flavors, thinking that doing so showed my sophistication.

Nery and I with Tío

Tío took Nery and me and my two cousins to his beach club frequently. After the official beginning of summer, before Nery and I left for vacation in Santiago, we went with him to the beach almost daily. He was a member of *el Casino Español*, one of the classy clubs in the beach district of the Havana suburbs. In Havana, access to beaches was controlled by private clubs that jealously guarded the entrance to their patch of sand and all water entertainment in their assigned territory. Membership in a club was a condition of access to the beach. Some of these clubs charged rather steep prices for membership. People who could not pay for a club went to public beaches that did not have the same quality of sand or were near reefs that could be dangerous because of the high waves. As was the case with so many other things, my parents could not afford membership in a beach club. But there was no way we would go to a public beach to mix with the riff-raff. Those who went to public beaches were the kind of people we did not associate with. Plus, given my parents' pride and need to keep up appearances, it would have been terribly embarrassing to let anyone know that we did not belong to a beach club.

One of my fondest childhood memories is walking into the white Casino Español building with Tío and being struck right away by the all-pervading smell of salty water. Whenever I evoke the vibrant smell of the sea at the entrance of the club, I feel it in my nostrils. Watching the water shimmering in the sun at the other end of the hallway where the building opened out on the beach, made me jump and skip with excitement. Delicious sensations were ever present at the beach in addition to the salty smell: the cool wind, the foamy soft waves, the feeling of water and sand rippling between my little toes.

When we arrived at Casino Español, I quickly changed into my bathing suit and walked out on the sand to meet the waves. I stayed close to the edge of the water because I did not know how to swim. Jumping sideways to be lifted by an approaching wave was a favorite pastime at the beach. With water up to my waist, I spent hours pulling up handfuls of sand, just to see and feel its texture as it trickled between my fingers and disappeared back into the water. From my tiny height, I looked down to the white sand, lightly distorted by the ripples of the soft waves. I didn't know then that the transparent water and powdery white sand in Cuban beaches are unique characteristics of the island.

In the 1960s, after I had left Cuba, when I flew over the island on my way back and forth between the U.S. and Costa Rica, I could not help but notice the distinctive turquoise color of the sea around the Cuban coast, so different from adjacent waters and even from the colors of the coast line of other Caribbean islands. I realized then that it was not just my childhood imagination that made Cuban beaches unique.

After we had spent a while playing with water and sand, Tío, probably slightly bored watching children's games, would ask, "How about a boat ride?" To which my cousins, Nery, and I immediately answered, "Yay! Boat ride! Boat ride!" Tío went to the pier where row boats were kept in waiting, signed for one of them, piled us on the cross benches, and rowed the boat away from shore. No matter how long or how far we went, our ride always felt too short. After the boat trip, it was usually time to shower, put our street clothes back on, and return home. I was tired, but I would have loved to stay longer. Going back home to Calzada de Reina was not something I ever wanted to do.

Tío encouraged my achievements even more than my father did. Did he see in me the child he wished he had? He clearly wanted to have a hand in helping me flourish. He knew my parents could not afford to develop whatever gifts he thought I had because of their tight financial situation. Whatever the reason, like Papi, he made me feel I was a worthwhile little person. I became accustomed to his attention and encouragement at a very early age and accepted it as a given.

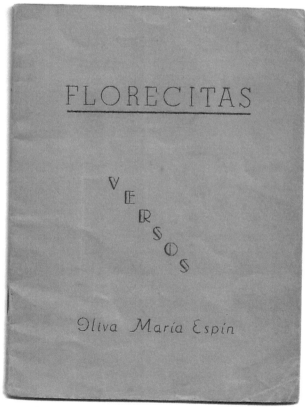

My childhood poetry published by Tío

Most remarkably, he collected, arranged, and published my poetry when I was just ten years old. Holding in my hands the blue booklet in which my childish words were printed, I felt important and capable of remarkable things. In his foreword to the small book, he explained that I had started reading at five or earlier and that my poetry, written since I was eight, was "the reflection of that reading." He also wrote he had no doubt I would be a great poet.

Life proved him wrong.

Instead of poetry in Spanish, I have written academic books about the psychology of immigration, psychotherapy, Latina women, gender and sexuality, and other topics. In English. But reading his foreword and my own verses I, too, am surprised at what I find. My childish poems celebrate the Three Kings from the Orient, who bring gifts (*Los Reyes Magos que traen regalos...*); the bells from the nearby church's steeple (*Campanas del campanario / que lindas y bellas son, / y repican a diario, / alegrándome el corazón*), a girl called Pilar who I do not remember, although I say she is beautiful and she is my friend. There are also poems about children's stories I had read and also some poems dedicated to my mother, my grandmothers, and several religious figures I was reading about in school, such as Moses. I have no doubt the publication of this booklet, as well as Tío's praise and recognition, were significant in shaping who I am. Because if Tío believed my words were good, I must continue writing. If he and my father gave me attention, I had to live up to their expectations and behave less childishly than my sister and cousins.

He not only encouraged me to read and recite poetry, but he also lent me and bought me books of history and works of literature. One surprise gift he gave me stands out: When I was in third or fourth grade, Tío took me to an evening of poetry recitation by Berta Singerman at a Havana theater. Singerman was a Russian immigrant to Argentina who had become famous reciting the works of renowned poets from Spain and Latin America in a dramatic, intense style that was then considered the most sophisticated form of interpreting poetry. The occasion was made even more extraordinary because it took place on a school night.

On that Thursday, when I arrived home from school, my parents startled me by saying, "Get ready for a big surprise." I took off my school uniform, showered, had a light early dinner and put on a pink cotton dress with a lace ruffle around the neck and a big bow tied at the back of my waist. Shiny black patent leather shoes, tiny earrings, a bracelet, and a small ring with a star on top, all in gold, completed my outfit. Once dressed, I waited impatiently for Tío who had finally phoned to tell me where we were going.

I had heard of Berta Singerman as the greatest *declamadora*. I could not believe I was really going to see her perform. At the theater, with the program in my hand, I sat very straight almost holding my breath in awe and excitement. I leaned forward to listen better, my legs that could not reach the floor crossed at the ankles. I felt grown up attending an evening performance with Tío, who was clearly pleased at my reaction to his surprising gift; he was delighted at my enchantment with the performance.

For each poem she recited, Singerman transformed her appearance. She stormed around the stage, expressing an almost violent passion through the force of her voice, facial expression, and arm movements; or she stood completely still, while her low voice conveyed the intensity of pent up emotions. She made her long beige silky dress into different outfits by rearranging two gauzy shawl-like pieces that started at her shoulders and extended to the hem of her dress. These shawls fluttered about her, rested on her head or twisted around her body. Or she folded them in her arms as if she were holding a baby.

Singerman recited poetry from memory for more than two hours. Her voice and the power of her performance made her seem taller than she was. In *Los Caballos de los Conquistadores* by Peruvian poet José Santos Chocano, I could feel the gallop of the conquerors' horses in her voice and in the movements of her arms. In García Lorca's poem about the death of bullfighter Ignacio Sánchez Mejías, she showed deep sadness by standing still with unmoving arms, her head lowered, her voice slow and deep. While she recited Neruda's poem, *"Puedo escribir los versos más tristes esta noche..."* there was a plethora of contained emotions in her slow, quiet delivery. I could hear the passion of a woman in love in her delivery of Juana de Ibarbourou's *"Prodigio, mis manos florecen..."* I was on edge at her ominous repetition of *"Dijo el cuervo: Nunca más"* in her interpretation of a translated version of Poe's *The Raven*.

The next day, Tío gave me copies of all the poems I had liked, written out in his careful handwriting, so I could read them again whenever I wanted to remember my experience of that incomparable evening we had spent together listening to poetry in the voice of the famous *declamadora*. Perhaps Tío believed I could one day be heiress to the Singerman tradition. But hers was a dying art. By the end of my adolescence no one was reciting poems in public, much less embodying them dramatically as Singerman and others like her had.

Abuela Boqui

On an early January morning in 1948, Abuela Boqui served me a breakfast of hot chocolate and crusty bread with olive oil in a room adjacent to the kitchen of her Almendares house that was always referred to as *"el comedorcito"*– "the little dining room." I had spent the night at her house. My parents would arrive later with Nery and baby Orlandito to spend the day as we did every Sunday.

Although we were not particularly close, I liked her calm demeanor and I liked how her bosom jumped up and down when she laughed. I enjoyed having Abuela Boqui all to myself that morning. We were alone in her house. My aunts had gone to church. My two cousins were sleeping. Tío was in New York on sabbatical.

Abuela Boqui, 1947

I noticed idly the unhurried movements of Abuela's round frame as she walked back and forth between *el comedorcito* and the kitchen, her white hair tied in a bun at the back of her head. She said something funny and when she laughed, her bosom moved up and down.

Abuela had just brought me something—a spoon, perhaps. She walked slowly back to the kitchen. And I heard her slide down and sit on the chair that was just on the other side of the door. It seemed odd that she suddenly wanted to sit. Then, she made a strange loud sound. Despite a mildly eerie feeling, I continued eating my breakfast, dunking my bread in the salty oil and sipping my chocolate, ignoring my vague sense of unease.

From my seat at the table, I could see only her legs—dark stockings, flat black leather shoes. She made the same strange sound again; it was a mixture of wheeze and growl. I got scared. After a few seconds, I quietly called out, "Abuela…" But she did not respond or move at all. I told myself that if she made that sound again, I would get up to see what she was doing sitting and making such strange noises. A moment later, the bizarre noise came again. Trembling a bit, I got up and went to look at her.

Straddling her feet to get through the kitchen door, I saw that her eyes were closed and her head was resting against the wall. The sound came again, her chest rising with it. Something was very wrong, although I did not know what. I needed to find an adult to help me.

Heart pounding, I raced down the long hallway from the kitchen to the front door on my short, shaky legs. The stained-glass of the Tiffany lamp that hung over the mahogany table in the center of the big dining room glowed brightly in the morning sun. The grandfather clock chimed eight o'clock in its Big Ben tones as I ran past it. Through the open door of a bedroom along the hallway, I got a glimpse of one of my little cousins sleeping peacefully.

As I reached the front door, I realized I needed a doorstop so the heavy wrought iron and glass door would not lock behind me. Somehow, I found something, secured the door, and stepped on the sidewalk. At that very moment, I saw my aunt Mamie turning the corner.

"*A Abuela le ha dado algo!*"— "Something has happened to Abuela!" I cried out.

She flew into the house, rushed to the kitchen, reached it in a few seconds, embraced my grandmother's slumped body and started screaming. By then, Abuela was not making noises anymore.

For the next few hours, the house was a mess of weeping adults, doctor, priest, family friends, neighbors coming and going, frantic phone calls to New York to locate Tío.

I just stood there, in the middle of the commotion, not knowing what else to do.

Before long, I found myself next door with my two little cousins and the neighbors who were trying to show us some picture books and tell us stories. After a while, someone took me back to Abuela's house.

She was on her bed, fully dressed; her apron was still tied around her, her face encircled by a big handkerchief meant to hold her jaw closed. She had been carried there from the kitchen, where she had died of a massive heart attack while I looked at her, not knowing that I was watching death. I had never seen a dead person, let alone see someone die. I had just turned nine years old a few weeks earlier.

The smell of the oil the priest had used to administer the Last Rites, the sacrament of Extreme Unction, as they called it then, filled her bedroom. It was like nothing I had smelled before. Oily, yes, but something more... like clay; not rancid, but "thick"—and yes, "sick" in a strange, frightening way. My nose has kept the memory of that scent for seventy years.

My aunts were standing next to the bed, weeping. The priest, a rotund short man with salt and pepper hair, was talking to one of my aunts in a low voice in his heavy Spanish accent. I was unsure of what to do besides stand rigidly by the bed. One of the adults in the room pushed me gently to go through the motion of leaning over Abuela's body and kissing her stiff cold cheek. I felt shaken, confused, nervous. I did not know what to feel or what to do next. Then, someone placed a hand over my shoulders and guided me out of the room.

My cousins were not brought in to kiss Abuela goodbye.

Why, I wonder still, was I put through this additional scary experience while they were not? Did no one think how kissing my dead grandmother after watching her die would affect me?

Later that day, I was taken home, where my aunt Marina took care of us until Abuela's funeral was over. Memories of the next few days are blurry. But there is one thing I remember: Abuela had died two days before Three Kings Day. The Three Kings, the Magi from the Orient, brought presents to children on the feast of the Epiphany. On that clear and chilly January morning, the Three Kings brought my siblings and me very few presents—socks and bags of candy. Marina tried to explain that the Kings were crestfallen and distracted because of my grandmother's death. Teresa tried to lighten the mood by saying that, once again, she had opened the door for the Black King and had told him that we were sad because of Abuela's death. She had told him not to leave toys this year because we were preoccupied with more important things.

I don't know if I still believed then in the nocturnal apparitions of *los Reyes Magos* carrying presents on their camels to reward children for good behavior. But I do know that in my mind there was some hazy connection between my slowness in responding to Abuela's strange sounds, her death, and the lack of toys from the Three Kings.

I could not sleep for days after Abuela Boqui's death. In the sleepless nights, I wondered if I should have done something more to save her. In a confused way, I felt guilty and responsible for my inability to prevent her dying.

For the next year or so, we continued to spend Sundays with my father's siblings at the Almendares house as we had done when Abuela Boqui was alive. Now, we were also leaving flowers for Abuela on the family grave at Colón Cemetery during the stop to change trolleys. My distaste for these weekly visits to the cemetery grew after her death. Someone I had known was inside that grave.

Every Sunday, when we arrived at the Almendares house, my aunts draped themselves around me, sobbing noisily. I stood rigidly and silently under their embraces. Tío—who had come back from his sabbatical, having lost both his mother and his dream of a year in New York—stood around with tears in his eyes. My father wept on my mother's shoulder. They were overwhelmed by their grief; so involved in their pain that they could not fathom mine.

My father adored his mother; while she was alive, he wrote or called her every day. Losing her devastated him. My mother was, as always, solicitous and mindful of my father's feelings more than anything or anyone. If he needed something, nothing and no one else mattered to her.

None of the adults—my parents, my aunts, other relatives on both sides of the family—ever asked me how I felt; no one made any comment about the possibility that I may have been scared or sad. Apparently, not one of them asked themselves what might be going on inside a nine-year old who had witnessed death—something most people do not see in their entire lives. They probably thought that children's emotions were like their frequently bruised knees—superficial wounds that heal quickly.

Their response seemed to be saying that I should not feel or express fear and pain. The jumble of disquiet, guilt, and sadness I felt need not to be taken seriously. Others could cry and voice their feelings, but I should not. I should just be proud that I had been so courageous and clever as they kept repeating. I'd handled the situation in such a grown-up manner as to appear invulnerable.

"How brave and grown-up of you," they all said, "to know what to do, to look for help outside the house, making sure the door did not close behind you."

I relished the praise, but it did not comfort me. After all, I had failed despite the celebratory comments about my adult-like equanimity. Abuela Boqui was dead; my father had lost his mother.

I will never know what this mixture of intense experience and conflicting feelings did to me. But I know something "turned" forcefully inside me. The messages that little girl received then are still with me. They became me. I was a feisty and resilient and strong girl as everyone kept saying. That was what mattered about me. I should be content and satisfied with that. Everyone would be disappointed if I wavered from being the little girl they praised.

Forty years later, during my first return visit to Cuba, I went to the Almendares house with Lilia, my mother's cousin. Carlitos, her nephew, was a good revolutionary, so he had been awarded the privilege of buying a Czech-made car. We drove in his car from my hotel in El Vedado to the other side of the river. When we arrived at what had been Abuela Boqui's house, I rang the doorbell and explained to the woman who opened the door that this had been my father's family home. I requested her permission to see the place again.

Abuela Boqui's house in Almendares

The mixture of familiarity and strangeness that had been present since my arrival in Havana hit me all over again. Tío's wooden glass door bookcases were standing along the hallway as they had been during my childhood and adolescence. The novels, history and poetry books he had lent me decades earlier were all there. However, the upright piano that had stood in the living room where my aunts, Tío, and Papi played during our Sunday visits was not. Neither was the Tiffany lamp my grandparents had brought from New York at the end of the nineteenth century hanging over the dining room table. I did not know who had taken these valuable objects and did not want to ask Alicia, the woman who now lived in the house, if she knew anything about them. I did not want to offend her in any way by implying that she might have sold them, although that was probably the case.

And then, unexpectedly, when we walked into the kitchen where Abuela Boqui had died, I looked at the corner where she had collapsed on a chair and started crying uncontrollably; my sobs shaking my body and startling Lilia and Alicia as much as me. When I finally could take hold of my dramatic explosion, still weeping, I explained to Alicia what had happened in that spot when I was nine years old. The grief held inside for several decades had erupted. The feelings unexpressed by the little girl I had been then, rushed out uncontrollably, intermingled with the other losses and sorrows evoked by this return.

Marisabidilla

Family lore had it that I could say the word *refrigerador* correctly when I was eight months old. Frankly, I doubt it, even though I heard it said many times. To my great smugness, mixed with embarrassment, my family repeated stories that proved how bright I was. Encouraged by the copious adult praise, I became excessively self-assured for my age. Almost inevitably I became a *marisabidilla*—a know-it-all, pedantic little girl.

When it was time for me to start first grade, my father, using his Church friendships and connections, managed to get me a scholarship to *Colegio del Apostolado*, a private religious school for middle-class girls. The next year, Nery started attending the same school. My parents wanted to preserve for us the middle-class opportunities that would have been ours but for arbitrary political events beyond their control. This *colegio* satisfied their need to keep up appearances. It provided us with the social standing that attending my father's school could not.

Hiding our precarious financial situation and maintaining our middle-class social standing despite financial constraints was my parents' goal, particularly my mother's. Her parents had raised themselves from poverty, but wealth did not equate a higher social status in this Cuban society that still, in many ways, reproduced the traditional Spanish European class stratification. Mami had married a lawyer and had believed herself secure as a middle-class wife because my father's was a patrician family even though they did not have as much wealth as my mother's. I learned very early to keep silent about this critical part of our lives.

Being a good student and an obedient girl helped me preserve my scholarship all the way to the end of high school. But attending this school required that I learn to live a double life. I lived among girls who, at four o'clock, went back to homes with the porches, patios, gardens, and garages that I pretended to also have. I made sure none of my classmates knew where I lived.

The girls who rode the school bus with us knew where we lived, but this did not matter much since they lived in the same neighborhood. And, in fact, they, occasionally, came to our place to play or we went to theirs. None of us was allowed to play in the streets. Only unruly urchins, all of them boys, were seen outside. No children played on Calzada de Reina, where the constant traffic was dangerous to pedestrians. The few girls who came to visit us were fascinated by the blackboards and desks in every room of the flat except the bedrooms. I, on the other hand, was mortified by their interest in these things that were always in my way.

Among the nuns at school, some showed me signs of approval and favoritism: intimidating old Madre María, who taught me the multiplication tables in her stern and forbidding manner; young and kind Madre Berta, who loved how I repeated almost verbatim the Bible stories she taught us, and Madre Teresa, who supervised all the elementary school activities. They choose me to recite poems at school events. They gave me little presents of rosaries and medals of the Virgin Mary as prizes for my good behavior and studiousness.

My first communion

Both Madre Berta and Madre Teresa were proud of my success in learning to write with my right hand. I was unquestionably left-handed when I entered first grade, but such a "deviant" behavior did not meet with my parents' or the nuns' approval. They set out to teach me to write and eat with my right hand. Each school morning, I stood for at least an hour by a high platform with notebook and pencil in hand, writing some words and phrases with my right hand. After a few months in first grade, I could do both without apparent difficulty, which won me more praise and more medals of the Virgin Mary from Madre Teresa and Madre Berta.

Luckily, I never stammered like many left-handed children forced to write with their right hands. I continued to do everything with my left hand when no one was watching. To this day, I sew, use scissors, brush my teeth and put on makeup with my left hand.

But some other nuns were not so happy with me. Madre Bértila, my sour second grade teacher, did not hide her impatience and her disapproval of my being ahead of others. When I explained to some of my classmates how to do double-digit multiplication before Madre Bértila got to it, her disgusted facial expression showed the effort she was making at containing her anger.

One of my lay teachers also showed displeasure at my airs of superiority. In our school, morning classes were in Spanish, usually taught by the nuns. Afternoon classes were in English, usually taught by lay teachers. I found Miss Ofelia's third grade class particularly boring. By then I had had my fill of Dick and Jane and Spot and Puff. Grammar exercises were tiresome. Once I had learned the rule, I did not need to spend what seemed like endless hours each afternoon repeating over and over exercises of correct usage and grammar.

Miss Ofelia's lackluster teaching and her repetitive instructions felt unbearable. "Girls, you have to use 'aren't' instead of 'ain't." "It is 'I don't know anything', not 'I don't know nothing'."

So, to escape the boredom, almost every day I asked her for permission to go to the bathroom and slipped away to Miss Rosa's fourth grade class, which was more entertaining. Miss Rosa did not keep the secret of my furtive daily presence in her class, though. Eventually, Miss Ofelia made it clear she knew what I was doing, and she was very unhappy with my preferring another teacher or a more advanced class.

"No more permission to go to the bathroom! I know exactly what you are doing!" she said angrily one day when I, again, requested permission to leave class.

Like the good girl I was, I quietly lowered my eyes and sat down at my desk. But I had to find a way of getting out of her monotonous class. So, when my tolerance for boredom had reached its limit I resorted to another trick: I was seized by the urgent need to visit students who belonged to the "spiritual treasures" group I led.

In small yellow charts, the girls in each one of the groups reported their prayers, little sacrifices, and other such pious activities labelled "spiritual treasures." At the end of each month, the group that performed the most of those "spiritual treasures" won some prize, like a medal or a holy card in addition to praise for being so dedicated to spiritual practices. Encouraging the girls in my group was my task as leader. Luckily these quaint "spiritual treasures" provided me with a great excuse to tell Miss Ofelia I had to leave her class to go and survey the prayer treasures charts. She could not deny me permission for this activity, but her facial expression as she gave her permission told me she was well aware that I had found another way to leave her tedious class.

My sneaking out of class whenever I could did not pass unnoticed to my classmates, either. I was conscious of not being liked by the other girls. A perfect little girl can be very irritating to other little girls. The more insecure I felt around my peers, the more I resorted to my *marisabidilla* attitude. I developed a haughtily adult way of speaking that further separated me from them. I knew my perfect-little-girl style would provide me with approval from most adults, which reassured me and made me feel appreciated. The reward of adult acclaim was too delicious to sacrifice in exchange for being chosen by my classmates to participate in some childish game or being invited to a silly afterschool party. I knew how to take care of my vague loneliness through reading or memorizing poetry or even composing poems or a few pages of some novel I fancied myself writing, modeled after the narratives I avidly read. But deep down I felt something was missing without quite knowing what that might be.

My classmates mostly ignored me despite the eagerness with which I told them the long stories I invented trying to engage their friendship. When they were friendly it was usually because they wanted to copy my answers in exams or get my help with their homework. I knew this was their motivation, but refusing to help them would have increased my isolation. On the surface, I was talkative and vivacious, but mostly I crawled inside myself. I grew more and more lonely, which made me crave more adult approval. I spent most of my time with my nose in a book; either my textbooks or *Las Niñas Modelo* and other novels of the

Countess of Ségur or whatever other books I could find in Tío's bookshelves.

Nery and I when we were beginning elementary school

Nery was better than me at dealing with peers. She was not a *marisabidilla* and made friends easily. One of Nery's classmates, Celita, was driven to school in her father's Cadillac by a uniformed chauffer. Almost every day, Nery came back home in Celita's Cadillac and, frequently, she was driven to school in it. Every so often, I was included in the luxurious ride. Celita did not seem to care where we lived and Nery did not care that Celita knew. But Celita and her driver waited downstairs; they never came upstairs. And then, every so often, my mother made a point of reminding us that Papi was a lawyer while Celita's father was only a merchant or had some other dubious means of making a living. We were superior even though we rode in public trolleys and busses rather than Cadillacs.

Obviously, it was not just the secret poverty that separated me from others. Being a *marisabidilla* had other causes. How is a lonely little girl to react to adult praise? I lacked the capacity for judgment at that age to realize that not all said by the adults was accurate, much less that there was a price to pay in exchange for this adult praise. Decades later, I realized that by making me an exception, the adults in my life trapped me in the joy of being special at the cost of being a child.

But then, that is not the whole story. The praise and encouragement I received from Papi and Tío and the nuns—who were the women I most admired—transmitted a message that became deeply engraved in my psyche: I was capable of much; I was not to become a useless young woman focusing all her energies on catching a husband; I could have a career and do remarkable things. In other words, I learned to believe in myself…at least in terms of my intellectual capacity. They—Papi, Tío, and the nuns—taught me to believe in myself and in my capacity to achieve much.

"Mastica y traga"

Nonetheless, the artificial adulthood in which I was immersed had a great deal wrong with it. The perfect-little-girl was needy and tired of being perfect. Something had to give.

So, I simply stopped eating. I did not decide to do this. It just seemed to happen. I'd chew each mouthful of food slowly and conscientiously, only with my front teeth, and did not swallow. Turning the food in my mouth, after chewing it for what seemed like forever, I waited patiently and when no one was watching, spit it back on the edge of my plate. Daily lunch and dinner battles over food set in. I was in control of my chewing and no one could make me swallow if I did not want to. The effort of not eating while being forced to do it became part of my daily routine.

My mother vacillated between getting annoyed with me and feeling alarmed. She took me again to see Doctor Tres Palacios, fearful that I would starve myself to death. While she was talking to the doctor, I just sat silently, my small frame again lost in a big chair in his office, indifferent to her worries, pondering once more the oddity of the pediatrician's last name. Despite the doctor's assurance that I would eventually eat when I felt hungry, Mami continued to badger me at every meal and to watch me to prevent my sneaky spitting out chewed food. I, in turn, continued to be completely uninterested in eating. Eating was a monumental effort that tormented me.

I now think this was the first and only rebellious act of the obedient girl I was then. But from my child's perspective, I was not a rebel; I simply found the taste of food and the effort of eating very unpleasant. I hated pasta and vegetables. Only fried plantains were tolerable. I could swallow rice and beans, in tiny amounts. Meat was the absolute worst.

We had a two-hour school break in the middle of the day to go home for lunch, which was the main meal of the day. We left school around 11:30, after the morning classes in Spanish; by noon the school bus deposited us at home. At 1:00 we were picked up again, to start the English afternoon session by 1:30. I dreaded the daily lunch break. Every minute of that lunch hour was torture.

By the time the school bus arrived to pick us up, Nery had long since finished her lunch and was ready to go, teeth brushed and haired combed. But I still had a full plate of untouched foods and a few mounds of disgusting chewed and spit-out food in front of me. I agonized about how to get rid of the heap left on that plate. Relieved by the school bus's horn, most days I grabbed my book bag and ran downstairs to the waiting bus, leaving behind a full plate and my preoccupied and irritated mother. I would have to deal with the difficult task of chewing and swallowing again in a few hours, but for the afternoon at least I could read about Dick, Jane, Sally, Spot and Puff, and whatever else we were studying in English and forget about the annoyance of eating.

To assuage my mother's frustration, but also out of concern for my puzzling behavior, Papi took upon himself the task of making me eat. Earlier he had used a little rhyme to encourage my eating *"el que acaba primero ayuda a su compañero"*— "whoever finishes first can help her buddy finish her plate." But it soon became very clear that if I was not interested in my portion, I was even less so in that of others. Far from being encouraging, sharing the mound on someone else's plate felt like a punishment. Papi changed tactics. Daily, when he had already finished eating like everyone else at the table, he would move his chair close to mine as I lingered, dumbfounded about how to consume the apparently enormous and inexhaustible amount that remained on my plate. He sat with a spoon or fork full of food in front of my mouth and repeated over and over, "Oliva María, *mastica y traga*" – "Chew and swallow; *chew and swallow*; CHEW AND SWALLOW."

While he was patiently repeating this sing-song, I kept chewing and not swallowing. The ritual became routine. It lasted several years. In my mind, I was busy constructing fantasies of princesses, castles, saints and heroes' adventures, or listening to Tarzan on the radio. As my father tried to persuade me to eat, I was in Tarzan's jungle, or on a distant shore converting heathens, or marveling at a miraculous apparition, or imagining something else, depending on the story I was concocting in my mind. If I had any conscious thought about eating it was something along the lines of *"Ay Dios! I hate food!"*

Chewing was mindless and mechanical; swallowing completely unnecessary as far as I was concerned. Only the spoon in Papi's hand, touching my lips waiting for admission into my mouth brought me out of my private world... and only for the few seconds that took the spoon to drop its cargo. Eventually, I distractedly swallowed some bits of food at lunch and went back to the afternoon school session or to the back rooms of our flat to do my homework in the evening with something in my stomach. Regardless of how little I ate, I always left the table feeling that I had been force-fed.

Mami, Marina, and Nery, their meals finished, got up from the table and went about their business. Sometimes, coming out of my reveries, I could hear Nery or see her from the corner of my eye playing with her dolls or running around the small apartment. I knew she was using her time in a more enjoyable way than me.

But I was obviously getting something out of my bizarre conduct. Getting attention for this form of "bad" behavior must have been worth the trouble. Strangely, at no point did my parents treat my not eating as disobedience. If I wanted them to see rebellion, I obviously did not succeed. They treated my behavior as a mysterious ailment. My reputation as perfect-little-girl was not tarnished in any way. The attention and concern I elicited with my silent and stubborn resistance to eating became a convoluted balance to all the-good-little-girl-who-never-disobeys conduct that I was so praised for. Apparently, no one seemed to notice that during the intervening summers in Santiago, I managed to eat by myself without anyone's help and eagerly consumed Abuela Fefita's meals.

Away from the dining table, while I sat on my small white rattan rocking chair reading incessantly or while I fantasized in some hidden corner behind a door or under some makeshift tent-like enclosure I had put together, I did not think about my perpetual, all-out, silent battle against eating. I was just glad I was not being pestered by the command to eat.

I was not conscious of the power I was exercising over the adults by my refusal to eat. I just felt tormented by the pressure to eat. My parents' evident worry and distress must have been reassuring. My father's undivided attention and patience was a powerful reward for my eccentric behavior.

I was even much less aware of possible hidden desires to be a little baby or of rejecting my mother by rejecting her food or of Oedipal feelings or whatever else might have been going on in my unconscious at the time. In hindsight, my behavior still leaves me puzzled. My guess is I was after some attention for simply being a child with childish needs, something I could not get by being intelligent and well-behaved, something I didn't have to accomplish through my efforts. But that is my psychology knowledge speaking now, trying to understand and explain my behavior. In fact, I remain perplexed by my strange refusal to eat. Particularly because as an adult, I thoroughly enjoy good meals and tasting new dishes is one of my favorite pleasures.

As abruptly as it had started, I finally stopped my resistance to food. I remember thinking one day, "*I have had enough of this silly behavior. It's about time I eat like everybody else.*" Around the time I turned eleven, when I was about to have an appendectomy, I started to eat by myself, and chewed and swallowed without my father's constant reminder. From that day on I ate normally. I never ate much, but I did it without any help.

Thinking back, I ponder how remarkable it was that I did not develop a full-fledged eating disorder in adulthood. Perhaps eating disorders were not "fashionable" yet. Perhaps I just needed to fulfill some hidden goal that had been achieved by the time I decided to start eating normally again.

"Do you want to be a hunchback?"

Around the time I stopped eating, other bodily issues came up. Once again, my body, its needs and insufficiencies, seemed to have provided me with ways to get the attention I craved without having to pay for it with perfection.

My mother repeatedly scolded me about my posture. "*¡Enderézate! ¿Quieres ser jorobada?*" — "Stand up straight! Do you want to be a hunchback?"

After her insistent commands failed to correct my bad posture, it became obvious that something was wrong with my back, and she took me to El Vedado again to see another doctor.

Like Doctor Tres Palacios, Doctor Arturo's office and clinic were at his home. He was a short, friendly man, full of energy and laughter. He was not a "real" doctor, though; he was a physical therapist who specialized in working with children. Doctor Arturo was called by his first name because he had a difficult German last name, even though he was Cuban.

Mami picked me up at school at 4:00 p.m. and we walked the few blocks to Dr. Arturo's home. The first time, Dr. Arturo asked me to take off my shoes and walk on long slanted wooden parallel bars that formed a triangle with the floor. I did so wobbly, pointing my toes to the top of the triangle and my heels to the floor as he had told me to do. He took a long narrow piece of wood along which moving pegs stuck out every inch or so and proceeded to place it at several intervals along my back.

"Stand up as straight as you can and don't move," he said. "This won't hurt; I just need you to stand very still."

As he moved the mysterious stick away from my back the pegs had shifted in and out and stood at different lengths. He meticulously marked some numbers on a chart that I assumed had to do with the length of the pegs. After taking a few other measurements, he talked to my mother for a while. He apparently told her that I had scoliosis, but it was early enough to be corrected.

From that day on, twice a week after school, I went with Mami to Dr. Arturo's clinic to do exercises that were supposed to straighten my back. It was nice to spend time with her these afternoons. My mother was never particularly interested in praising me. She never joined the chorus of other adults who celebrated my achievements. When someone said I was very intelligent, she replied, "She just has good memory," and changed the conversation. My physical problem offered me an opportunity to be cared by her. My brother Orlandito had been born a few months earlier; Marina took care of him while Mami took me to the clinic. I wonder if my mother was glad that my misshapen back was providing her with a break from household duties.

The exercises other children and I performed on the cement patio of Dr. Arturo's home were fun. His voice marked the rhythm, "Up! Down! Up! Down!" or "One, two, three; one, two, three." I also walked slowly on the slanted parallel bars holding a small bag of sand on my head while my back and head were aligned so the sand bag did not fall. Other exercises consisted of putting a bar behind my back and over my head repeatedly and performing movements that were supposed to contribute to straightening my spine.

As I moved around, following Dr. Arturo's instructions and performing the prescribed activities, I half listened to the mothers sitting nearby, embroidering or knitting, watching our performance while talking about politics. The mother of one little boy spent the children's exercise sessions knitting, always arguing in favor of President Grau's government and political party. Another woman always had something critical to say about him.

During my two years in treatment with Doctor Arturo, Carlos Prío was elected President. Both Grau and Prío were members of the same Auténtico Party that had defeated Batista in 1944. When Grau was elected in 1944, his election had raised people's hope. Many Cubans believed that all the reforms Grau had been unable to implement in 1933 because of the American interference that had emboldened Batista, would become a reality. However, Grau had not done much by way of reforms during his presidency; many people felt disheartened.

According to the 1940 Cuban constitution, presidents could not run for re-election immediately after serving one term. Grau supported Carlos Prío's bid for the presidency. Prío had been a student during the University protests against Machado in the early 1930s. Grau had been his professor. Prío was now the standard bearer for the Auténticos. He made pledges to respect all citizens and protect the public treasury, but corruption under his government continued unabated. Both Grau and Prío had disappointed the high hopes of many Cubans. A lot of the mothers' arguments centered on disappointment with these two presidents and their Party. But some still believed that the Auténticos were better than any other alternative.

While the children's mothers argued heatedly about the latest political news in Doctor Arturo's yard, my mother remained quiet, or at most, said, "I am not interested in politics." I knew she did not feel strongly favorable to any politician. I don't know if she voted for Grau in 1944. But I know she did not vote in the 1948 elections. She did not like Batista, of course, but by then he did not feel like a threat or even a presence in Cuban politics. He was a figure of the past. When I learned decades later that he had been elected Senator in 1948, I was surprised that no one ever spoke about that. He was simply irrelevant then. His name never came up anymore in the news. No one mentioned him in any conversation including the mothers' discussions while we exercised.

Invariably, the mothers talked about what Chibás had said the previous Sunday. Like most Cubans, they listened to Senator Eduardo Chibás's hour-long weekly speeches as my father also did.

Chibás was a passionate politician, who galvanized Cubans against government corruption and excessive U.S. influence in Cuban affairs. I still remember his thin squeaky voice, almost like a child's and the way in which he strained to make his points as powerfully as his voice allowed him to. Chibás had left the Auténtico Party, revolting against government corruption, and founded the popular Orthodox Party. Fidel Castro became a member of this party as a young man before he achieved political prominence in ways Chibás could not have anticipated.

If the exercises in Dr. Arturo's yard had been the sole remedy to my back problems, it would not have been so bad to have scoliosis. But in addition to the weekly exercises, Dr. Arturo prescribed two contraptions. One was a horizontal metal bar, hooked to a door frame by a chain. A leather band hung from the metal bar. Twice a week, after school and during vacations, I had to be pulled up, with my toes barely touching the ground, my arms bent at the elbows, my hands resting on the metal bar, my chin on the leather band. I had to remain in that uncomfortable position for half an hour. Supposedly this process would align my vertebrae. I believe it is now considered damaging for a child's body to be stretched so extremely. But then it was state of the art for correcting scoliosis. While I was hanging in that difficult and awkward position, Marina read aloud from some book she knew I liked so I would not get too impatient.

The other contraption prescribed by Dr. Arturo was worse. It was a metal corset extending from my underarms to my hips that kept my back straight. It laced up in the front of my body. Felt cushions on the inside were supposed to soften the edges of the metal, but in fact, contributed to the discomfort in the heat of the day. Sweating against the rubbing felt and metal irritated my skin and caused sore spots on my sides and shoulder blades.

I wore this heavy metal case to school every day, unless I succeeded in sneaking out with my uniform on without the horrible contrivance under it. Unavoidably, when I returned from school on a day when I had escaped from the metal corset's torture, my mother welcomed me with the same menacing question, "Do you want to be a hunchback?" And, invariably, I thought that the fate of a hunchback could not be worse than this daily physical torture.

At school, I was pathetically incompetent at physical activity or competitive games because I was rather uncoordinated and very small. The respect I could gain with my success in Math or Reading or History became mockery during Physical Education, or any sports played during recess. The captains of the sports teams always picked me last and begged each other to take me. It was humiliating to stand around, pretending I did not care.

I ran here and there sometimes during recess playing a game of tag I had invented that I called *los Buenos y los Malos*—the Good Ones and the Bad Ones. Every so often, while playing *los Buenos y los Malos*, if any girl happened to touch me or to try to grab me, she would hit her hand against the hard metal of my corset and say, "Ouch! What do you have inside there?" This added embarrassment to my physical discomfort and made want to avoid physical games altogether. I couldn't explain to other girls that I needed to be encased in metal to straighten the curve in my spine. On top of my arrogant *marisabidilla* attitude, my shame about our hidden poverty, my avoidance of touch games and physical ineptitude created additional barriers that contributed to my lack of friends at school.

At least in Dr. Arturo's back yard, I was doing something that felt like playing with other children and enjoying some physical activity. In Dr. Arturo's games being selected was never an issue. All of us were there precisely because something needed to be corrected in our bodies. I was not different from other children in his clinic. This was an equal opportunity place. My sense of isolation at school did not change, but, in a paradoxical way, the strange contraptions and the exercise sessions meant getting attention because of something completely unrelated to anything I accomplished. My imperfect body was counterbalancing my perfect-little-girl attitude.

After more than a year of Dr. Arturo's exercises and contraptions, I was finally freed from the torture instruments, despite the threat of becoming a hunchback. I think I had grown and needed a new corset to fit my body. The expense was probably too much for my parents. Or perhaps Mami and Marina were tired of the daily struggle to make me wear the corset and hang from the metal bar. Possibly my back was better and it did not seem necessary to continue the treatment. In any case, I was delighted to not have to wear a corset to school every day, although for the rest of my childhood and adolescence, my mother never stopped saying, every time she looked at my posture, "Stand up straight! Do you want to be a hunchback?"

Saints in the Cuban Heat

At school or at home, I continued retreating easily into my fantasies. Becoming a saint became one of those fantasies. My favorite one, in fact.

Early in my childhood *los Tres Reyes Magos*—the Three Kings—had brought me a small book, *Niños Santos* that contained the stories of holy children. A film on the life of Rose of Lima, the first canonized saint of the Americas, had become a popular hit in Latin America when I was about eight. *Rosa de América*, a black and white feature film, triggered even more of my fantasies about sainthood. Glamorous Argentinean actress Delia Garcés played the role of Rose of Lima. Her beauty made sainthood seem attractive. Her dark curly hair, so much like mine, made me think I could be like her if I tried to behave like her.

Rosa was Latin American, not European like the other saints I was reading about. This made her particularly attractive. The incessant tremors of Cuban political history, the distant echoes of life and death dramas in other Latin American countries, were ever-present during my childhood, even though I did not have a clear understanding of those events.

Trying to imitate Rosa's masochistic and self-torturing behaviors, I filled my school shoes with beans, knelt on pebbles to pray, and went long hours without drinking water in the Cuban heat, while dreaming about founding a religious order named after Rose of Lima. I spent hours designing the habit my nuns would wear, making it as beautiful as possible: white pleated chiffon, trimmed with black velvet at the neckline, the sleeves and the waist, silky black veil. I wanted to be a fashionable saint!

A few years later, during Christmas vacation, I saw the now legendary film in which Ingrid Bergman played the role of Joan of Arc. For an eleven-year-old girl already half aware of the limitations awaiting her in 1950s Cuba, imagining being Joan of Arc even for a fleeting moment meant that anything might be possible.

My mother had four sisters, my father, three. All of them were over thirty. My mother's beautiful sisters were desperate to get married. They were unlike my father's sisters who wore shapeless dresses that made them look like the pious spinsters they were. Cubans called women who looked and acted like my paternal aunts "cucarachas de sacristía"— "sacristy cockroaches." None of these alternatives appealed to me. Nor did becoming a woman in a society where girls and women weren't supposed to be too smart, where adolescent girls never went out without chaperones to watch over them because women who were not virgins would not get married, and where women anticipated infidelity in their husbands as the price to be paid for financial security.

I spent the rest of that Christmas vacation and many weekends after that, when my father's students were gone, being Joan of Arc. Valiantly straddling desks, jumping over tables and chairs and whatever other pieces of furniture happened to be in my way, I carried my banner, an old piece of cloth tied to a broomstick, held in my hand a ruler that was my triumphant sword, and set out to climb castle walls and conquer fortresses. I imagined that if I became a Cuban Joan of Arc—*Santa Oliva de Cuba*—I might be able to put an end to the political dramas and perhaps even restore my father to his position as Teniente Auditor of the Navy.

I had read other stories and fairy tales and seen other films about young female heroines. Indeed, Disney's *Snow White* was the first film I saw. But the stories of young women devoted so deeply to God that they reached the Catholic Church's pinnacle of sanctity, truly captivated my imagination.

And yet, I find it amusing that my wanting to be a saint and imitate these women did not interfere with other not so saintly activities. Around the time, I saw the film on Rose of Lima, I discovered that lying on the bed on my stomach and rubbing against the mattress gave me a delightful sensation *down there*. I did not have any sense of this being a sexual activity or something sinful. I would not have known what "sexual" meant. But I vaguely knew that I should not be doing this and that no one should know what I was doing. In any case, the sensation was delicious and I did not stop practicing this activity almost every night while I continued praying and hoping to become a saint.

II

Santiago

O monja o artist/A nun or an actress

Every summer, Nery and I left behind the two bedrooms in the back of the flat that housed my father's school in Havana and went to Santiago de Cuba in the Eastern part of the island. We spent three months in the house where my mother's parents and siblings lived together as they had for several decades. In Havana, I lived walled in by asphalt and cement; in Santiago, open spaces where magic and freedom bloomed along with luscious vegetation welcomed me and gave me the chance to enact my fantasies and become the characters I read about in books.

More than in the bustling Havana streets, the Cuba of the 1940s is encapsulated for me in the daily routines of life in Santiago. My childhood memories are full of the charms of the provincial city; the steep streets, balconies, and portals; the distant mountains of the Sierra Maestra that could be glimpsed from my grandparents' dining room windows; the waters of the Santiago Bay—where in 1898 Spain lost its last battle for Cuba and the few remnants of what had been the largest empire in history. *Santiagueros* were proud of their city, which had been the first capital of Cuba and the birthplace of all struggles for Cuban independence. I, too, was *santiaguera*; I had been born there and loved Santiago. I was proud of its rich colonial heritage, its vibrant music scene, and the transparent water of its beaches.

Memories of the long trips to get there, of what I lived through and savored during those summers in Santiago, of the neighbors and childhood friends, of Carnavales, evoke for me what my country was then, with all its limitations and beauty.

The sound of distant trains still fills me with excitement. Trains meant escaping the cramped space of our Havana flat. The train ride itself was a treat—the beginning of vacation; a first taste of the open world that awaited me in Santiago. Cuba was one of the first countries in the world to have a railroad system in the nineteenth century. Trains were comfortable and efficient. In addition to regular seats, they had private compartments with tiny bathrooms at both ends of each wagon. When I was little, we travelled in one of those compartments.

Papi took us to the train station every year in a taxi cluttered with suitcases. Mami travelled with us to Santiago. Nery and I, dressed in blue overalls with colorful, short-sleeved T-shirts, jumped up and down on the train corridor between the seats while the suitcases were being carried into the compartment by Papi and a porter. Papi joined us in Santiago about a week later and both of my parents returned to Havana together a few days after that, leaving us behind to enjoy our stay. One or another of my mother's sisters brought us back to Havana at the end of summer.

The train ride between Havana and Santiago took about twenty hours. As the train lurched at a snail's pace along the 540 miles that separate the two cities, almost the full length of Cuba, we passed endless cane fields interspersed with *bohíos*, the huts made of boards thatched with royal palm fronds where the peasants lived. Looking out of the windows I saw uninterrupted green expanses of vegetation go by. Thick *ceibas* and other towering trees, tall royal palms, trees full of avocados or guavas, horses or cattle, wild flowers. Occasionally, a thunder and lightning storm could be seeing in the distance.

The changing scenery and shifting views outside the windows usually provided enough amusement, although occasionally we would sit back to play a board game—Chinese checkers, dominos—but not for long. It was not easy to keep the pieces in place in the moving train. Mostly, I enjoyed looking out the window at the moving countryside that kept going by during the many hours of the train ride, reluctantly going to sleep in my berth only when it was completely dark outside. I did not want to miss anything. The train ride was our first taste of open space.

Idle peasants—*güajiros*—sat at the door of their *bohíos*. They would not have paid work until the *zafra* in January, when all hands were needed to cut cane during the first three months of each year. Most of the land was owned by the large sugar conglomerates and nothing but cane was cultivated. The *güajiros* were unemployed nine months of the year. If they owned any land, it was a tiny plot behind their *bohíos* where they could grow a few vegetables and keep a few hens or, if they were lucky, pigs or a cow.

The passing train barely drew the attention of the *güajiros*, although when it stopped in the towns along the way, they swarmed it trying to sell fruit, vegetables or sweets. The little money they got from selling stuff to the passengers was probably their only source of income during the hot and rainy summer months. Not aware of the pitiful condition of the *güajiros*, I liked what their presence added to the picturesque landscape.

Later, when I was about ten, we started going to Santiago by bus, which was faster; it took only fourteen hours. One of my mother's sisters came to Havana to pick us up and to bring us back at the end of summer. Sometimes their cousin Lilia went with us. One summer, Nery and I, full of fear and excitement, were sent alone by plane.

Santiago was paradise: a huge house with many rooms where I could hide to read all day undisturbed, a patio full of shrubbery and flowers, several doting aunts, new dresses, gifts from visiting relatives, smells of garlic and oregano exuding from the kitchen, my grandmother Fefita's stories about Spain, playmates among neighborhood kids, evenings in Parque Céspedes in the center of the city. I relished spending my summers in that house at the other end of Cuba.

My mother had lived in that house since the early 1930s, leaving only to marry my father. My last surviving aunt died in that house in 1996. Whenever I think of Cuba, or of happy childhood moments, the image of that house is present in my mind. And, specially, its rectangular central patio, the interior courtyard which was the universe where my childhood fantasy life flourished.

Santiago-The patio

Sitting in that patio or in one of the empty rooms, I read voraciously—from children's books to adult novels, including authors like Emile Zola, who my father would not have allowed me to read at that age. The many bushes and tall fruit trees provided little nooks and hiding corners where each childhood summer I was Robin Hood or Lady Marian, Ivanhoe or Joan of Arc or some other saint or hero. In that patio, I could become as daring as those legendary figures. I thought I could be a famous person of some sort, perhaps a miracle-worker saint. I could become a writer. Or an actress like Ingrid Bergman or Argentinean Delia Garcés or Imperio Argentina, the beautiful Spanish singer who appeared in the black and white films I went to see with my aunts. With so many interesting and challenging possibilities, I had trouble deciding which path to follow.

When my aunts asked what I wanted to be when I grew up, I always responded, *"O monja o artista"*— "A nun or an actress." My response provoked great hilarity because of the apparent contradiction of my intended professions, but I remained determined to be one or the other or preferably both. In Santiago, reading stories and fantasizing for long hours in the patio seemed to make it all possible. Even though my aunts teased me, in Santiago I felt free to say what I wanted. In Havana, my mother would have called me silly, an edge creeping into her voice, and she would have commanded me to perform some chore or another and forget my childishness.

I lived those summers surrounded by brightly colored vegetation and tropical foliage the whole gamut of green. Red hibiscus, light blue plumbago, and other flowering plants grew all over in the patio, competing for space with several varieties of ferns and climbing vines and pots where basil, oregano, and other herbs grew. A universe of birds, lizards—*chipojos*, as they were called in Santiago, instead of *lagartijas*, their usual Spanish name—worms, and insects as well as the occasional stray cat profited from the shrubbery as shadow or food, and shared the space with me, Nery, the other grandchildren and our neighborhood friends. I do not think it was a coincidence that the cats I saw walking on the red tile roof of the house in Santiago never scared me as the cats in Havana did. Buzzards—*auras tiñosas*—glided slowly above as if stationary in the blue sky.

Hallway, Santiago house

A long veranda corridor ran along one side of the patio and ended in a huge open kitchen at the patio's edge. Light bounced off the white and red shiny tiles behind the big coal stove with its massive chimney where Abuela Fefita prepared delicious food; I loved the smells that wafted from that cooking.

My grandfather's and my uncles' bedrooms opened into the veranda. The two rooms closest to the kitchen were used for food storage, unwanted items, and trinkets. The doors of these two rooms usually remained closed unless Abuela Fefita or the maid or one of my uncles went in there to look for something.

Door to Abuelo Candido's room, Santiago house

The windows of a large dining room looked into the patio on the same side as the living room. Together, living and dining room formed an L-shaped angle with the veranda. At the front of the house, beyond the dining and living rooms were my grandmother's and my aunts' bedrooms. During our summer stays, Nery and I slept on cots, under mosquito nets, in a corner of my grandmother's bedroom.

Living room, Santiago house

Division between living and dining rooms, Santiago house

Sample of mosaic floors in the Santiago house, typical of Cuban houses

A plain iron fence divided the central patio from a dirt-and-cement walled backyard, *el traspatio*, with no flowers or plants. The *traspatio* was inhabited by a fierce, terrifying guard dog, appropriately named León. He had the coloring and the face of a yellow Labrador, the size of a Great Dane, and the temperament of neither. Against the back wall of León's kingdom leaned the old carriage house, where horses and coaches had been kept a half century before I was born and now served as depository for unwanted pieces of furniture and other junk. A large cement-floored covered space, where all laundry was still done by hand, and a tool shed were also off the *traspatio*. These structures separated the property from several small dwellings from which we could hear the constant conversation or singing of neighbors who lived in what must have been the servants'—or perhaps slaves'—quarters in the nineteenth century when this house was the mansion of a rich family. The nooks and crannies were endless.

Façade of my grandparents' house in Santiago

Instead of a front porch, my grandparents' house had five small wrought-iron balconies along the front that were closed at night with wooden shutters that let the breeze in. During the day, the wooden shutters were folded back and kept open. Because the street sloped sharply down along the front of the house, the first balcony was almost at street level. The last two balconies were one story high. Beneath these two higher balconies that provided light and fresh air to my grandmother's bedroom, lay a wide door that was never opened, *el portón*, big enough for a horse carriage, which is probably how it was used in the nineteenth century. El *portón* closed off a porch-like area with beautiful tiled walls and floor. A small door, a segment of *el portón*, served as the entrance and led to a short flight of stairs that gave access to the house.

Every summer morning, I descended the wide red-brick steps that led to the patio, after going through a wrought-iron gate that separated the patio from the living room. I plunged into the vegetation of my private jungle with its splendid trees; the fantasy world I owned during those summer days. Hibiscus adorned my hair to make me look like a Spanish gypsy. Little plumbago flowers in aquamarine tones hooked together to become necklaces and bracelets of precious stones. Tall ferns formed woods where I roamed looking for hidden treasures and dangerous creatures.

The most important occupant of this, my fantasy forest, was a soaring *mamoncillo*, a tree that produced small round green fruit with a big pit and tough skin similar to lychees. Several tall fruit trees grew around the patio, but the *mamoncillo* stood alone in one corner. On its rough bark, lizards crawled undisturbed. Bits of grass fought their way out of the cement cracks left by the unruly growth of the *mamoncillo's* roots. The thick tree trunk, several feet wide, grew many meters high, surpassing the roof of the house, its many limbs and branches growing high in all directions. One branch, a foot wide or so, grew out sideways at about my height before taking a vertical turn. On this branch, three knots created the illusion of a face: two eyes and a mouth, slightly above my own, smiling at me. The knotted branch became an ideal boyfriend for my imagination. I stepped into place next to my beloved, pretending that we were taking a stroll together, holding hands. I embraced and kissed the wooden mouth with all the passion I had seen actresses do in the movies, and I spent hours in conversation with my invented *novio* or fabricating stories about our undying love.

Where my tree friend used to be

My attraction to my tree boyfriend did not go unnoticed.

Nery, who thought I was mildly "cuckoo" because of all my imaginary adventures would dissolve into laughter when she saw me kissing the tree. Every now and then, one of my aunts would reprimand me: "What do you think you are doing, kissing a dirty tree? You can catch some illness doing that. Stop it!"

Undeterred, I continued talking to myself and loving my tree. And I continued reading the stories that fed my fantasies. Nery, meanwhile, played at mothering her dolls like most girls did.

On most summer evenings, after showering and getting into fresh clothes, Nery and I went with one or another of my aunts, to the center of Santiago to walk and play among the laurel trees in Parque Céspedes, as so many other *santiagueros* did, trying to escape the heat of the summer nights. Parque Céspedes is framed by Santiago's City Hall, the Cathedral where my parents married, and the Hotel Casa Granda, a grand establishment that dates from 1914. The evening outings to Parque Céspedes were full of adventures running around with other children.

Parque Céspedes

About once a week, my aunt Mercedes, her boyfriend Jorge, Nery and I boarded a big motor boat that provided public transportation to points inside the Bay like the tiny Cayo Smith—El Cayo for short—a key in the middle of Santiago Bay where Jorge owned a house. From the pier in the city where we boarded the steam boat to the small pier of El Cayo the ride was about a half hour. The smell of sea salt surrounded us. Shrieking seagulls and other sea birds encircled the boat but abandoned pursuit as soon as they realized that the big launch carried humans, not fish.

El Cayo

Jorge owned a small rowboat with an outboard motor that Nery and I commanded while Jorge and Mercedes, sitting on the front of the boat, watched us and talked. We circled the Santiago Bay in this small boat, making sure we did not approach the narrow entrance where the waves became too strong and there was danger of capsizing. Nery and I took turns steering the boat into the many little coves that cluster inside the Bay like curls on a mane made of water. Slowly, we went by the cliffs and reefs, observing the vegetation and the birds soaring over our heads and admiring the beautiful houses on top of the hills that surrounded Santiago Bay.

But what we loved most was playing with the dolphins. At some point during our boat rides, a couple of *toninas*—as the dolphins were called—dark and shiny, with beautifully pointed snouts, jumped out of the water in front of our boat. They were unmistakably inviting us to pursue them by repeatedly shooting up ahead. Enthralled by their presence, Nery and I pointed the small boat in their direction, laughing loudly every time they avoided us by submerging themselves, only to appear again on the surface a few feet ahead. And, to our great amusement, as if by magic, a few more *toninas* appeared to the left or the right of the boat, joining in the game, jumping and glistening in the sun. The thrill of pursuing the beautiful animals lasted until Jorge or Mercedes would tell us that they were getting dizzy with so much swerving. After a few more sharp turns, we stopped our game. Otherwise, Jorge would have taken over the tiller and Nery and I would have lost the chance to control the boat.

The dolphins continued leaping out of the water in front of the boat for a while, but eventually left when they realized the game was over, perhaps looking for other playmates in other areas of the Bay.

Despite so much playing on water and beaches, despite growing up in an island, neither Nery nor I ever learned to swim. Once, a swimming instructor in Ciudamar, one of the beach clubs in Santiago, had tried to teach me. His lessons consisted of lowering children into deep water tied with a rope around our waist with which he held us from above. As he walked the length of the pier moving the rope along, he just ordered, "Paddle!" But I was too terrified that he would let go of the rope. Rather than trying to swim, I thrashed the water with such desperation that he raised me up, untied me as soon as my wet feet touched the pier and yelled, "Next!" A little boy came down strutting and boasting that he would not be afraid to be in the water like girls were. I walked away wet, embarrassed and humiliated. I never tried to learn to swim again.

Abuela Fefita and Abuelo Cándido

By the time I was ten or so, only Abuela Fefita, three of my aunts, and Candito, the youngest of my uncles, who was deaf, lived in the very large house. My grandfather, Abuelo Cándido, was there only part of the time. The rest of the time he lived in his small farm in the town of El Cristo, about seven kilometers from Santiago. Regardless of who lived there, without doubt, the house was first and foremost Abuela Fefita's kingdom.

She ruled her household with an iron fist, always yelling about one thing or another, barking orders at someone whose behavior displeased her. She would deliver incessant commands, trying to control everyone.

"Don't run in the hallway!"

"Stop that loud laughter!"

"Close that door!"

"Don't use so much soap to wash your hands!"

"Don't make so much noise!"

"Be silent during meals!"

"This plate is not cleaned properly!"

"That is not the correct way to iron clothes!"

Luckily, the house was big enough and, with a little practice, I learned to ignore her ill-tempered voice while I was reading or playing. Lots of enjoyable activities overshadowed her grumbling.

Each one of my unmarried aunts was assigned a specific chore that she had to perform daily. The intricately designed tile floors were swept, mopped, and polished bright by Mirita. Celia dusted the furniture and the picture frames and trinkets on top of each table, the frames of the mirrors and paintings on the walls; she then applied wood polish to each chair and table. Mercedes watered the plants in the patio and spent the rest of the day sewing dresses for Nery and me or for herself or her sisters. These tasks were performed every single day, which made me wonder how it was possible that floors needed mopping and furniture needed dusting with such frequency. But there was no questioning Fefita's orders.

One of her daily orders was that Nery and I should eat our meals without drinking any water. If she caught us trying to have some liquid in the middle of a meal, she ordered us to leave the table hungry. More than once in one of her fits of rage she said that it was no wonder Abuela Boqui had died because Nery and I were such bad girls that we probably had killed her. Not what I needed to hear!

If she had had her way, her daughters and grandchildren would have sat still all day, in silence, doing nothing, unless we were performing tasks she had commanded us to do… and doing them in the exact way she thought they should be done. I wondered then and still wonder now what made her so angry and impatient all the time. Perhaps she had felt so frustrated all her life that she needed to lash out. Perhaps she had some mental illness.

My mother and aunts, who had suffered her tyranny, never dared voice anger toward her even when they were adults. My mother was the only daughter who married young. Two of my uncles married soon after and left to live with their wives' families. Marina moved to Havana with us. The other daughters and my deaf uncle stayed in the house until they died.

Fefita woke up every morning at five and sat on a cane-back Cuban style rocking chair in a small foyer by the entrance door, impatiently waiting for everyone else to wake up. At seven, she would start yelling that it was late enough and everyone should be up. Her daughters got out of bed quickly. Nery and I lingered for as long as we could, until her loud commands made it impossible to sleep any longer. Only my deaf uncle, who could not hear her shouts, slept undisturbed for as long as he wanted.

When she woke up, Fefita brewed coffee and put it in a big pot with three times the amount of milk and a lot of sugar. The mixture sat on the stove for several hours, so by the time Nery and I had our breakfast only the buttered slices of Cuban bread, sometimes covered with brown sugar in addition to the butter, compensated for the horrible taste of the coffee mixture. If one of us commented about the taste of her *café con leche*, Abuela had an immediate response,

"Wake up earlier and you will get a better taste."

She spent her mornings cooking in the open kitchen on a big brick stove topped by a huge chimney that drew up the smoke of the coal fire. She did not trust the maid or any of my aunts with the cooking. After lunch, she supervised the maid who washed the dishes and pots and hovered around the woman who boiled and laundered by hand the clothes of the large household. Fefita believed no one could do anything as well as she did. And, in fact, the meals of black beans and rice, pork or beef, plantains and *yuca* she had learned to cook throughout her decades of life in Cuba, were delicious despite the primitive stove she used. The smell of spices that lingered through the house while she was cooking is one of my fondest childhood memories. It provided the sense of warmth she could not bring herself to convey.

The kitchen, Santiago house

Sometimes she cooked *caldo gallego* or *fabada asturiana*—substantial garbanzo or white bean soups with pieces of chorizo and ham and a lot of garlic that were typical of either Galicia or Asturias, the regions of Spain my grandparents had come from. I loved the taste of these thick soups although they made me sweat profusely because they had not been intended for the Cuban climate.

Lunch was served at noon sharp when the loud wailing of the Bacardí rum distillery siren could be heard all over Santiago. At the loud sound that announced to the workers that it was time for the lunch break, Fefita expected everyone to be at table without a minute's delay. We had to stop we were doing, wash our hands, and go to the dining room immediately or risk Fefita's rage.

My aunts, my uncles who usually came for lunch even after they were married, and grandchildren would wait for Abuela and the maid to bring the big platters of food along the veranda that separated the kitchen and the dining room. Nery and I sat on piles of *Vanidades* magazines placed on the seats of grown-up chairs to help us reach the table.

In the mornings, until lunch time, Abuela Fefita smelled of garlic, spices, and smoke. In the late afternoons, after she took her daily shower, she smelled of Lifebuoy soap and cologne, and did not go near the kitchen until the next day. She washed her long white hair daily, so it would not smell of cooking smoke, and rolled it into a tight bun fastened with long hairpins at the back of her head. After the evening meal—that usually consisted of previously made soup, cold cuts, bread, vegetables and fruit—she sat and read the newspapers. For the next hour or so at least, she was silent, probably as spent from her day's yelling as we all were.

Abuela Fefita softened only when she told stories about Spain. This usually happened in the early afternoon, after lunch, when everyone else was taking a *siesta*, and Abuela was supervising the maid who washed the lunch dishes. Fefita's stories about the Spain she had left when she was a child and visited only briefly in mid-life were always idyllic. In Spain people were always nice, meals were always delicious, hot chocolate was thicker and tastier, chorizo was yummier, relatives loved each other unconditionally, everyone was respectful, and women wore hats that made them look elegant.

Abuelo Cándido had regularly sent money to his siblings, nieces, and nephews in Spain. In the late 1920s, when my mother was fifteen, he engineered a trip to his hometown for the entire family. He wanted to show his wealth to all the relatives left back in his native region of Asturias. He wanted to show his children where he had come from. By then Fefita and Cándido had lived in Cuba for fifty years or so. During those decades they had never been back to the Spain they had left as children.

My mother's family right before leaving for Spain, 1927

This trip, when she visited her country of birth with Abuelo Cándido and their eight children, her only time in Spain as an adult, was the source of Abuela's tales about the country. The thick, tasty hot chocolate, the elegant women, and all the rest that made Spain marvelous came from that visit. From her glowing stories, Spain grew to be a legendary and extraordinary place in my child's mind. I could not grasp then that most of the anecdotes she told were idealizations of a country she barely knew. Memories of the Galicia of her childhood were too blurry or too dreary to be remembered or recounted.

Fefita had arrived in Cuba in the nineteenth century with her mother and siblings when she was nine years old and Cuba was still a colony of Spain. Her baptismal certificate describes her parents as illiterate peasants living in a small hamlet in Galicia in the 1870s. I don't know why my great-grandmother Matilde came to Cuba with her children; I never knew who paid for their voyage. Probably, Matilde came to work as a maid to escape the poverty of rural Spain. She and her children were among the half million Spaniards who emigrated to Cuba during the last third of the nineteenth century, counting on the advantage their Spanish birth gave them in the island colony—the same reason why many citizens of European powers have moved to their colonies through the centuries. Matilde needed to make sure that Josefita, her eldest, was married to someone who could support her. She chose Cándido, another Spaniard, to marry her daughter because in her mind, any Cuban, no matter how educated or how well-to-do, was inferior to any Spaniard, a belief held by my most of her countrymen and women.

Mixed with Abuela's daily afternoon stories about the wonders of Spain were angry tales about my grandfather. She complained that he made her work at one of the machines in his printing business when she was five months pregnant with one of my uncles. She repeated this and other stories as proof of his lack of consideration. By the time I was born, my grandparents slept in separate bedrooms even when Abuelo Cándido was in town from his farm. I always knew there was no love lost between them.

Abuela Fefita's accent was thick; it underscored her peasant roots and her lack of education. Her Cuban grandchildren laughed behind her back and imitated her thick accent. Our sneering was a small revenge against her domineering and unpleasant ways. In fact, we never laughed about Abuelo Cándido's accent, which—although slightly less marked because of his years of involvement in business—was not much different. As children and grandchildren of immigrants have for generations, we were both embarrassed and fascinated by the accents of the old country we had never seen and Abuela herself only vaguely remembered. Her quirky accent also included words and ways of saying them we never heard from anyone else. For example, when she stubbornly refused to have a shot for any medical treatment, she called the doctors prescribed injections, *enyeciones,* rather than *inyecciones,* the correct Spanish word.

About three-years-old, with Abuela Fefita

I felt somewhat guilty mocking Abuela because I knew I was her favorite grandchild. She seldom left the house, but when she did, she always took me with her. On the rare occasions when she said something nice about someone, it was usually a word of praise for me. She made no attempt to hide her favoritism. Years later, when I went to Spain for the first time, she sent me as a gift a ring my grandfather had given her—a diamond mounted in platinum with an elaborate Victorian design. This was the ring I smuggled out of Cuba in the hem of a dress. I still own it. Nery never received such a gift and rarely even a nice word from Abuela.

Once, when she was about ten, at the smell of the accumulated stuff in one of the storage rooms near the kitchen, Nery blurted, "*¡Qué peste a viejo!*" — "What an unpleasant smell of old things!" Abuela Fefita was just walking down the corridor. She assumed my sister was making a disparaging comment about her and proceeded to grab Nery by the arm, slap her, and punish her by having Nery sit for three days in the kitchen, where Fefita could watch over her and make sure she did not leave her chair for anything but eating and going to the bathroom. Despite Nery's many protestations and explanations about what she had said and despite the many pleas of my aunts to release her from this punishment, Abuela Fefita did not relent. And I was caught between my empathy for Nery and my desire to be thought of as the better child. I knew the punishment was extreme but felt relieved to be safe from Fefita's anger. I was afraid of receiving some arbitrary punishment myself if I dared antagonize Abuela or tried to change her mind. I basked in my status of favorite grandchild that protected me from her anger. I also felt vaguely guilty for the undeserved punishment Nery was getting; in some formless way I felt my good standing with Fefita was equally undeserved.

Abuela Fefita was very proud of her methods for disciplining children; making her children stay in an enclosure of chairs all day long, belting them whenever they transgressed or disobeyed her orders. Insistently, she recommended her disciplinary methods to her two daughters-in-law. My guess is they went back home understanding better their husbands' coldness.

When we reached adolescence, Nery and I could not talk to a boy without Abuela going into a tirade about not talking to *mozalbetes*— her own peculiar word for young men. One of the *mozalbetes* happened to be my boyfriend, a gentle and bright boy who had the most beautiful dark eyes and long lashes I had ever seen. I knew my heart would be broken leaving him at the end of summer. I was in love with him as only adolescent girls can be. Once, Abuela abruptly and unceremoniously closed the balcony doors on my face while I was talking to him, embarrassing me and my shy boyfriend. I retorted, "But you were married at fifteen! How did you marry if you did not talk to guys?" My question made Abuela even more furious. She warned me not be fresh and disrespectful, and continued yelling for another half hour while the balcony doors remained closed.

As an adult woman, I can see that Abuela's experience of marrying at fifteen a man ten years older because she was ordered to do so by her mother, and then having twelve children in rapid succession, only eight of whom lived to adulthood, had nothing to do with my desire to talk to boys or have a boyfriend. Nery and I saw it as freedom and enjoyment; she probably saw it as danger and future constriction. Women of her generation and background had one child after another, frequently from loveless marriages, because both the knowledge and availability of birth control were extremely limited or non-existent. In retrospect, I think she might have been trying to shield us from a fate she had suffered and feared for us. But her harsh style made it difficult to understand her motives. Abuela Fefita's approach to everything was so different from Abuela Boqui's kind gentleness that more than once during my childhood and adolescence I wished that Fefita were the dead Abuela.

Despite her unpleasantness, I knew she was delighted with our yearly visit. She made a point of cooking what we liked. She encouraged my aunt Mercedes to sew us new dresses. Many other little things showed her pleasure at our presence during those three months every summer. I, in turn, learned early to ignore Abuela's irritation and ranting. Her bad temper became only a minor annoyance in the larger picture of Santiago's delights.

Abuela Fefita died in Cuba a few years after we had left the country. By the time she died, she had lost her memory—but she had continued to yell nonsensical orders at the top of her lungs all day long. My mother and aunts, who never dared raise their voices to her when she was alive, did not express relief when she died. It was Abuelo Cándido who spoke for all of them. He said to my mother on a long-distance phone call, "She is not the only one who is at peace now."

Abuelo Cándido never minced words.

When I was twelve years old or so and talking to a tree or playing at being a hero, a saint or a hermit were no longer appealing, a new attraction appeared in the patio. Abuelo Cándido, who had lived in his farm outside of Santiago for most of my childhood, sat there every day surrounded by his newspapers, always ready for storytelling and conversation. I was an enthusiastic listener. Like Abuela Fefita, he was full of stories, most of them rather different from hers. Abuelo Cándido's stories about his childhood in Spain and his many decades in Cuba were far from idealizations. He talked about the deprivation he had experienced in Spain; about the long hours of arduous work he had put in to make a living in late nineteenth-century Cuba.

With Abuelo Cándido when I was a baby

Cándido had come to Cuba from rural Spain in the early 1880s. His baptismal certificate states that he was born on September 2, 1870 in the tiny village of Colloto, near Oviedo, in the province of Asturias. My aunts said he had been sent to the island as a *quinto*—a military conscript—when he was fifteen years old. My mother said that Cándido's father had sold a cow to buy him a third-class ticket on a ship. But, sitting in the patio, he told me he had come as a stowaway because he could no longer tolerate the poverty and exhausting physical labor he had to endure since he was a child. Apparently, the only job available to him in rural Asturias was carrying big stones on his back for the construction of coal mines. He could not bear this heavy labor that provided only a meager income, so he left his parents and five siblings, and went to Cuba.

I suspect that if he had been sent to Cuba by the Spanish government as a *quinto*, to fight against Cuban independence, he might not have wanted to talk to me about that. Indeed, he did not talk about the last few years of the nineteenth century, before U.S. intervention in Cuba, when the war of independence was raging and most Spaniards served in the Volunteers Corps—the *Voluntarios*, a vigilante group—fighting against Cubans. Only once, in passing, did he mention that he had served as a *Voluntario*. He probably knew that his eight Cuban children and his grandchildren would not take kindly to this involvement. More than fifty years after these events, he probably had little desire to refer to it. He had decided to stay in Cuba after it was no longer a colony of Spain. He had learned to keep a low profile after Cuba's independence. He died a citizen of Spain in 1970s Cuba—his statement of where he thought he still belonged.

Either as a *quinto*, a paid passenger, or a stowaway, Abuelo Cándido had not passed up the opportunity to leave Spain's rural poverty and try his luck in Cuba. He took advantage of his position as a Spaniard in the colonial social structure. In Spain, he was just another poor peasant. In Cuba, he was one of the *peninsulares*, born on the Iberian Peninsula, therefore entitled to more rights and privileges than anyone born in Cuba, even highly educated *criollos*—Cubans who had Spanish parents or grandparents—such as my father's family.

"When I was sixteen, after several months in Cuba," he told me once in his calm voice, still thick with the accent of his native Asturias, even though he had lived in Cuba for more than six decades, "I started working at a jewelry store owned by another Spaniard, guarding the store at night. During the day, I swept the store, cleaned the glass counters with a rag, scrubbed and polished the wooden frames of cabinets and counters."

Although he did not say it, I knew he had gotten this position, despite his youth, because he was a *peninsular*; his birthplace opened doors for him as he had expected. If he had come to Cuba as a *quinto*, his military superiors might have "rented" him out to the business owner—a widespread practice then. The owner would not have trusted a Cuban to be alone in his store at night. No Spaniard could trust Cubans while they were trying to become independent from Spain.

Abuelo's first job in Cuba at this jewelry store provided a space under the counter where he could sleep after the owner and the employees had left. His duty as a night guard did not pay money but gave him shelter. "Only a strong sixteen-year-old could tolerate the uncomfortable sleeping space," he chuckled. "But it gave me a place for the night. I didn't have anywhere to go and didn't have to pay to stay there."

There, he taught himself to read and write. During the day, young Cándido collected newspapers left behind by customers or employees. Before the end of the workday, he approached the owner or a sales clerk, showed them one or two words on the newspapers that he could see had some similarities, and asked them to read the words for him.

"I would show them words that look similar, say, *'casa,' 'cama,' 'hamaca;'* and then I repeated the words to myself so I would remember the combination of letters with which the sounds were written," he told me. In the evening, after the others had left, with the help of a candle, he looked at those words, repeated them, and copied them, drawing the shapes of the letters with a pencil on the empty margins of newspaper pages.

He knew the meaning of most of the words he was learning to read and write, but others, like *economía—economy*, he also had to ask what they meant. Slowly, after months of laborious evenings, spent learning more and more words, Cándido could read whole pages of newspapers. He went around the store reading to himself the descriptions and prices of the jewelry kept inside the locked glass and wood cabinets.

The store owner noticed his newly acquired ability as well as his eagerness to learn. In a year, he was promoted to cashier, and after another year of sleeping under the counter, saving every penny he earned during the day, he left the jewelry store and settled himself independently.

The illiterate peasant who had taught himself to read and write had gone from cleaning the shop and being the night watch boy to owner of his own small business. As the decades rolled by, his business savvy helped him continue to increase his wealth. Abuelo Cándido succeeded in owning several establishments—installing glass panes on homes and store windows, printing children's books, labels and tobacco rings. He bought blocks of commercial property in the center of Santiago that he rented out. He amassed a fortune that made his children forget they might have been poor peasants in Spain.

These tales of exile and migration for political or economic reasons, followed by stories of patriotic or financial success were part of my early consciousness through my grandparents' and my father's stories. Long before I could anticipate I would also live most of my life away from my country of birth, I had heard innumerable stories on both sides of my family about longing for a distant place. No wonder studying migration narratives has been the main focus of my professional career.

When Abuelo Cándido retired, he bought a little farm near the city, in the town of El Cristo, a short ride outside of Santiago, where he lived by himself. Whether he wanted to go back to his rural roots or to keep distance from Fefita by moving to this farm after retirement, I never knew.

Before he retired, Abuelo distributed the bulk of his money among his eight adult children. He didn't want them to wait for his death. My mother received a chunk of money and the ownership of my grandfather's printing shop. In my father's inexpert hands, the money disappeared slowly, lent to people who never repaid him. The printing shop was sold to my mother's cousin. The profits from this sale went the way of everything else.

Although Abuelo owned the farm where he retired and other properties in the city, the large family house where I spent my summers was rented. It did not become family property until the advent of the Revolution, when people were allowed to claim ownership of the places where they lived.

Abuelo Candido's farm house in El Cristo

A visit to Abuelo Cándido in El Cristo was always an enjoyable adventure. Nery and I went with my aunt Mercedes by public bus from Plaza de Marta in Santiago to the gate of the farm. The ride took about forty-five minutes. As on the train from Havana, we saw sitting *güajiros* and thatched roofed *bohíos* as the bus rode on the rural roads. When the bus stopped for passengers to get on or off in the small towns along the way, street vendors were waiting. We purchased green coconuts with a little hole at one end from which a straw protruded, and we drank the cool coconut milk, a viscous and sweet tangy liquid, a delicacy that tasted better than any other juice I knew.

On the porch of the farm house in El Cristo

At the farm, Nery and I rode on horseback, both of us together on the grayish mare Abuelo Cándido owned. We steered it this way and that. After an hour or so of horseback riding, we stopped to watch my grandfather and his one farm worker pull pineapples and *yuca* roots up from the ground. The worker handed us ripe *guayabas*—guavas— from one of the trees while we sat on the cool porch floor of the ramshackle farmhouse. At the end of the day we went back to Santiago telling stories about the outing to the aunts who had not accompanied us.

Abuelo was taciturn, soft-spoken, and somewhat aloof. His tall stature and erect back, his starched shirts, and his calm, confident air gave him an elegant appearance that belied his poor origins. He did not need to raise his voice to establish his authority. The only time I saw him come close to losing his temper was once when Fefita was, as usual, scolding one of the grandchildren sitting at the table. With his habitual composure, in a steady voice, he said firmly from the other end of the table,

"Woman, if you say one more word, I am going to turn over this table with everything on top. Anything, so I don't have to hear your irritating nagging any longer!"

For once, Fefita was silent for the rest of the meal.

As he read his newspaper on the patio, under the shadow of the tall fruit trees, Abuelo commented on what was happening throughout the world. He had acerbic views about Cuba's politics. By the time I reached adolescence, he had witnessed the political transformation of Cuba from a Spanish colony, a U.S. occupied territory, a republic, and a dictatorship. Years later, he would also witness Cuba's transformation into a communist country. Spain's governments did not fare much better in his view. Franco had thwarted hopes for change. Abuelo detested Franco as much as his royal predecessors. The one thing Fefita and he had in common was their disdain for everything and anything associated with Franco or Spain's royalty, particularly religion and the church. Both Fefita and Cándido were unbending about their disgust with anything religious. No wonder my mother had no use for religion.

Abuela Fefita contributed regularly to some nuns who took care of the elderly and infirm, but her donations were motivated by her desire to help good people who helped the poor, not by religious feelings.

"Everything ends after you go under the ground," she told me once in her customary abrupt style, after the nuns who had come to collect the monthly donation had left. "I give money to these nuns because of their good work, not so they pray for me. In any case, there is no God; so, no one would listen to those prayers. And I will never give a penny to a priest to say their Latin mumbo-jumbo for me. They are all crooks."

In this household, much to my chagrin, no one except my aunt Mirita went to church on Sundays. She went to mass at six in the morning. If I wanted to attend church during my summers in Santiago, rising at dawn to go with her was the only possibility. Moreover, Fefita would not let anyone back from a later Mass have breakfast; if you were dumb enough to go to church, you paid the consequences. I went to Mass with Mirita most Sundays despite having to wake up so early. I prayed for all the others who stayed behind, including Nery.

Abuelo Cándido never spoke much about religion, though; no need to waste time on this ridiculous nonsense. He was glad to have my attention during those summers while he talked about his life and about his views on many things. I had always liked Abuelo Cándido's self-possessed and quiet way of being in the world. Those engrossing summer conversations brought a new closeness between us. I could see why his daughters loved being around him.

I could also recognize his great sorrow. A freak accident had incapacitated him physically. One night in the early 1950s, Abuelo Cándido, who was then eighty-two years old and living alone on the farm, had heard a noise that might have signaled an intruder. He took his handgun and went to find the cause of the noise. But he tripped and the gun went off, shooting him in the right leg.

If there had been an intruder, he probably disappeared at the sound of the shot. But Abuelo had to attract the attention of his closest neighbors across the rural road to get to a hospital. He shouted with all his strength for almost an hour until they finally heard his cries. The neighbors wrapped his bleeding knee in a towel and drove him to a hospital in Santiago in their truck. But by then, he was weak from the loss of blood and an infection had started to set in.

A few days after the accident, he lost his leg to gangrene. The doctor had recommended amputation to soften an inescapably painful death; better to be a one-legged corpse than a two-legged one blackened by the invading gangrene. My mother and her siblings agreed to the amputation and waited for their father's death. But, instead of dying, Abuelo Cándido, recovered from his accident and lived for another twenty years with only one leg. That is why he sat in the patio every day then rather than be out riding on horseback or cultivating vegetables in his farm. He died peacefully in his sleep, years after the beginning of the Revolution, when he was over 100 years old.

The Neighborhood

Besides Abuelo Cándido, my beloved tree with its nooks and crannies, and all the shrubbery I cherished to hide or dream under, the patio of the Santiago house held other attractions. It functioned as an auditorium or a collective community center. You could hear without effort the neighbors' conversations from all nearby dwellings. The houses in that urban neighborhood were attached wall to wall. Their central patios converged, separated only by concrete walls that were not taller than the one-story houses.

Summers in Cuba bring unrelenting waves of heat, alleviated only by the ocean breeze and the furious, almost daily afternoon rains. Santiago, deep in a valley surrounded by mountains, is particularly hot. You spent the day fanning yourself with anything you could find, from elegant Spanish fans to pieces of cardboard. Outside, you suffered under the relentless scorching sun. Inside, you were deprived of the cooling breeze unless you kept all windows and balconies open. To balance the effect of the torrid humid heat, most houses in Santiago had front porches and central patios surrounded by roofed verandas into which living rooms, dining rooms and bedrooms converged. Patios and big porches were the best safeguard against the heat at a time when no one had air conditioning. Amidst their shading vegetation of tall trees and red, orange, and purple flowers, patios were the centers of life during the day. Only gigantic drops of summer rain pushed all of us back into the verandas that surrounded them. In the evenings, people moved cane-backed rocking chairs to the sidewalk, outside their doors, and had long conversations in loud voices, while fanning themselves. My grandparents' house, with its large patio, allowed us to open the inside doors and the wooden blinds of the street balconies to let the breeze circulate without needing to sit out in public. The doors and windows to the central patio were left open at night to let the light breeze come in accompanied by the persistent buzz of the unavoidable mosquitoes streaming in through the unscreened openings.

Against the backwall of the house, the former servants' quarters that had been converted into tenements opened to the parallel street behind *Calle Trinidad* where the house was. From the kitchen and the bathroom, through the back wall, we could hear the neighbors' incessant chatter or singing.

As Fefita was teaching me to bathe by myself when I was five or six, commanding, "Behind your ears!" "Under the arms!" I could hear a blaring radio and a woman singing along at the top of her lungs. *"Por alto sea el cielo en el mundo, por hondo que sea el mar profundo, no habrá una barrera en el mundo que mi amor profundo no rompa por ti..."* ("As high as the sky might be, as deep as the sea might be, there will not be a barrier in the world which my love for you will not break...").

I wondered what the neighbor was doing as she sang: *Was she ironing? Sweeping floors? Washing clothes? Cooking?* I asked myself. *Probably not laundry; that was usually done in the mornings. Too early to cook. It was*

barely four and no one ate dinner before seven. But maybe she only had a
kerosene two-burner; perhaps she needed to start early.

And so I went, picturing in my imagination what the woman on the other side of the wall might be doing as she sang, until my grandmother's firm voice brought me back saying, "Between your legs!" "Don't forget your toes!"

On one side of the patio, we could also hear the neighbors in the house next door that was barely separated from ours. One of the people in that house was a swarthy young man nicknamed *Majo*. He was probably not older than twenty, but to me Majo seemed a big adult man. Majo took his daily shower around four in the afternoon, like most Cubans did. People showered in the late afternoon or early evening, when the heat subsided slightly and you could wash off the sweat of the day. What made his shower time unlike others was his habit of yelling when he finished: "*¡No miren que voy 'esnúo!*" to inform his two older sisters that he was about to go across the patio completely naked and they should look the other way as he went by. His yelled warning, mispronouncing the word *desnudo*–naked, was heard through all the nearby patios every afternoon. He had to have known it. Clearly, he wanted to announce himself to the neighborhood, not just his sisters.

My aunts and other neighbors shook their heads making it clear that his daily warning to not look, "*No miren…*" was in poor taste. But Nery and I and other young girls giggled mischievously every time we heard Majo's daily broadcast of his nakedness. We would have loved the chance to take a peek.

Majo was the son of Mercedes, *la Panadera*, a widow who owned the bakery shop where everyone in the neighborhood bought their fresh bread daily; her nickname was a reference to her business. Her two daughters were close in age, just a few years older than Majo, but they were quiet and mousy. I never learned Majo's real name. But I do remember his booming voice. The only one in the family who could match Majo's voice was Mercedes, who was at work in the bakery when Majo bellowed his daily announcement. When she came to visit the neighbors, including my grandmother and aunts, no one mentioned her son's behavior. However, behind her back, Mercedes was blamed for having raised Majo so badly and doting on him more than on her well-behaved daughters.

On the other side of my grandparents' house lived Cucusa and Chichita together with their parents and several siblings. We played together frequently. Cucusa's real name was the same as her mother's, Chichita also had an adult name, but no one ever called them anything but Cucusa and Chichita. Their father was the conductor and owner of a well-known musical band, Pancho Portuondo y sus Muchachos, that played in theaters, at public dances and at large private parties. Mr. Portuondo made a comfortable living playing his music.

My cousin Grisel, Cucusa and I in Santiago, 2011

The Portuondos would be considered black by U.S. standards, but in the Cuban context of the 1940s and 50s, they were just somewhat darker but not quite black. We knew they were not white, but they were middle class and lived comfortably. And in Cuba, despite the undeniable racism, class was always more important than race, particularly when multiple skin shades were present in one family. Although Nery and I were not allowed to go alone to other houses in the neighborhood, it was always fine to go play at the Portuondos' house because Señora Portuondo—a beautiful and elegant caramel-skinned woman—was always home and all the children were *bien educados*—well-brought up and well-behaved; more than what could have been said about some of the other kids in the neighborhood. Nery and I grew up playing every summer with Cucusa, Chichita, their brothers, and other girls. We played hide and seek, tag, spin the bottle, and other kissing games. But most important, Cucusa and I, who were the same age, played "movies" by ourselves.

While the adults sat in other rooms of either her house or my grandparents,' Cucusa and I developed our own "screenplays." The details of each "movie" plot varied, but at some point, one of us would lie down on a sofa or bed, either dying or enduring some serious suffering of one sort or another. The other leaned over and started kissing the cheeks of the suffering one while saying as passionately as she could, "I love you! I love you!"

Slowly, the kisser kneeled closer to the sofa or bed as the "I love yous" became more hushed and passionate, and the kisses moved closer to the mouth of the sufferer. When both mouths touched, the movie ended, leaving both of us excited and elated about our beautiful story. We had no idea of how the movie should continue. Neither of us knew a thing about what might be behind our interest in those "movies."

But then, it was Cucusa who, sitting by one of the balconies in the living room of my grandparents' house in the early 1950s, narrated for me the story line of the 1931 German film "Maidens in Uniform." The movie had been shown in Santiago earlier that year for the first time. This iconic lesbian film is set in a Prussian boarding school for the daughters of officers and the bourgeoisie. It follows the story of Manuela, whose crush on a kind and beautiful teacher infuriates the cruel headmistress. The headmistress sets out to destroy the girl, who slowly begins to contemplate suicide as the only escape from her constant punishments. In one version of the film, Manuela commits suicide; in another she doesn't. Cucusa had seen the one that ended in suicide while Manuela weeps and repeats "I love her! I love her!" The film is a heart-wrenching love melodrama, fitting with the tone of our own "movies."

I don't think either one of us consciously knew what the film was about, but this did not diminish Cucusa's or my fascination with the story. Perhaps most telling is that the vivid memory of Cucusa's narration of the story in this film is still with me after more than half a century. I guess it touched a nerve in both of us. We were unconsciously attracted to it by something we could not describe. Decades later, it became evident why this film and my games with Cucusa touched a deep chord in me. My life course and choices had already started then without my knowledge. Eventually, I embraced my love for women, and it became central to my life. However, when Cucusa and I played movies, one of us was always the boyfriend, usually the one doing the kissing. All our "movies" were heterosexual love stories. Neither of us could have imagined another possibility.

Our summer days in Santiago were punctuated by the voices of the *pregoneros,* the street criers who passed by each day, always at the same time under the wrought iron balconies of the house. They came up and down the steep slope of Calle Trinidad, bellowing their offerings of goods or services. I found the daily procession of vendors fascinating because nothing like this ever happened in our neighborhood in Havana.

Early in the morning, if Abuela Fefita had not succeeded yet in getting us out of bed, we were awakened by a tall black man announcing in a loud characteristic sing-song, *"¡Se atesan bastidores!" "¡Se ateeesan baaastidores!"*— "Iron bedsteads tightened!" Around four in the afternoon, a fat middle-aged black woman with the white dress and white scarf of Afro-Cuban *santeras* went by yelling in a booming voice, *"¡Eh, la merienda!"* She balanced a wooden tray full of homemade sweets on her head, crying out for people to buy their *merienda* treats from her. Everyone called her *La Merienda*— "The Afternoon Snack"—none of us knew her real name. Even if we did not buy anything, when we heard her voice, we knew without consulting our clocks that it was time to take our daily shower and have a snack.

Between the man who tightened iron bedsteads and La Merienda several other vendors came by bellowing for us to buy their goods or skills. Fruit and vegetable vendors, knife sharpeners, and peanut vendors paraded by throughout the day.

Among the daily cries of the vendors, twice a day we heard the mailman's distinct whistle. The mailman was a tall, uniformed black man who was always smiling. At the sound of the whistle, everyone opened their balconies or leaned on their porch railings to wait for whatever letters he might bring for them or for anyone else in the neighborhood. The missives the neighbors received were the object of everyone's curiosity. The mailman was always welcome, and everyone knew him personally, chatting with him as he walked by carrying his heavy sack full of letters.

One vendor, whom everyone called *Marchante,* because that is how he called out to his customers, came by every Tuesday morning bringing his vegetables and fruits on a cart that consisted of a big wooden platform, covered with burlap and thick discolored canvas sacks that long ago had served to transport sugar from the nearby mills. Marchante walked alongside his makeshift cart, prodding his tired horse to pull it up the steep slope of Calle Trinidad while watching carefully to make sure that none of the produce fell off the back and slid down the hill.

As horse and cart clambered up, Marchante recited a litany of produce at the top of his lungs, encouraging women to open their balconies and porch doors, hopeful they would buy from him rather than from the nearby *bodega* or other stores. He called out to his customers in a characteristic sing-song as he climbed, "Marchante, here I am, bringing your mangos, *aguacates, plátanos...*"

Marchante's merchandise included bright orange carrots, dark green avocados, green and ripe plantains, root vegetables like *yucas, malangas, ñames, boniatos* and potatoes, onions and garlic, papayas, guavas, bananas and other tropical fruits such as red *mameyes* and yellowish brown *nísperos* whose thick peel looked like kiwi's. He also carried several varieties of mangoes. *Mangos de corazón*, big and heart-shaped, that I poked at one end to squeeze the dark yellow pulp out without peeling them to avoid getting stringy mango fibers between my teeth; *mangos de bizcochuelo*, thin and long, with a smooth sweet pulp that I ate with a spoon right out of the peel; *mangos de Toledo*, very small and round, the size of plums, with a bland pale yellow pulp; narrow *mangos filipinos* that, as their name implied, had come from the Philippine islands when both the Philippines and Cuba were colonies of Spain.

Marchante was sinewy and wiry like most Cuban peasants, his face and hands tanned from his daily work under the sun. He had a thin dark moustache. He wore a straw hat pulled down to his ears, dark pants, and an impeccably clean starched white shirt with rolled-up sleeves.

My aunt Mirita waited for him every Tuesday morning. Whatever vegetables and fruits she bought from Marchante's cart would later be found in the meals Abuela Fefita cooked that week. Vendors never entered the house. All transactions with them were conducted through a balcony. Mirita and Marchante, exchanged fruit, vegetables, and money through the lowest balcony of the house, closest to street level, while his horse whinnied softly and flicked his tail at the flies that wanted to get on him.

On Fridays, another wiry farmer, this one wearing dirty and smelly clothes, came to pick up cans of rotting food to feed his pigs. Once or twice a week a cow horn blared in the middle of the afternoon. It could be heard from a distance of two or three blocks. At the sound of the horn, the women in the neighborhood started calling out, "¡La basura! ¡La basura!" to announce the trash collectors were approaching in case anyone had not heard the horn. Hurriedly, big trash cans were pulled out to the street through *el portón* from the kitchen in the back of house. The trash collectors hoisted them up by sheer human strength, hurling the contents into the open truck.

Finally, around six every evening, a boy who could not have been older than fifteen, ran down the hill, passing balconies and porches, yelling "¡*Oriente!*" and "¡*El País!*"—the names of the local and national evening newspapers. Again, my aunt Mirita would go to the balcony closest to the street and lean forward, give the boy some coins, and take the papers that would be passed from hand to hand by the adults that evening after dinner.

After 1959 it became illegal to go around the streets of a Cuban city announcing your goods or your skills. Too much private enterprise. And in any case, if newspaper boys still existed, they would be selling *Granma,* the official government paper, named after the boat in which Fidel Castro arrived in Cuba in 1956 to create the rebellion that would topple Batista three years later.

¡*Temblor!* ¡*Temblor!*

Life in Santiago never lacked for surprises and interesting things to do.

Walking on the steep streets. Climbing the steps of Padre Pico street. Going with my uncle Candito, who had been deaf since childhood, to places like the anthill *loma de San Juan*, made famous by Teddy Roosevelt, or to the Bacardí Museum.

The Bacardí Museum had been created at the beginning of the twentieth century by Emilio Bacardí, the patriarch of the rum family. The Museum was full of historical artifacts from Cuba's Independence Wars. But the most exciting artifact in the museum was not Cuban. It was the mummy of a young Egyptian girl that Don Emilio had brought back to Santiago from one of his many trips. Going to see the Egyptian mummy was a highlight of each summer. She fascinated me, swathed in yellowing white wrappings, a painted mask on her face—*was this how she really looked when she was alive?* —At her feet were a small cat mummy and other mummified objects.

Egyptian mummy, Bacardí Museum, Santiago

One afternoon in the summer of 1949, I was reading a story about the young English princesses Elizabeth and Margaret that had been written by their long-time governess. I was lying on the cold tiles of the floor, at the door to one of the rooms along the veranda that overlooked the patio. These rooms that had been occupied by my mother's brothers and her male cousins when they were young were now empty because four of them had gotten married and left. Nery and I had been flower girls in these weddings, and I loved the pictures of us with our long dresses and made-up faces that I imagined had made us look like the British princesses.

I was absorbed by the story, my body under the door frame, only half inside the room to catch the breeze from the patio. I was in my favorite reading position: on my tummy, elbows on the side of my head, cheeks resting on my hands, knees bent, ankles crossing in the air. Suddenly, I felt a little dizzy and heard the voices of aunts Mirita and Celia, yelling, "*¡Temblor! ¡Temblor!*" followed by rapid footsteps running out to the patio. Startled from my reading, I looked up and saw my grandmother, my three aunts and Nery standing in the patio. With a frightened look on her face, Mirita started beckoning me with hand gestures and repeating even more frantically, "*¡Temblor! ¡Temblor!*" I was not sure what she meant, but I understood I was supposed to get up quickly and join them in the patio. I scrambled to my feet and ran to the patio, still feeling dizzy. A few moments later, after the earth tremor ceased, I realized my dizziness had been caused by an earthquake.

I had never had this experience before: no earthquakes or tremors rattled Havana. I had heard stories about a very serious earthquake in Santiago in 1932 that had left a pile of debris, the marble ruins of Hotel Venus, across from Parque Céspedes. Supposedly, my youngest uncle owed his deafness to the fright he had experienced as a child during that earthquake. My mother's family had moved to the house where they now lived after the 1932, with its big patio, because their previous house was too hemmed in, making it difficult to avoid falling debris.

Although the tremors of 1949 were not of that magnitude, the first tremor was followed by frequent aftershocks over the next several days. The open space of the patio, unencumbered by electrical wires, walls or anything that could tumble and hurt anyone, provided a sense of safety that other houses in the neighborhood did not offer. Neighbors started arriving at our house that evening and installed themselves on the patio to spend the night in safety. They came with cots, mattresses, cushions, rocking chairs—anything that helped make it possible to rest and pass the night. Our patio became the neighborhood haven. Some of these neighbors were people we barely said hello to in passing. Others were well-known to my family and visited frequently. The adults still remembered the power of the 1932 earthquake. Nery and I and the neighborhood kids had heard many stories about it. We were all frightened, and the aftershocks exacerbated our fear of what could happen in the middle of the night.

Mercedes *la Panadera* and her three children came together. Majo was surprisingly quiet; he probably didn't want to admit that he was scared. He carried in a big rocking chair for his mother, who sat on it to rest and snored noisily whenever she fell asleep. Cucusa, Chichita, their parents and siblings were also there, her brothers sleeping on mattresses on the ground. Nery and I slept together with the other neighborhood girls on cots assembled by the brick steps at the patio gate.

On the other side of the iron fence that separated the patio from the *traspatio*, León, the fierce dog I so disliked because he usually barked furiously at me, acted in an unusual way. Despite the strange smells and the low rumbling of hushed voices so close to him, he did not react. Under other circumstances he would have hurled himself against the fence, barking incessantly to scare away the unfamiliar company. Instead, he sat quietly next to the fence, as if searching for the comfort of human presence. Then, quite suddenly, he jumped to his feet and started running in circles and barking with what seemed like extreme anxiety. A minute or so after his performance started, another aftershock would shake us, waking those who had been dozing off in the intervals. By the third time León did this, we all understood the meaning of his reaction and whenever he started to bark, we huddled together, holding our breath, in anticipation of yet another rumble. For the first time, I felt León's presence as protective rather than scary. He was showing the wisdom of animals.

Once, I was startled awake upon hearing León's bark. I jumped the brick steps down to the patio. When the tremor passed, I found myself sitting in the lap of Romeíto, an adolescent boy who lived across the street from us. His chair was just at the bottom of the steps, and he had been sound asleep when I jumped into his lap. We both laughed a little nervous laughter, somewhat embarrassed at finding each other in such an unusual position. I quickly climbed back to my cot and did not look at him for the rest of the evening.

At dawn, although there were still some aftershocks every few hours, neighbors began collecting their belongings and heading home. During the day, tense and tired, I tried to go back to reading about the British princesses. As night approached, neighbors returned to our house. Fewer of them came this second night because the frequency of aftershocks had subsided. On the third night, no neighbors came, the aftershocks had ceased, and we all went back to sleeping in our beds.

Santiago, or even Cuban culture itself, cannot be fully described without talking about the *pregoneros* or without the intricate everyday connections among neighbors that punctuated the rhythm of our months and years. Shared festivities, earth tremors and other unanticipated events knitted the fabric of Cuban life and identity. They built community, gave meaning to what it meant to be Cuban.

Over the years, I have experienced earthquakes in Costa Rica and California. They always scare me. Earthquakes demonstrate the instability of all we think is solid, both literally and figuratively. They provide an apt metaphor for the unexpected shakes and transformations of life and the shaking of certainties, of our understanding of truths we had previously considered stable realities.

Arrupe

On some evenings in Santiago, instead of staying in Parque Cés-pedes, we went around the corner, to the Lyceum. The Lyceum had begun as an officers' club for the American military based in nearby Guantánamo Bay during World War II. Upper- and middle-class *seño-ritas* went to dance there with American and Cuban Navy officers, a refined environment much appreciated by my maternal aunts, Marina, Mercedes, Celia and Mirita. After the war, the sophisticated *señoritas* transformed the old Anglo-American Club into a membership-only women's club—sort of a finishing school for adult women—and re-named it Santiago Lyceum.

There, my aunt Celia learned to make artificial flowers. Celia's cre-ations of beautifully shaped and brilliantly colored amaryllis, camel-lias, and carnations were displayed in the living room of my grandpar-ents' house. Once, Nery and I went to the Lyceum with my aunt Mer-cedes, who wanted to learn how to make cucumber and green pepper juices in the newly invented Osterizer blender. I could not take my eyes away from the whirling machine that liquefied vegetables in sec-onds even though I didn't like this strange concoction. I preferred the better tasting fruit refreshments we had in the Lyceum while my aunts played *canasta*, had coffee, or gossiped with their friends.

In the middle of the Lyceum's central patio was a well. I was fasci-nated by its depth and the shiny dark color of the water flowing at the bottom wondering where the underground current was flowing to. The Lyceum building is now part of the government-sponsored Colo-nial Museum in Santiago. The elegant and elaborate exhibits of this Museum are stocked with the furniture, dinner services, porcelain sculptures, paintings and other works of art abandoned by the families that left Cuba since the beginning of the Revolution. The well is still in the center of the patio, a romantic stone and iron structure in this house of memories.

By the well in the Lyceum, 2011

For me, anything that happened at the Lyceum was delightfully in-triguing: watching my aunt Celia dip small pieces of crinkly paper des-tined to become flower petals in warm wax, marveling as Osterizer blenders liquefied cucumbers, or simply looking down the well's shaft.

On a sultry August evening, a few years after the end of World War II, when I was ten or so, I went with Nery and my aunts Celia and Mercedes to the Santiago Lyceum to hear Pedro Arrupe, a Spanish Jes-uit priest who had lived in Japan for many years. I don't know if my aunts were aware of the topic of the lecture scheduled for that evening. I suppose so. I, on the other hand, went to the Lyceum that day as I had so many other days, looking forward to drinking cold icy lemon-ade and hanging out in the attractive colonial building or gazing into the mysterious well.

Typical Cuban medio punto stained glass over doors

On that evening, Father Arrupe sat on a small platform inside the open gallery that surrounded the Lyceum patio. Behind him was a cream color wall with four tall windows topped by *medio punto* stained glass arches in bright-colored geometric designs, typical of Cuban colonial architecture. A small table covered with a delicate lace cloth was in front of him; his notes were on top of the table. He wore a black cassock, the standard garb for most priests in those days. His sharp profile and his distinct Basque-Spanish accent commanded attention as soon as he spoke. Celia and Mercedes, Nery, and I sat on the Lyceum patio, our backs to the well, to listen to Padre Arrupe.

Arrupe had been the Superior of the Jesuit house in Hiroshima when the atomic bomb was dropped. His visit to Cuba was part of a world tour he undertook to warn the world about the dangers of atomic war. Several decades later, he became Superior General of the Jesuits and was a powerful influence on the Order's involvement in social justice issues all over the world, particularly in Latin America, during the 1970s. He is now being considered for canonization to be declared a saint of the Catholic Church.

Padre Arrupe started his talk describing the morning of August 6, 1945 in Hiroshima. That morning, he told us, a few more reconnaissance planes than usual flew over the city. The inhabitants of Hiroshima, as well as the priests living on a distant hill on the outskirts of the city, wondered idly about the additional planes. But they went about their daily business, as normal as daily business could be in a time of war. And then, all of a sudden, there was an enormous explosion. In the Jesuits' house on the hill, Father Arrupe was surprised by its magnitude. The bright light and the cloud it produced were visible in the distance from his window. He knew this explosion was stronger than others they were used to by then. But, like everyone else, he could not tell then what made it so different.

Father Arrupe was a physician, and the Jesuit house he supervised served as a hospital for the city of Hiroshima. The building was not damaged by the explosion because of its location outside the city. Soon after the blast, the wounded started to arrive and slowly but surely, the magnitude of the disaster became painfully obvious. Of the many descriptions of the horror in Padre Arrupe's talk, one stood out for me—perhaps because it did not fit anything I had seen in war films or newsreels. A day or two after the explosion, several parents appeared at the hospital on the hill bringing children who cried loudly and complained of sore throats. Father Arrupe, and the rest of the hospital personnel, overwhelmed by the wounded, had no time or patience amid the tragedy for minor complaints such as the sore throats of spoiled kids. They told the parents they could not attend to sore throats in the middle of so many other serious injuries and asked them to go away with their troublesome children so hospital personnel could take care of the wounded. But more parents came with their children complaining of sore throats in an equally persistent manner. Tired and exasperated, Father Arrupe told one of the crying children to open his mouth. When he looked into the boy's throat, he could not believe his eyes. There was total destruction inside that throat; he could not understand how this child was alive. Feeling concerned about all those he had turned away believing they were complaining of common sore throats, he started to ask children and adults to open their mouth and found himself confronted by the same level of mutilation. No one really knew then what effect radiation of this magnitude could have on human beings. Pedro Arrupe felt totally helpless to do anything for these victims. That is why, a few years later, he traveled all over the world to warn people about the horrific devastation that atomic weapons could wreak, describing in detail what he had seen.

In my mind's eye, I could not stop looking down the throats of those Japanese children who were more or less my age. I felt thirsty in the heat of the evening. I was fanning myself to avoid sweating too much. How would it feel to be not just parched because of heat and thirst but to have your throat burned by some strange force that, apparently, had not even touched you?

Recently, as I thought of writing what I remembered about Padre Arrupe's talk, I started doubting the accuracy of my memory of the stories I had heard on that evening seventy years ago. Searching, I found the text of the talk Arrupe had given all over the world. And there, in black and white, was the narrative about those children's throats I so vividly remembered after more than half a century. His description had been engraved in my memory. Another form of radiation had imprinted the horrific details on it.

As Father Arrupe described what he had witnessed, I did not fully understand the implications of what he was recounting. Nor, I suspect, did the women around me. The atomic bomb had ended a cruel war just a few years before; therefore, it had to be good. I had watched a black-and-white American film in which Chinese children were saved from Japanese bombs by a singing actress, as well as lots of newsreels and commentaries about Japanese cruelty during the war. How could they be victims?

How could my child's mind reconcile the war ending that everyone had celebrated so joyfully singing "*¡Pin-Pin cayó Berlín! ¡Pon-Pon cayó Japón!*" with the horrible pictures Father Arrupe was presenting? I think this was the first time that I had an inkling of the blurry and complicated nature of the good and the bad, of the precariousness of absolutes. It may have been the first time I realized that "good people" from "good countries" do not always do "good things" to others.

Carnavales

My aunt Mercedes and her boyfriend Jorge with whom I enjoyed the waters of the Santiago Bay, never married. She died of breast cancer in her thirties. By then, my parents had decided that it was too expensive to send us to Santiago every summer. But in the summer of 1953, a month after Mercedes's death, I went to Santiago with Mario, my youngest brother, who was then a toddler and very vivacious, to distract Abuelo Cándido from his grief at the loss of his favorite daughter.

My aunt Mercedes, 1952

Despite the family mourning, I was glad to be in Santiago for *Carnavales*, which were always one of the best parts of summers in Santiago.

Each year during our childhood summers there, Nery and I waited for Carnavales with excited anticipation. Most evenings during Carnavales we went to the terrace of Hotel Casa Granda, across from Parque Céspedes, to watch fireworks spit out from the roofs of City Hall and the Cathedral. Sometimes, we went during the day to watch the parades from bought seats on the bleachers.

The *Carnavales* in Santiago are famous. They were celebrated every July 25th to honor *Santiago Apóstol*—Saint James, the patron saint of the city. For days at the end of July, Santiago filled up with visitors from other parts of Cuba and abroad to participate in the fun. *Santiagueros* are known for their readiness to have a good time. Afro-Cuban music and musicians are a vital element of Santiago; they became even more so at Carnavales.

What started in colonial times as a religious procession to honor *Santiago Apóstol* followed by dancing black slaves became a three-day city-wide celebration that involved all social classes. Festivities were non-stop from July 24th, Santa Cristina's feast, and the day after St. James, July 26th, Santa Ana's day. Endless parties in private homes and public venues featured performing groups and improvised revelries. Dancing groups called *comparsas* prepared all year for this event. *Comparsas* and individual revelers marched dancing to the sound of drums or other *conga* music instruments and competed for prizes with their costumes, music, decorations, execution of intricate steps or choreographies.

Celebration flooded the city. Aside from the official celebrations and marching *comparsas*, at any hour of day or night, anywhere in Santiago, people might start playing drums, singing and dancing *conga* together along any city street. Although Calle Trinidad was not a parade street, improvised congas passed by several times a day during Carnavales. Groups of people went by the house, singing, swaying hips, jutting shoulders, and shuffling feet rhythmically in a style called *arrollando*. At the sound of a conga group coming, we ran to the balconies of the house to see groups of men and women go by *arrollando* up the hill of Calle Trinidad keeping up with the beat of a drum and the tempo of their own voices. The feet shuffling and the conga rhythms disciplined the anarchy and drunkenness of the improvised parties that went by. The revelers were often followed by a few stray dogs barking.

Nery and I never tired of watching the congas go by.

No matter how many times we had seen them, we waited at the open balconies for the sound of coming congas with their shuffling feet and chorus, "*¡Mírala qué linda viene! ¡mírala que linda va! ¡La comparsa de Los Hoyos, que se va y no vuelve más!*" — "Look how beautiful it comes! Look how beautiful it goes! The comparsa from Los Hoyos that will leave and won't return!" Los Hoyos was a poor, mostly black neighborhood in a lower part of the city. The comparsa from Los Hoyos was always the best. Even if they were not the ones passing by, singing voices kept celebrating them and their prowess. We would hear the sound of music and people coming up or down the street, the sounds of shuffling feet and singing voices getting closer and whoever was coming the song was the same, "*¡Mírala qué linda viene! ¡mírala que linda va! ¡La comparsa de Los Hoyos, que se va y no vuelve más!*"

Carnavales was a time for poor blacks to celebrate who they were, to forget poverty and hardship and become the center of attention. Slum neighborhoods competed through of elaborate costumes and the complexity of dancing steps and choreographed performances. This was also a time to render tribute to some of the *Santería* deities that embodied their African heritage. It was a time when white Cubans followed them, enjoying themselves and forgetting class differences, enthralled by the frenzy of drums and sweating bodies.

Participants in the official comparsas spent the year saving for their flashy costumes and rehearsing dancing steps. On Santa Cristina's day, the city's trash collectors, vendors, street sweepers, and other laborers, many of whom lived in Los Hoyos, came to the house to collect their tips for Carnavales. On Carnavales, rather than their regular clothes, they wore colorful costumes. Costumes were made of shiny satin in bright yellow, white, lime green, baby blue or pink; their tall plumed hats matched. Toño, who on regular days swept the streets in the neighborhood, always stopped by in his shinny white costume during Carnavales. Mirita and Mercedes gave him big coins: silver pesos or dollars and attached them quickly to his costume with a few wide stitches to little ribbon "nests" that were already sewn onto the costumes. By the time he got to our house, he usually had his chest covered with donations. Only men came for tips, but in the comparsas, scantily clad women with tall plumage on their heads, dressed in color-coordinated outfits, shuffled, sang and danced together with the men.

Some costumes were individual creations, creative combinations of clothes, hats and painted faces. Nery and I were delighted and surprised when we saw one man who wore a black short sack with fake wings over his body and painted his shaved head, neck, and feet bright red to make himself look like one of the *aura tiñosas*—the buzzards that were constantly flying over Santiago. He got a prize that year for his original outfit. I heard later that he had some serious health complications from all the red paint that he had to remove with turpentine at the end of the three days.

The colorful costumes and dances of those Cubans of African descent existed side by side with the rage and frustration created by racism and discrimination. When the Revolution came, the Afro-Cubans trusted that it would put an end to their disadvantaged position in society. But despite official statements, the promises of Fidel Castro's revolution remain unfulfilled after decades of a government that continues to show its racism despite words to the contrary. Even though it is considered counterrevolutionary to say there is racism in Cuba, prejudice and discrimination are ingrained in Cuban society. Black Cubans know it is still there.

Most Cubans living in Cuba today are not white. But Cubans of African descent are mostly absent from positions at the high levels of government and from managerial positions. They are systematically excluded from jobs in the tourist industry. Black Cubans have been less able to start businesses under the recent laws that allow and encourage small private enterprise because they seldom have relatives in foreign countries who could send them the needed funds. They are still relegated to poor housing and are more likely to be imprisoned.

Carnavales are still a major event in Santiago, now mixed with political commemorations of the 26th of July attack on the Moncada. Nowadays non-white Cubans express their disappointment through rap music. Other forms of protest against racism are non-existent and even dangerous because the government has declared that the issue of race has been solved by the Revolution. The accumulated discontent and resentment still seethe under the masks and costumes. I cannot avoid wondering if they will ever explode.

The fact is that the world changes when you are not watching. Apparently solid realities are always fragile and beliefs always contestable. During Carnavales in 1953 when I was in Santiago with my brother Mario to help Abuelo Cándido deal with his grief over Mercedes' death on one of the Carnavales nights, a month after my aunt's death, hoping that drunkenness would dull the soldiers' alertness, Fidel Castro and his companions tried to overcome the Moncada Barracks. The attack in the early dawn of July 26th was poorly planned. The attempt resulted in carnage and death. But the movement Fidel created after this failure was named for that catastrophe that brought him into national prominence—*Movimiento 26 de Julio*.

All over Santiago, I heard terrified whispers and fearful rumors about the cruelty of Batista's military to the small group that had attacked the *Cuartel* Moncada under cover of darkness during Carnavales. Fidel and his brother Raúl and a few surviving collaborators were imprisoned. Only the intervention of the Archbishop of Santiago, Monsignor Enrique Pérez Serantes saved Fidel and Raúl from certain death at that time.

That summer, I constantly heard that Fidel was a hero, that his dead companions were martyrs. The next time I went to Santiago, in 1959, he was already in power.

Several decades later, in 1984, I returned to the house in Santiago where I had spent so many summers during my childhood and adolescence. Again, I slept in Abuela Fefita's bedroom, this time on her massive mahogany bed rather than a cot covered with a mosquito net as I had during my childhood visits. I ate lunch and dinner at the long dining room table. Now, as in my visits to Santiago during my adolescence, I no longer needed a pile of magazines to reach the table. Mirita, my only surviving aunt, was delighted to see me. She now looked more like Abuela Fefita than her own younger self. Mirita lived in the enormous house with my deaf uncle and the man she had married after Fefita's death, when she was already middle-aged. The others who had lived in that house when I was a child were now dead.

Mirita had made a bonfire of old papers and photographs in the middle of the patio soon after Marina's death. My adolescent diaries had gone up in flames a few months before my arrival, much to my deep disappointment. I could not recover them. But I did recover contact with people who had been important for me. I saw Cucusa, her sister Chichita, and their mother, who were still living next door. By then, Cucusa was married and had several grown children. We talked about her life and her children; nothing terribly profound. I have no idea what meaning, if any, the adult Cucusa gave to our "movies." And I didn't know if I wanted to tell her that I was enacting in my real life, the love scenes she and I had played in our "movies."

Cousins, other relatives, and childhood friends came to visit during those days, including one of my adolescent friends, now bald with belly bulging—looking more like Pumarejo, the TV show host, than himself. Neither Mercedes, *la Panadera,* nor her children lived in Cuba any longer. Other people lived in their house. No one yelled, "¡No miren que voy 'esnúo!'" in the afternoons. But the patio and the everyday familiar noises of neighbors were still very present.

During that week, I walked Santiago's hilly streets and went to Parque Céspedes. The tall laurel trees in the Parque were there waiting for me as they had every summer during my childhood. And so was the well in the old Lyceum, now transformed into the Colonial Museum.

I sat for hours next to the stump of what had been my beloved *mamoncillo* tree. Sitting there, remembering what had been, I became painfully conscious of the life I had been denied. But I also smiled at my childhood self that is forever entangled on the vines and shrubs of that patio.

Santiago de Cuba Cathedral (and a corner of Parque Céspedes)

III

Mysteries of Life:

...pedazos de la vida...

A *"Particular Friendship"*?

I was in sixth grade, twelve years old at most, when I became aware for the first time of the magnetic presence of another girl. Her name was Oneida and she was a few years younger than I; my guess is she was in second or third grade. Her hair was black and straight, just short of her shoulders. Her skin was pale, almost translucent. She always kept her eyes down, but I knew they were dark with long lashes. Oneida was painfully, excruciatingly shy. My contact with her was limited to two rides a day on the school bus each morning and afternoon. She and her sister stayed at school for lunch. For some reason, her silence and shyness incited the malice of some older girls. They tormented Oneida during those rides with the refined cruelty that children can display. They pinched her, whispered insults in her ear, and in all possible ways made her time during those bus rides as miserable as they could. She reacted like a trapped bird, shrinking back from the bullying by hiding even deeper in silence and reserve.

While the girls who used her as a target to relieve the boredom of the school bus rides relished every minute of their viciousness, I was secretly enraged with them and indignant with her older sister, who did nothing to protect Oneida from her tormentors. But, of course, neither did I. I was already isolated enough from other girls at school. Indeed, I wouldn't have known what to do to protect her from the malicious jokes and taunting behavior of the other girls since I did not know very well how to do that for myself. However, I knew that the disdain the more popular girls showed me for being obedient and studious did not remotely compare with the treatment Oneida received. In the mysterious ways in which hierarchies of power operate among children, I knew I did not have enough status to influence their behavior toward her, but I also knew they did not have the power to harass me into submission the way they did her. The nuns would not have allowed it. But the nuns did not seem to know what was happening to this girl on that bus.

We always had an adult monitor in our school buses. They were middle-aged unmarried women—spinsters or widows—hired to watch over us and to do other monitoring tasks during the school day. Our school bus monitor was Señorita Pilar, a woman in her forties or fifties who dressed in a style older than her years, always sack-like dresses and "sensible" flat shoes tied with laces, her short gray hair held in place by a thin net. We were supposed to ride the school bus in complete silence, so any misbehaving on the bus was always done quietly. The gossiping in whispers, the excited gestures whenever we crossed or rode alongside a boys' school's bus, happened behind Señorita Pilar's back. The pinching, hair-pulling, and murmured insults directed at Oneida were a few of the many hidden activities that seemed to escape the attention of Señorita Pilar.

Some days I managed to cleverly maneuver so when Oneida got on the bus, Señorita Pilar would tell her to sit next to me. At those times, while my racing heart wanted to leap out of my chest at her proximity, I acted consciously as a barrier between her and her abusers who, at least during that one ride, could not reach her physically and mostly opted to ignore her then. Oneida did not seem to notice the reason she was not enduring the usual torment on those rides. Señorita Pilar, more aware than we thought about the goings on behind her back, was obviously unaware of my ecstatic adoration of this girl and counted me among her harassers. She made a point of not letting the same girl sit next to Oneida all the time. I suppose she intended to distribute evenly the amount or type of cruelty Oneida would have to endure. And, I did not dare tell Señorita Pilar that I would never join in the nasty treatment to which they subjected her and that in fact I yearned to protect Oneida from it.

Oneida and I never spoke. She did not say a word or direct a look or a gesture at anyone, ever. She just sat stiff, mute, eyes lowered, probably waiting for another assault. I delighted in my luck on the few occasions I sat next to her or looked at her from a few seats away, pained at my impotence to interfere with what the particular tormentor of the day was making her endure, paradoxically content that I could at least look at her.

Then, the school bus routes were changed, and Oneida and her sister were assigned to a different bus. Nery and I and the other girls in our neighborhood stayed on the same bus with Señorita Pilar and a new driver. Oneida was assigned to a bus that served other neighborhoods, with Antonio, our old driver, and a new Señorita, taller and thinner but otherwise looking more or less like Señorita Pilar. I was devastated.

Oneida lived in a building with beautiful glass doors called *El Palacio de Cristal*; it boasted one of the first elevators in a private dwelling in Havana. A friend of my maternal aunts, who had a very long Basque last name, had lived in the same building. A few times, when my mother's sisters had come to visit from Santiago, Nery and I had gone with them to *El Palacio de Cristal* and ridden in the metal cage elevator with its accordion-like grid door that seemed so luxurious for a building located in the center city. But these visits had taken place some years earlier, before Oneida started riding the school bus with us. By then, my aunts' friend no longer lived there. Going to *El Palacio de Cristal* hoping for a glimpse of Oneida was not an option.

Because she was a few grades below me, her classroom and recess yard were in another section of the school. Now that there were no more bus rides together, there was no possibility of crossing paths. So, I enlisted Alicia, one of my classmates, a very kind girl, one of the few with whom I got along, to help. I suggested we might want to pay a visit to the younger girls' area during recess to bring them some candy. Innocent of my true reason for wanting to visit the younger girls' area, Alicia acquiesced easily; the idea of making some little girls happy by bringing them candy appealed to her. The next day, during mid-morning recess, Alicia and I were on our way to the other end of the school property, our pockets full of hard candy. As soon as I entered the perimeter of the younger girls' recess yard, I spotted Oneida. She was on a see-saw playing with another girl, and I think she was smiling broadly. My heart was beating so hard I was almost dizzy. Alicia and I walked toward them.

With a big smile, she extended her hand full of candy to both of them and asked, "Do you want some? You can take as much as you want!"

The girl who had been playing with Oneida, took a handful of candy with another bright smile while saying, "Thank you!" She was probably flattered that some "big girls" had come to their recess yard to give them candy.

As flustered as I was, I gathered my courage after a split second of hesitation, and following Alicia's example, I extended my hand full of candy to Oneida. But to my horror and desolation, she recoiled from me, shaking her head no. She jumped back, the same look of fear I had seen on her face when she climbed the steps of the school bus. *"But,* no!" I wanted to scream, "*I am not one of them; don't you remember the few times I sat next to you?*" Obviously, she did not; frozen in place she resembled a caged animal terrified of a coming attack. Unable to withstand my hurt and disappointment, I turned around, clutching in my hand the candy I knew I would not eat, my eyes brimming with tears I could not understand.

Pretending everything was fine, I sauntered back with Alicia to our area on the school property and without thinking, blurted, "Well, anyway, I know I should not feel like this for anyone."

Alicia gave me a puzzled look and asked, "Feel what? Why shouldn't you?" Her question made me face another: *How did I know I should not feel this way?*

Although I did not know how or why, I also had some indefinable awareness that I should not talk about these intense feelings, some vague sense that if I told anyone I would be condemned or censured. Not even Nery heard anything from me about this. Although I could not tell what, if anything, might be wrong with these feelings for Oneida and my wanting to protect her from abuse, I *knew*, somehow, that my feelings were out of bounds. Ignorant of what my emotions might entail, nonetheless, I grasped that *something* in them was not what it was supposed to be. Something was *wrong*.

My hunch is I may have heard some nun talk about the danger of too much closeness between girls—*particular friendships*, as they were called. In fact, at the end of every school day, before returning home for the day, we were supposed to make an "examination of conscience" regarding our daily activities to repent from whatever misbehaviors we had engaged in during the school day. One girl was assigned in each classroom to read aloud a catalogue of possible faults and wrongdoings of varying degrees of gravity. On that list, together with transgressions like disobeying, lying, not paying enough attention to our lessons or school duties, not respecting our teachers, there was always a mysterious question: *"Have I had particular friendships with any of my classmates?"* I was always puzzled about the meaning of the term "particular friendships." *Of course, I liked some of my classmates better than others; Alicia, for example… Were those "particular friendships"? And if so, why was that wrong?"*

I suspect anyone who went to Catholic school at that time or even later, heard about the mysterious "particular friendships" we were supposed to repent from at the end of each school day.

Whatever I sensed about my reaction to Oneida, my foggy awareness that others would disapprove of this imprecise yearning did not qualify as knowledge. However, somehow, I sensed the words "particular friendships" referred to the feelings I had for her. I knew these feelings were different from liking Alicia or some other girls. My reaction to Oneida had expressed *something* about me, *something* powerful and unacceptable, but whatever that *something* was I was not sure.

I was not even sure why I had blurted those words to Alicia. Oneida's reaction to my candy offering demonstrated what I guessed my feelings deserved. But that was all: a vague, imprecise, nameless longing that I should keep to myself.

I had felt utterly alone at that moment in the school yard. As I had learned to do so well at moments of deep insecurity, I became intellectual and pretentious and hid behind my academic prowess. I turned to Alicia and answered her question pompously, mumbling something about the "spiritual imperfection of human attachments." I didn't understand that statement well either, even as I was uttering it, but I guessed it would sound "elevated" and elegant and would stop Alicia from asking any more questions. In fact, Alicia was the only one of my classmates to whom I had confessed that I wanted to be a nun. I imagine she understood my convoluted statement as the result of my deep spirituality. And, to some extent, I also thought it was, precisely because I could not explain what I was feeling. By then, I had learned that aspiring to sainthood and "intellectualizing" was the way of avoiding questioning anything, including my pervasive feelings of loneliness and my mysterious yearning.

Cigüeñas y Sangre/Storks and Blood

It may seem rather strange that I did not know what sexual intercourse was until I was about fourteen years old. Or what "sexual" meant, for that matter. I found out that babies were not delivered by storks when I was about twelve, and I learned even later that babies came to be because of something men and women did together. But what that might be remained a mystery for some time still. By then, I had had two boyfriends. One had lasted longer than three months, a record for most girls my age. But we never went beyond kissing... and that with lips closed.

One of my brothers was born when I was eight, the other when I was almost twelve. Both times, months before they were born, I knew my mother was "ill," and Nery and I needed to be careful not to bother her too much. I could see her belly growing and took it as a symptom of her "illness." Then one day she was so sick that she had to go to the hospital. Later my father told us that "the stork had brought us a little brother." Why had the stork delivered the baby at a hospital where my mother was sick rather than at home was never explained. Neither was it clear why she had been cured of her illness at the same time. I can see now that there was something amusing about believing in the stork—like the kid who still believes in Santa Claus when most children have stopped believing the legend.

Whatever I learned about anything remotely related to sex came from information Nery whispered at night before we fell asleep. Nery and I had grown up almost as twins, dressed alike, and doing everything together. From early childhood to when we left Cuba in our early twenties, we slept in parallel beds and shared a wardrobe and a chest of drawers. When we were very young, we were put to bed around eight o'clock. As soon as the lights were turned off, one of us reached her arm out through the perilous distance between our beds. The unstated question "*¿Tienes miedo?* — "Are you afraid?" floated in the air. We were fearful of anything as harmless as a cat; no one could convince us that there were no monsters living under our beds, waiting to leap up and carry us away. We devised a meticulous system, alternating our nights of stretched arms across the gap and of holding the other's hand firmly in the safe territory of our own bed. We held hands tightly until one of us fell asleep. Most of the time it was Nery. If it was my turn to stretch my arm across the dangerous divide, I stayed awake until Nery fell asleep before I moved my arm back into my bed. If it was her turn to face the monster, I waited until her stretched arm relaxed and fell from my grip, signaling that she was asleep, and then I carefully folded her arm back on her bed. I frequently lay awake into the night, vigilant about the monsters.

By this time, we were no longer holding hands to protect each other from monsters that lived under our beds, but we had long talks every night. She clearly knew a lot more than I did about some crucial matters. She made comments like, "Men have a long hard thing that goes into women down there." "Women feel things in their breasts when that happens." "When girls grow up they pee blood." And other similar remarks.

She was proud that she knew things I was completely ignorant about. Mostly, I thought she was making things up. I only half believed her accounts about all these mysteries, but it progressively became evident that she knew some important details about forbidden topics that I'd do well to learn also. Just in case, I tucked the information away in my brain.

That Nery, who was a year younger than me, was my source of information reveals how "out of it" I was. But it was also a sign of the complete silence on all matters sexual that surrounded us in 1950s Cuba; this was in sharp contrast to Americans' opinions about Cuba. The erotic world, the sexual paradise sought by tourists who visited Cuba, was not our world.

Although I may have been more in the dark than other girls, most of us were extremely ignorant about "the facts of life." There was a pathetic lack of information about anything sexual. Nery knew more than I because she made it her business to find out things that adults did not want us to know. She participated in conversations with "savvy" girls. She also listened to comments made by the maids at home and older girls at school; her ears perked up for the benefit of both of us. Our whispered conversations were full of factual errors. But despite holes in her knowledge, the forbidden information became essential during my adolescence.

Nery on the day of her graduation from middle school

On the January day when my period arrived without warning, I went to school as usual. With the clarity with which one remembers what one was doing at the precise instant when momentous historical events happen—when Kennedy was shot, when the Twin Towers fell—I remember the moment when I realized something unusual was going on. The teacher had called me to the blackboard to write down the grammatical forms of the three singular personal pronouns when I noticed that I needed to go to the bathroom immediately.

Yo, mi, mío, me; Tú, tu, tuyo, te; El, Ella, su, suyo, se, le, la, lo, I wrote, finishing my blackboard demonstration as quickly as possible. Then I asked permission to go to the toilet. When I saw my blood-stained underwear, the vague memory of night conversations with Nery resurfaced in a flash. That memory held me back from screaming and making a fool of myself in front of my classmates. I remained silent despite the terror I felt. Nery's comments were my only inkling that this blood was not a sign of approaching death.

I anxiously waited for the end of the school morning session, sitting sideways to keep the white cotton school uniform from telling the tale of what was happening. Riding the bus home at lunch time also required some careful and discreet gymnastics to avoid telltale red stains.

As soon as I arrived home I went to find my mother and said, "I need to talk to you…"

She smiled in a puzzling way and responded, "I have been waiting to talk to you, too."

Apparently, although I had succeeded in saving my white uniform from blood stains, I had left proof of my new state on my bed sheets. Orlandito, one of my little brothers, now slept on his small bed in our bedroom. Nery and I always dressed in the dim light of dawn, almost still night, and got out quickly and noiselessly, so we would not disturb his sleep. Dressing in the dark I had not noticed anything that morning. My mother had been waiting for me since she made the bed that morning after we left for school. But even though she had been waiting for me "to talk," she only said, "This happens to all women, wear this," while she handed me a sanitary napkin and belt and showed me how to hook them together.

She had never said a word to help me anticipate this strange event that "happens to all women," which seemed to have caught both of us equally by surprise. I was left to figure out what this new thing my body was doing might mean; its connection with sex and babies was still non-existent.

Sometime after, I finally figured out that babies came from inside women's bodies rather than from storks dispatched to deliver them to families. But I still did not know how they got "in there" and did not connect this new knowledge with the presence of the blood oozing from my body every month.

One thing I knew: I was not supposed to ask questions about these topics. Those night conversations with Nery in our dark bedroom were my only source of information. But even though she was taller and stronger than me and knew all those forbidden things, we both knew I was the older sister: I had to take care of both of us.

Decades later, during the last two years of Nery's life, I desolately remembered all that we shared, including my commitment to taking care of her. In the end, I could not protect her from the insidious monster that grew in her brain. Progressively, her memories disappeared. She stopped talking. She was transformed from a beautiful woman into a stolid old hag. And all I could do was look at her helplessly, trying to keep those early memories alive for both of us, talking about them when I visited her even though her only response was a blank stare.

But while we were growing up, Nery ate heartily and ran and played as soon as she finished her lunch or dinner. I brooded in front of my plate. She played physical games at school and even at home in our restricted quarters. She had friends and lived like a child. She seemed to feel free to disobey, while I was always as obedient as I knew how to be. I am sure it was not that easy for her to be my sister. At some level, I envied her, and wished I did not have to be so good. But every time I tried, either the nuns or my parents shamed me into obedience by reminding me that perfect little girls like me did not do any of those wicked things.

As we grew into adolescence, Nery got into trouble with greater frequency at home and at school. Yet, her trust in me never abated despite some of my supercilious attitudes.

If her trust remained strong, so did my fierce loyalty to her. I protected her from my mother's fury, and less successfully, from my father's indifference. Whenever she was scolded about something she had done, instead of acting repentant, Nery made some defiant noises and turned away— "frying eggs," my mother used to call those noises. This behavior earned Nery the few slaps any of us ever got from my mother. Whenever she made these noises, Mami slapped her, yelling, "Stop frying eggs with your mouth, *falta de respeto*! Don't you dare be disrespectful, *malcriada*!"

By the time we were adolescents, when we worried about boyfriends, not about monsters, I still did my best to protect her. I could not prevent the punishment that followed Nery's defiant gestures and noises. But I could cover up for her in front of my mother.

When she was barely twelve, Nery had a boyfriend, a fourteen-year-old boy, who lived one block away from where we had recently moved in El Vedado and walked to his school on a route that overlapped with ours. In our newly acquired status as walking rather than bus-riding students, we ambled to school and back home twice a day in the company of other girls who lived in the area, surrounded by boys from nearby schools, who also lived in the neighborhood.

Mami caught on quickly to the fact that Nery had a boyfriend among those boys. She decided that this was completely inappropriate for a twelve-year-old and forbade us to walk in this boy's company on our way home from school. We were to avoid him by turning at different corners and approaching our house by other streets. Neither Nery nor Ramón had the slightest desire to follow my mother's orders.

Almost every day after school, Mami asked me, "Did you walk with Ramón today?" and she usually added, "I won't believe Nery's answer. She will probably lie. But I know you will always tell me the truth."

Although aware that I was not supposed to lie because it would endanger my perfect-girl status, there was no way I would betray Nery. So, with a very straight face and my very best good girl demeanor, I would answer my mother, "No, we did not. We walked a different way than he did."

The matter would have stayed there had it not happened that Orlandito, who was now going to kindergarten at the same school Nery and I attended, decided to be a good boy and tell the truth.

"We walked with Ramón today," he reported without being asked. Furious, my mother marched into our bedroom with him in tow and asked her question again.

"No, we did not walk with Ramón," I insisted. Turning to Orlandito, who was then about five years old, with a straight face, I said, "Shame on you! Don't you know you are not supposed to tell lies?"

I knew I was confusing and embarrassing him and possibly earning him some scolding from my mother. But my loyalty to Nery was more important than anything else, and if my good girl reputation could shield her from my mother's punishment, I did not hesitate to compromise my integrity for her sake.

More or less consciously, I knew that all the praise I received as a child had a strong deleterious effect on her self-confidence. We went to the same school, she was a grade below me, but she did not have a full scholarship as I did because she was not considered a good student. She suffered regular comments from nuns and lay teachers who asked why she was not as good, as studious or obedient as I was. Growing up in my shadow, being constantly told that she could never be as good as her sister, stunted her sense of what she could have been. In truth, I believe she was as intelligent as I was. Probably if my father had not been so busy praising me and ignoring her, she might have been the lawyer he had hoped for, but never got from me or my brothers. Instead of trying to garner whatever praise was left over after being lavished on me, she disobeyed and misbehaved. Her rebellious behavior was her way to make the adults look at her, if only to express disapproval. To be scolded for not being more like me was better than being ignored.

It is a tribute to Nery and to the strength of our connection that we remained friends. However I may have flaunted and even abused my privileged status in my immediate and extended family or at school, I always knew that Nery was essential to my life. But this awareness of how much I needed and loved her, did not fully prevent me from doing everything I could to preserve my superior status. Probably, protecting her was another way of keeping that status while trying to compensate her for it.

I took only one vacation in childhood without Nery. When I was thirteen years old, as a prize for my good grades in the high school admission exam, my parents agreed to send me to Santiago for summer vacation once again. As Nery's punishment for not studying hard enough, she stayed in Havana that summer. It was the most boring vacation I ever had.

El Vedado

A few months after I got my first period, we moved to a dilapidated three-bedroom house in El Vedado, where our school was. Most of our classmates lived El Vedado. Doctor Tres Palacios and Doctor Arturo had their offices there. El Vedado had been a private hunting preserve for Cuban aristocracy in the nineteenth century. Its name literally means *the forbidden*. In the first half of the twentieth century, elegant apartment buildings and houses with tiled front porches, graceful columns and bas-relief details were built in El Vedado. Luscious vines growing in the front gardens entwined the columns and gave the houses an almost mysterious air.

I am not quite sure how my parents were able to afford the rent. Our financial situation had not improved. I guess my parents had decided that continuing to live in the back of my father's school would not help the social life of two daughters who were entering adolescence. Sometimes Nery and I could not participate in social activities with our classmates for lack of cash or clothes. At those times, we pretended to have other obligations. But, no matter, Nery and I were delighted to be living in El Vedado and away from the flat on Calzada de Reina. We were happy to be living a normal adolescent life in a normal house full of normal furniture in a normal neighborhood.

The house on Calle C (2011)

At 13, right after we moved to Calle C

We now lived in a house where all the rooms were available to us, not just two bedrooms in the back of my father's school. Only bedroom furniture had been in use in those rooms in the school flat. Now, the living- and dining-room furniture my parents had bought when they got married was back in use. They unpacked their Baccarat crystal wine glasses and placed them in a glass-doored cabinet in the dining-room. I loved the tinkling sound the glasses made when touched lightly with the tip of a fingernail. Furniture, dishes, and decorative objects were brought from the garage of my father's family home in Almendares where they had been stored for more than a decade.

And Mami was delighted that this house had a gas stove. The fire could be turned on and off in a second. No more cooking on coals; less pressure from daily meal preparation.

Our new home in El Vedado, was on a side street, rather than on the wide avenues that ringed its perimeter. On those avenues, luxury hotels opened their doors to tourists and Cubans alike. The Hotel Nacional built on a hill overlooking El Malecón in the earlier part of the twentieth century was the most beautiful of them all. Memories of the bloody battle against officers of the armed forces that had taken place in the Hotel Nacional in the 1930s were mostly gone by then. Other modern hotels were built in El Vedado during my adolescence. The Riviera and the Capri with their gambling casinos that I learned years later had been owned by the Mafia. The Habana Hilton rose at the busy intersection of L and Twenty-Third Streets with its walls covered in murals by famous painter Amalia Peláez. The Hilton—renamed Habana Libre at the beginning of the Revolution—topped *la Rampa*, the steep wide extension of Twenty-Third Street that ended at El Malecón, where huge waves crashed, soaking sidewalks and passing cars alike.

Hotel Nacional

El Malecón

El Malecón

With Nery, Orlando and Mario, early 1950s

El Malecón runs from the entrance to Havana Bay, across from the Morro Castle, all the way to the Almendares River, at the edge of El Vedado. It is a showcase for the Havana skyline. During my elementary school years, I loved riding the school bus on El Malecón, screaming with joy when the waves splashed the windows we quickly closed to avoid getting wet. Now that we lived in El Vedado, there were no more bus rides by the waves of El Malecón. Our new home was walking distance from the school Nery and I had attended since first grade.

The flooring in the house and the porch were made of beautiful tiles with elaborate designs typical of Cuban houses. The columns and the ceiling's edge at the façade had bas-relief details like most houses in this neighborhood. A small garden patch full of flowers sat between the porch and the low wrought iron gated fence that separated the house from the sidewalk. The pungent sweet smell of white *galán de noche*, night blooming jasmine, filled the air in the evening—an enormous difference from the fumes of cars, trucks, and buses that we had lived with in Calzada de Reina.

Nino and Chicha, two mentally disabled adults, lived in the elegant house next door, watched by their old parents and a widowed sister. Chicha was very quiet; she looked at us, smiled shyly and went back to whatever she was always doing with her hands. But Nino was very talkative and spent hours walking around in the neighborhood. Even though his speech was not clear, people loved talking to him and hearing whatever stories he wanted to tell when he approached them. I can still picture his small frame clothed in shirts and pants that were always too big for him; his mouth moving in circles trying to form the words. His tales usually did not make much sense. He endeared himself to us and, rather than being taunted, he was cherished by the neighborhood kids who enjoyed hearing his barely intelligible stories.

On the other side of our new home, Belén, a middle-aged widow, lived with her son and a maid who had worked for her longer than Teresa had for us. Belén had been a student in the same school Nery and I attended. She was delighted at the coincidence and so were we.

The day we moved into our new place, I was startled while taking a shower by the voice of an old woman yelling "¡Socorro! ¡Socorro!" — "Help! Help!" at the top of her lungs. I quickly dried myself and got out of the bathroom, only to realize that the screams were coming from a parrot in Belén's house. Others in my family who had also been startled by the screams were standing in the yard, by the wall that separated the twin houses, laughing at the parrot who was now saying, "Canta, lorito, a ver..." — "Sing little parrot, let's hear you..." Belén apologized for the scare the parrot had given us. We talked on our adjacent porches frequently after that first day.

The best thing about having Belén as a neighbor was that the walls of her living room were covered with bookcases. And I was welcome to use her vast library. Her books ranged from popular fiction like Henry Morton Robinson's *The Cardinal* or romance novels by Spanish writer Corín Tellado to Tolstoy and Dostoyevsky, Vicente Blasco Ibáñez, José Mármol and other Spanish and Latin American writers. Belén's library kept me occupied on vacations and weekends for the six years we lived in that house.

During our first year living in El Vedado while, like a typical adolescent, I was mostly interested in myself, political troubles kept brewing in the background. After years of Sunday speeches, in 1951, long after I had stopped attending Dr. Arturo's classes and overhearing the mothers' political discussions, Chibás, while still standing in front of the microphone at the radio station, shot himself at the end of his weekly speech. The radio audience heard the shot and his parting words, "This is my final knock on Cuban consciences..."

Chibás was a senator of the Republic. His body lay in state in the Capitolio for an entire week. Long lines of people came to pay their respects. All over Cuba, women and men wept and looked at each other from reddened eyes. I did not understand why Chibás had killed himself. Neither did the weeping adults. Some said he had not been able to prove his accusations about some corrupt politicians. Perhaps he had simply lost hope. But, whatever his motivation, his suicide left me with a foreboding feeling about the destructive power of Cuban politics.

Dalia, a nice friendly woman in her mid-twenties, who lived on the top floor of Nino's house with her parents and her younger brother Guido, knocked nervously on our door very early one morning. In a frightened voice she told us, "Batista ousted President Carlos Prío in the early dawn, and no one knows what might happen next! Stay indoors! God knows what can happen."

The day was March 10, 1952.

Soldiers marched idly up and down the street, and we were aware of a larger than usual police presence even around our quiet street. Nothing else seemed to be happening; still, we heeded Dalia's advice. At a time when most Cubans did not own a TV and depended on the radio for information and entertainment, when we turned on the radio that day, we heard only classical music, no news at all. Obviously, whoever was in power wanted to keep people confused and ignorant about what was happening.

As if to underscore that everything was completely normal, the ice-cream vendor went by that afternoon as he did every day. He came up *calle C* riding his cart, a motorcycle that had an icebox attached to the front. He rang a metal device that sounded like a doorbell and announced his merchandise by yelling ¡Heladeeroo! ¡Helaaaaados! The *heladero* was a short chubby man who dressed in a white uniform and wore a flat sailor cap and eyeglasses. He sold *Helados Hatuey*—the brand named after the Taíno chief who led a rebellion against the conquering Spaniards in the late fifteenth century. A stylized head of Hatuey was painted on the sides of the ice cream cart. The *heladero* sold popsicles in fruit flavors, chocolate or vanilla for five cents; a vanilla popsicle covered in chocolate was ten cents. The greatest delicacy was called *coco glacé,* coconut ice cream inside a coarse coconut shell that cost twenty cents. I saved my pennies to have a *coco glacé* every so often, even though that meant forgoing chocolate popsicles for several afternoons so I could afford the more expensive delicacy. On that March 10, I made sure I had a *coco glacé* to soothe my apprehension.

My family had already suffered the consequences of Batista's actions during his first term as president. My parents didn't say much about their obvious dismay at having to live under Batista again. They may have wanted to avoid verbalizing any opposition or their trepidation and anxiety in front of the children. You don't know what children may repeat in public. Or they may have been so despondent that they couldn't even talk about it. They prepared for the worst while pretending that nothing had happened. No one knew what the future under Batista would bring. All of us kept to our routines and tried to forget the new disheartening political situation, even though one of the ministers Batista appointed soon after the *coup* lived in a big house at the end of our block and there was always a police detail standing at that corner.

Further down the block from our new home, across from Batista's minister, lived Gracielita and Albertico. Their house held the greatest attraction on the block: a black and white television their parents had bought before anyone else in the neighborhood had one. Every evening, even on weekdays, after homework and dinner, we were invited to watch TV at their place. Everyone was excited by the novelty. We watched live Cuban television—several variety shows, the plays of Antonio Buero Vallejo and Alejandro Casona, performed by handsome actors Manolo Coego or Jorge Félix, as well as dubbed American programs like Perry Mason or *Patrulla de Caminos*—Highway Patrol—in which dubbed Raymond Burr and Broderick Crawford spoke Spanish with Mexican accents. We were required to be completely silent during the whole show as in a movie theater. If anyone said a word or commented aloud on whatever we were watching, Gracielita's mother produced a furious *SHHHH!!!* that immediately restored the silence.

After we had our own black and white TV, in addition to watching the same evening programs, in the late afternoons, I watched Mexican and Argentinean films with Dolores del Río, Jorge Negrete, Delia Garcés and others. My little brothers watched cartoons featuring Mighty Mouse or Woody Woodpecker and Mami watched Nitza Villapol's cooking show, trying to find new ideas for the daily meals.

On the porch of the house on *calle C* where we spent our adolescence, Nery kissed her *novios* surreptitiously while I spent my high school vacations reading books from Belén's library, sitting in one of the cane-back rocking chairs that furnished the porch.

It was on that porch that Nery and I had our diminutive *quinceañeras* celebrations because my parents could not afford anything else. There, we held other dances with school and neighborhood friends, celebrating whatever occasion we could find for a party. The shiny tile floors made it easy to dance. Using a borrowed record player that looked like an attaché case, we played 78 and 45 rpm records, and danced to American music like "Good night, Irene...I'll see you in my dreams," Glenn Miller's "Moonlight Serenade" and Cuban songs like "La Engañadora," a new and popular *cha-cha-chá*, "Almendra," and other traditional *danzones*. Records of other popular musicians such as Benny Moré's orchestra, Pérez Prado's mambos, and slow *boleros* sung by other musicians also played at our parties. Elvis Presley was not very popular; rock-and-roll was difficult for us to dance to.

I loved dancing and had a *novio* among the boys who came around after school under the pretext of hanging out with Guido, our next-door neighbor. I kept it a secret because my mother would not have approved. We were not supposed to have boyfriends before we were at least fifteen. I didn't want to battle my mother like Nery did.

Francisco, my boyfriend, was a handsome sandy-haired fourteen-year-old. When I had to sing my little brother Mario to sleep, I always sang a song about Spanish bullfighter Francisco Alegre—a message to his namesake that I would be out on the porch as soon as my brother fell asleep. In a muffled voice, hoping the baby would doze off fast, but loud enough so Francisco would hear, I repeated, *Torito bravo, ten compasión que entre bordados, lleva encerrado, Francisco Alegre y olé, mi corazón* ("Brave bull, be compassionate, because under his glittering outfit, Francisco Alegre y olé, hides my trapped heart"). I kissed Francisco once, when my mother was not home. We managed to hide behind a tree up the block, around the corner. I was thrilled about having been kissed, but secretly thought, "What's the big deal about kissing?"

Garzas y Danzas

Memorizing and reciting poetry as dramatically as Berta Singerman did is now outmoded, but it was a highly appreciated art in Latin America when I was growing up. I regularly recited poems at school events. Tío wanted me to become more skilled at "*declamación*." He had taken me to a Singerman's performance a few years earlier to encourage me. When I turned thirteen, he arranged for me to take private poetry recitation lessons.

At elementary school events, I had recited simple poems such as

Bandera de mis amores
tan gallarda, tan bonita
pareces una cestita
de las más pintadas flores

(My beloved flag
so graceful, so beautiful
you look like a little basket
of the most colorful flowers).

Or long poems such as "Los Zapaticos de Rosa" by José Martí, the poet and architect of Cuban independence, that started

Hay sol bueno, mar de espuma
y arena fina y Pilar
quiere salir a estrenar
su sombrerito de pluma.

(The sun is shining, the sea is foamy,
the sand is fine powder and Pilar
wants to go out wearing
her new feather hat for the first time).

My instructor, one of Tío's "bohemian" friends, a tall, wiry man who looked very gay even to my naïve eyes, introduced me to serious poetry, poems that were more elaborate and more difficult to interpret. From him I learned about the poetry of Argentinean Alfonsina Storni, focused on the meaning and pains of womanhood. Under my instructor's direction, I memorized Felipe Pichardo Moya's "La Garza" and performed it many times.

He matado una Garza
lo confieso, Señor
En el cristal del aire
toda blanca y como transparente bajo el sol
yo la vi que pasaba
y la maté, Señor

(I have killed a white heron
I must confess it, Lord
In the glass reflection of the air
all white and translucent in the sunlight
I saw her fly by
and I killed her, Lord).

I am not sure I fully understood the meaning of this sad poem about regretting mistakes when it is too late to choose a different course, but I could feel then—and still feel—a deep sadness at the heron's heartrending death whenever I uttered those words.

My teacher would throw back his mop of dark curls to emphatically demonstrate the gestures he wanted me to master, what he expected of my stage presence. "Back straight, chin up, arms moving slowly; gestures precede the words you want to express, not follow them."

He focused on my posture, "Feet in fifth position, tight together;" on the inflection of my voice, "Up at the last syllable of the verse, down or flat on the previous one;" and on my comprehension and empathy for each poem, "Can you feel what the hunter must have felt when he saw the heron falling to the ground?"

He insisted that posture, gestures, vocal inflections, and understanding would improve my interpretation, and they did. The constant repetition of the same verses was never boring. I could tell that I sounded better with each new attempt.

When he visited during my lesson, Tío sat in the living room watching me perform under the skillful direction of my instructor while the rest of my family went about their daily activities. His pride was evident.

At school, the nuns gradually assigned me more difficult poems. When I was about fourteen or so, I was taken by one of the lay teachers, with my parents' permission, to recite some poems to incarcerated felons in *El Castillo del Príncipe*, one of Havana's prisons that was located on a hill a few blocks from where we lived in El Vedado.

Looking at the sea of prisoners' faces from the stage where I stood alone made me nervous. Their faces would have frightened me if I had encountered them anywhere in the city; their fierce expressions, even their smiles, were intimidating. In El Príncipe prison's courtyard, standing on the stage, I could hear my voice reverberate against the high gray walls as I started reciting my first poem. It was *"Muerto,"* a poem written by José Martí in 1875. His only religious poem. I had memorized it for a school event a few months earlier. The long blank verses in which it is written, and the complicated metaphors and allusions did not make for easy recall. I suppose the choice of that poem by whoever put my program together was meant to inspire some religious feelings in the prisoners and some repentance for their sins through the contemplation of Jesus's death and Mary's suffering.

As I started to recite it, I started to falter. I repeated the first stanza twice, but the rest of the words escaped me. The buzzing in my head repeated the words of the first stanza over and over but no other words would come out. Acutely embarrassed and humiliated by my failure, I stopped after my third failed attempt at going beyond the first stanza and in a shy, shaky voice whispered into the microphone,

"I am sorry, I do not remember the rest…"

Much to my surprise, unexpectedly, I heard big tough hands clapping. They gave me a big ovation thanking me eagerly for taking the time to perform for them. The previously fierce, frightening prisoners seemed to me now as if they were kind and gentle men, forgiving my terrible muddle—which was nothing, I suppose, by comparison to theirs.

My fiasco at the prison notwithstanding, it became increasingly clear that the private lessons were teaching me more than just how to memorize and recite poetry. The sense of mastery created by my performances as well as the content of the poems had a subtle impact on how I felt "about things" and perhaps on my sense of self. My recitation lessons were transformative in more than one way. They made me feel more adult.

In addition to paying for these lessons, Tío also helped me check historical facts for my school papers, helped me revise the poems I continued to write, and gave me his poems to read and critique.

As I stood in the middle of Tío's room in the Almendares house near his massive desk, trying to understand what he had written, I frequently felt confused. His poems were not made for recitation or for clearly grasped meaning, either. They were full of the intricate and obscure metaphors and symbolism so in vogue in 1950s poetry. Reading his poems made me anxious because, for the most part, I did not understand what Tío wrote. I knew he was going to ask me questions after I read them—and I was going to feel embarrassed and flustered not knowing what to say.

Once, while he was sitting almost hidden behind the voluminous stacks of paper piled up on his desk, he showed me a new poem, "La Gota Azul" (The Blue Drop). His blank verse described arbitrary colors and shapes such as *amarilla canal del aire* ("yellow canal of the air"). It continued attributing other capricious colors to seemingly unrelated objects. I read the poem silently several times but could not make any sense of it. Tío sat hunched in his chair, watching my facial expression, waiting for my reaction. Finally, he said, "Well…?"

I stammered, uttering something like, "Lots of colors but nothing about the blue drop of the title…"

"Oh," he said in a dismayed voice, "but all the color progression is there to recover the blue drop!"

Perhaps he was disappointed in me because I had not been able to figure out the essence of the poem. Perhaps he was frustrated that his poem did not convey the intended meaning. Perhaps he was trying to advance my education and good taste by sharing this intricate poem. Whatever his intent, I was frustrated by not being able to rise to his intellectual level.

Poets of Tío's generation in Cuba and all over Latin America—published, renowned, and celebrated—took pride in writing what they described as "difficult poetry." Tío won a modest place among them with poems like "La Gota Azul." One of his published poems was about José Martí on the centennial of his birth in 1953. Another one, *Yo la he Visto Empinarse Largamente*," loosely translatable as "I Have Seen her Rise Up," was written in honor of my cousin who became a nun at fifteen in the mid-1950s. Both poems were loaded with abstruse symbolism. Tío was never a very successful poet, but he did achieve some recognition, and he shared his nocturnal literary café life with Havana's well-known poets, novelists, and essayists.

One of the many things I learned from Tío and from Papi, and others of their generation was a profound love for Cuba: its heroes, its history, its geography. They were the first generation born after independence and they cherished the country their parents had fought to free from Spain; they respected and venerated those who had and still continued to struggle each day to make it a better place for all Cubans; they celebrated Martí's creativity and Félix Varela's carefully crafted political philosophy; they resented U.S. interference in Cuban affairs that had so impacted the early development of the Republic; they gloried in the beauty of Cuban beaches and mountains. In everyday palpable and subtle ways, they showed their pride in the country, and believed in its potential while being aware of all that still needed to be accomplished.

In my most recent trip to Cuba, I was appalled by the ignorance displayed by young Cubans concerning anything before the Revolution that does not fit the narrative of salvation by Fidel. Of course, Cuba was a poor country. Though never in the same category of extreme poverty as other countries in the world, social injustices were rampant, particularly in rural areas. There was much that needed to be done; but there was also much that had been accomplished in the short life of the Republic. Life expectancy and literacy were among the highest in Latin America. Labor unions were a major force protecting workers; there was a solid middle class, at least in the cities.

For Tío, the thirst for improvement of Cuba's social conditions and his thirst for knowledge went hand in hand. When I was about fifteen or sixteen, a junior in high school, Tío took a continuing education course on Cuban geography and geology. The academics who participated in the course took field trips to different areas of Cuba during the year-long program. Frequently Tío invited me, the only young person among all the adults. After participating in those tours, I knew a lot about Cuba's mountains and plains, rivers, coastlines and sea currents. I could recognize the signs of earth movements in rock formations and layers, and I could also identify different geological periods; the word *Jurassic* was meaningful to me decades before Steven Spielberg's film made it popular.

The course followed the steps of German Baron Alexander von Humboldt, who studied Cuba in detail in the eighteenth century. Humboldt traveled extensively through Latin America and loved Cuba best of all—confirming, much to Tío's pride, Columbus's comments in 1492, "This is the most beautiful land that human eyes have ever seen."

Half a century after my excursions across Cuba with Tío, I saw a statue of the Baron in East Berlin, at the gate of Humboldt University, which he and his brother founded in 1811. An inscription in Spanish on the pedestal startled me, *"El pueblo cubano agradecido al segundo descubridor de Cuba"* ("The grateful Cuban people to the second discoverer of Cuba").

One of those tours following Humboldt's steps took us to the Ciénaga de Zapata, the shoe-shaped peninsula on the southern coast of Cuba at the heel of which is the Bay of Pigs. Zapata is an enormous swamp teeming with life forms but few human inhabitants, an inhospitable area of the island. In 1961, it was the site of the failed invasion organized by the CIA, sending Cuban exiles to battle Castro's army— an incongruous choice of location for an invasion of a country that boasts such a long coastline.

During my week-long visit to the Ciénaga with Tío, about a dozen female and male professors and the crew of five or six men glided slowly among the mangrove swamp canals. There was barely enough space for all of us on the old steamboat. We observed and studied the lush vegetation, the wildflowers hanging precariously from tall branches. Birds that flew overhead, perched on nearby tree limbs or stood still in barely dry spots—white *garzas* among them. As I looked at the beautiful white *garzas*, standing on one foot in shallow water or flying over the boat, I remembered the poem I had learned and understood better the regret of destroying one of those beautiful creatures. The reptilian fauna included frogs, turtles, and several scary alligators. We also caught glimpses of a few *jutías*, large rat-like mammals native to Cuba, eating their meals on the high branches of trees.

We also watched the magnificent sunsets and basked in the clear starry nights, heard the constant murmur of the water under the boat, the rustling of the leaves and the calls of the animals. We ate fruit we grabbed from the trees as we glided past them, together with rice and canned beans. We feasted on lobsters and shrimp caught in front of our eyes, prepared by the crew on the two-burner kerosene stove. Strangely enough, I don't remember many mosquitoes around. But I do remember that I got badly sunburned, an unavoidable consequence at a time when no one used sunblock. The deck was unprotected from the sun. To be under cover in one of the two cabins below meant missing the spectacular flora and fauna we passed. The sunburn took more than a week to heal when I returned to Havana; it was small price to pay for the opportunity to visit a part of Cuba most people had never seen.

During the trip, the professors and crew members enjoyed telling dirty jokes; at such times Tío sent me to the other end of the boat: I sat alone while they laughed at each whispered joke. Although mortified by being excluded, I welcomed the time for solitary observation. Sitting alone on the deck, I watched the scenery drift by, floating above the marsh waters and reflected by them. I never got tired of the jumble of greenery, vines, exposed roots, trunks, branches, birds and other creatures. Interspersed with subtle rustling sounds of unseen animals or the distant call of birds I could hear the laughter of the adults. I shook my head at their silliness, missing all this beauty huddling inside laughing at dirty jokes. I was delighted enjoying this natural paradise undisturbed.

Besides these educational activities and his many ways of encouraging my creativity and intellectual curiosity, Tío taught me to dance. He was an excellent dancer and wanted to share his skill with me as he had supported my literary and academic interests.

In the central hallway of the house in Almendares stood an old upright RCA Victrola purchased in the 1920s. A big horn, like the one on the classic RCA phonograph ad, crowned the Victrola. Tío would open the lower storage compartment and take out a 78-rpm disc from a beige paper sleeve with a round hole in the center through which you could see on a red circle the name of the single piece of music and its interpreter. After placing the disc on the turntable, he would hand-wind the Victrola, setting the needle's arm carefully at the edge of the fragile shellac surface. As the scratchy notes of "The Blue Danube" or another Strauss waltz filled the living room, he would start swaying back and forth and gyrating while counting "*one*, two, three, *one* two, three." First, I was to look at his feet and his turns conscientiously, then I was to imitate them, my movements parallel to his. Finally, he would put one arm around my waist, hold my hand, rest my other hand delicately on his shoulder, and we would start rotating together, still counting, "*one*, two, three, *one*, two, three."

After I had mastered the waltz, we tackled more complicated ballroom dance styles. Initially, our moving to the rhythm of the music made me feel clumsy. But eventually, I stopped feeling self-conscious and started feeling more confident about testing my newly acquired dance skills with others. For a bookish adolescent girl, becoming a good dancer was a priceless gift. It showed me and others that I was more than a brain. Thanks to Tío, I learned to perfection how to be led in dancing. At parties and balls, I was sought out by boys who were skillful dancers and knew they would get a pliable partner and thus show off their own virtuosity.

One of those boys, Alfonso, became my constant dance partner for several years. More than once, Alfonso and I were given the whole floor, to waltz or to perform Spanish and Cuban dances. Other young people and the adult chaperones who accompanied us to parties and nightclubs enjoyed watching our show. Mami, who always accompanied Nery and me as a chaperone was surprised and proud watching my performances and hearing the congratulatory comments of the other chaperones. This attention was an additional debt I owed Tío. My mother did not care much for my intellectual pursuits. Impressing and getting praise from her was rare, but she understood and enjoyed my dancing prowess.

Alfonso guided me slowly in the traditional *danzones* that required exact, languid steps, marking a small square on the floor or speedily, as the rhythm of Spanish *pasodobles* required. *Pasodobles* were one of our remarkable successes. My wide skirts twirled and turned about me, as I moved back in a straight line in my high heels and then forward, when it was Alfonso's turn to move back with quick steps. I was never interested romantically in Alfonso, but I enjoyed the flair of our dancing together; I felt the music of the *pasodobles*, *mambos*, *danzones* or *boleros*, delighted in following the rhythms, and was aware of every muscle in my legs and arms and in touch with every fiber of my body in a way that I never felt before or after. Without Alfonso as a partner,

I could not have been so competent. If I'd had to dance alone I would have felt lost. My dance talent was in following, which was what Tío had taught me. I have never done much following in life—and, in fact, have tended to move to my own internal music. But dancing with Alfonso and other boys was a joy.

Tío

As an adult, I have frequently wondered whether Tío might have been gay. This possibility was unmentioned and unmentionable. In 1950s Cuba, if the topic of homosexuality was ever brought up, it involved snide remarks or disparaging comments about blatantly effeminate men and masculine women—*pájaros* or *maricones* and *marimachas* as they were called—who deserved rejection because of their contemptible or aberrant behavior. A few effeminate performers who were known homosexuals were forgiven their shameless conduct in exchange for their artistic contributions. Bola de Nieve and Luis Carbonell, one a pianist and singer, the other reciting poetry that imitated the accent and dialect of black Cuban women, were both very successful while displaying effeminate mannerisms in their performances. Others like Ernesto Lecuona, the foremost Cuban composer, always displayed appropriate masculine behavior in public. The lives or activities of respected professionals who behaved in a masculine manner were never questioned or scrutinized—at least not in front of adolescent girls. Even though supposedly there was a vibrant gay life in Cuba in the 40s and 50s, the only homosexual I knew of, besides my apparently gay recitation instructor, was Roberto, the brother-in-law of my uncle Rogelio. Their mannerisms made their gayness obvious. I knew enough to know this meant they were homosexuals, although I am not sure I knew what that meant. However, if there were questions about Tío's sexual preferences I was never aware of them. His behavior, like Lecuona's was always culturally masculine, which meant heterosexual.

Everyone understood that because Tío was unmarried and had no children, he focused his attention and financial resources on his nieces and nephews. But my siblings and cousins were aware that no one got more attention from him than I. In turn, I was aware that Tío's and my father's expectations led me to excel.

The Dark Side of Magic

My father cherished me even more than Tío. And I adored him. I thought he could do no wrong and, apparently, he thought the same about me. During my childhood and adolescence, he made me feel there was nothing I could not do. Mostly, I believed his assessment of me and saw myself through his eyes, which was not always good for me.

He demanded that I be extraordinary. But his expectations were always presented in a very gentle way.

I had an appendectomy when I was eleven years old. A few days before I went to the hospital my father asked, "You can do this with only local anesthesia, can't you?"

His question made it apparent that having surgery under general anesthesia was beneath me. There was no way I would willingly disappoint him. Therefore, the evening before the surgery I informed the anesthesiologist who visited my room to talk about the preparations for the surgery that I wanted only local anesthesia. He gave me an amused smile and said firmly,

"No, that is out of the question."

He probably left my room thinking that this petulant little girl was out of her mind. Mami, who was sitting by my bed during this conversation with the anesthesiologist, did not say a word. Fortunately, I didn't feel I could contradict him and was secretly relieved that I did not have to stay awake while some doctor was cutting my belly.

The next morning, after the surgery, I came out of the anesthesia whimpering and feeling sick. The ether had nauseated me, and the six-stich incision—too big by today's standards—hurt with burning pain. But all I could think in the middle of my fog was that my father would be disappointed I had acquiesced to the general anesthesia.

What motivated my father's wish that I be so heroic I never knew. I doubt it had anything to do with concerns about the dangers of general anesthesia. Such knowledge was not widespread then as it is now. To my eleven-year-old self this request felt as if my father thought, once again, that I was capable of the most astounding feats. No wonder I believed I was unique and better than others!

At twelve, I took the national official high school admission exam and got a grade of ninety-seven over one hundred. When I received the call with the results I ran to my father, who was sitting at lunch and hugged him screaming with delight.

"Ninety-seven! Ninety-seven! I got in! I got in!"

He smiled with a mixture of astonishment and pride.

"I got eighty-six in mine," he said. "Congratulations! That is an amazing result. What do you want as a prize?"

I had found the exam very easy and couldn't understand how my wonderfully intelligent father had not aced it. I concluded that the exams must have been more difficult back then. But his comment suggested as well that he did not feel he was as first-rate as I was.

In my fourth year of high school, the equivalent of junior year in the U.S., I fell from a horse at a farm near Havana two days before the official exam for first semester Physics. I was badly bruised. My whole body ached. My jaw and other muscles were inflamed and painful. I couldn't concentrate to study for the difficult exam and received a barely passing grade. Even if I succeeded in getting a perfect 100 in the second semester exam, my official grade for Physics could not be more than a B. This B would tarnish my otherwise perfect A high school record, no matter how well I did in all the other exams during my fifth and last year. I was disappointed and ashamed and swore not to go horseback riding ever again.

The humiliation I felt at my first low grade ever was compounded by my father's reaction. He could not live with this blemish on my academic history.

"Why don't you nullify this first semester grade by taking a final exam for the whole year? It won't be that difficult for you," he suggested.

In fact, keeping up with Physics a semester at a time was very difficult for me. I hated the subject matter; I had trouble understanding optics and solving intricate problems involving electricity. The thought of having to deal with all this material in a double dose felt overwhelming. But, could I live–could my father live–with a B in my impeccable A record? Could I risk the possibility of a C if I got less than a perfect 100 in the second semester exam? Could I stand my father's disappointment?

I waged an internal battle for a couple of months that interfered with everything else I was doing or studying, including Physics. Finally, as June approached and with it the second semester official exams, I decided that struggling with the Physics material for second semester was hard enough. I said no to my father's suggestion.

"It's OK," he said when I told him. "It was always your decision."

But I could see the letdown in his eyes and hear it in the tone of his voice.

I did get a perfect 100 in the second semester Physics exam. At least the feared C was avoided. But, in the following months, once or twice, he said, "You got 100, you could have taken the final exam for the year-long material if you had not been afraid." And I knew I probably could have. But I would have been a sixteen-year-old with no other life but optics and electricity. For once, perhaps for the first time ever, I did not think that pleasing him was more important than anything else.

Did I understand his lofty expectations and lavish praise when I fulfilled them or the thinly disguised sadness and disappointment when I didn't, had to do with his missed chances to live as he had dreamed? In his eyes, life showered me with possibilities. He wanted to share in my luck and be proud of me in ways he could not be proud of himself. I can see now that my apparent perfection and success compensated for his evident failure. Most parents hope their children will live the dreams that escaped the parents. But not all parents lean equally heavily on their children to live their unlived lives for them.

Perhaps my father needed me to live his dreams for him more than other parents because he felt more of a failure. Life's possibilities had been wide open to him in his youth. Batista had shattered those. And Batista was in power again. Any chance of rebuilding his life was now more unreachable than ever. But I had my life ahead of me, and so far, it seemed as if I could accomplish anything I aimed to do. No wonder he placed so much hope on my anticipated success in life.

Looking back, I know I had a persistent vague sense that all was not right with my father's expectations and praise of me, but nothing more. I was not consciously aware that they were having a subtly burdensome impact. My father was my idol, and he thought I was great. What was not to like about that? It was easy to dislike my mother for her constant nagging. It was easy to forgive my sweet father for his endearing vulnerability.

Despite the contradictions, I cannot imagine my life without the strength I derived from my father's encouragement. Though mixed with his neediness, his love and caring were undeniable; he showered me with respect and appreciation. I know that he believed in me. His belief in my competence and his respect for my intellect helped me take for granted that I had the right to be whatever I wanted to be and that marriage and children did not need to be my only goal in life as they were for most girls in 1950s Cuba.

Being taken seriously at such an early age by my father and Tío was the all-important initial push toward who I have become personally and professionally. And I have wondered if their encouraging reaction and affirmation of my interests was influenced by the strong women's movement in Cuba when they were students at the University of Havana.

The feminist movement of the late 1920s and early 1930s in Cuba had significantly influenced public discourse. Women's activism had resulted in changed divorce laws, fostered discussion on lesbianism and the legitimacy of children born out of wedlock, and it advanced several women's political careers. It also influenced wide participation of middle class women in the professions. The movement had inspired my aunt Mamie, my father's oldest sister. She became a pharmacist in the 1920s and worked doing lab research all her life.

Nuns and Books

While I was in high school, girls around me, including Nery, were preoccupied with boys. I did have a couple of boyfriends in my teens besides Francisco, and had some more kissing experiences with a few of them, but mostly I found boys boring. They were interested in talking about sports I did not care about or boasting about something, trying to impress each other or the girls. Sometimes they did not say much but silently tried to put their hands where they did not belong—on my breasts or between my legs. At one excruciating party, I was paired with a boy who did not say a word and did not even try to touch me. It was as if I was not there. And, frankly, I wished I were not. Most definitely, books were more attractive to me than boys.

The idea of spending my life with one of those boys, as some of my classmates fantasized, was not appealing at all. I knew this was not what I wanted to do, although I had trouble conceptualizing alternatives. It took me several decades to become aware of other reasons I may have felt boys were boring and found women and girls interesting. But at that time, I knew for sure that the possibility of spending my life learning new things and teaching them to others, surrounded by intelligent women, was a lot more attractive than taking care of babies.

At school, the nuns and lay teachers, all of them women, taught math, physics, chemistry, biology, zoology, literature, languages, history, geography, philosophy and other subjects. Talking to my teachers was engaging. And the girls who were my classmates were more appealing when they were talking about school subjects than when they got silly about boys. Most of those girls became professional women: architects, engineers, pharmacists, lawyers, dentists or physicians. They took for granted that they would have careers, but their favorite topic of conversation was boys.

I had been a devout girl since childhood. Amusing as it may sound now, I had told my aunts in Santiago many times that I wanted to be a nun or an actress. Reciting poetry in public had taken care of the actress part. But I still really wanted to be a saint. Being a nun seemed the easiest avenue to reaching sainthood, given that martyrdom or conquering castles and crowning kings as Joan of Arc had was no longer an option.

I sensed that my attraction to convent life was similar to what it had been for some of the saints I had wanted to emulate since I was a child. For centuries, convents had represented for women a space for intentional or unacknowledged resistance to the institution of marriage and its limiting effects on women's intellectual pursuits. I knew the convent could offer me what marriage could not, even though I may not have been fully conscious of such thoughts and could not articulate my desires that clearly. I wanted to follow the path of some of my favorite saints, particularly Teresa of Avila, who admitted she had entered a convent because she did not want to be a married woman, facing early death in childbirth as her mother had. What she really wanted was to pray, read, and write in the company of other women. Although the danger of dying in childbirth was minimal now, four centuries later, the dependence on a husband's will that Teresa had written about had not changed enough for my taste. And I did want to read, write, and pray in the company of like-minded women.

In our yearly, silent retreat, doing the Ignatian Spiritual Exercises, guided by Jesuit priests, I had reflected intently all through high school about what I wanted to do with my future. I had concluded several times in these retreats and in other moments of prayer that life as a nun was what I wanted and what God wanted for me. So, when I was sixteen, finishing my junior year of high school, I decided that on the fall of my senior year I would enter the convent of the nuns who had taught me since I was a child.

The Superior General of the nuns pins one of my medals at graduation

The congregation of the Apostolado del Sagrado Corazón de Jesús—the Apostleship of the Sacred Heart of Jesus that ran my school, had been founded by Jesuits in nineteenth century Cuba. As Jesuit priests usually do, these nuns focused intently on learning. The nuns were mostly serious and aloof, intent on teaching us to be good without being sentimental. They saw intellectual and spiritual endeavors as interconnected. They made us think seriously about what God wanted from us, and they encouraged reflection on the direction of our lives and ways in which our efforts could help create a better world. Although it was assumed that, as proper young women of the 1950s, we would become wives and mothers, it was never assumed that that meant ignoring our intellectual lives. Our teachers taught us cooking and other domestic skills, but they simultaneously prepared us for attending university and becoming professionals.

The Mistress of Novices—the nun who oversaw the education and formation of young nuns in this congregation—was then Madre Berta, my beloved first grade teacher. Studying again with my favorite childhood teacher felt also like an attractive prospect.

On a Sunday afternoon in early summer 1955 I visited Madre Berta in the Novitiate and told her I was firm in my intention to enter the convent in September. "Good," she responded, "We would be delighted to receive you. Now, you must tell your parents. They need to sign a written permission because you are a minor. The sooner you tell them the better, so they can use the summer months to adjust to the idea of your leaving home."

I knew this was not going to be easy. But I knew I had to do it. I don't remember exactly when or how I told my parents. However, I do remember the reactions that followed. My parents responded in character.

My mother was furious. "Those nuns are selfish and sneaky, like all priests and nuns are," she said over and over, her anticlerical, antireligious upbringing coming out in full force. "They want to recruit young women to go live the stultifying lives they live without considering what they are stealing from those young lives. They live miserable lives and want to impose on young girls the same frustrations they suffer. Misery loves company!"

How could I tell my mother that far from being boring or frustrating, I thought the nuns' lives and choices were more appealing than hers? My mother did not read much and did not comprehend my fascination with studying. She never understood that my many hours with books were the best times of my life. Religion was a nuisance to her. She accepted it in my father as she accepted everything else from him. But she was not about to accept that my whole life would be centered on something she perceived to be useless and even harmful.

Because she saw religion in a negative light and could not comprehend the value of books, the idea of my entering a convent seemed to her like an abandonment of the potential my life held. I suspect that she was also worried that the anticipated financial help I could provide upon finishing high school would not materialize if I went into a convent. I could not blame her for the expectation that I could help improve the family's financial situation. Our economic difficulties grew worse each year. Even though the nuns had given me a free education since first grade, my mother was not about to let them profit from it instead of benefiting the family.

"Come September you are going to a non-denominational school with lay teachers to finish your senior year," she said firmly. "Enough of this nonsense. You need to be away from nuns so they don't continue to *comerte el cerebro*—eat your brain."

My father's reaction was also a reflection of who he was, but not quite what I had anticipated. When I started talking his face had taken an expression of hesitation, of not wanting to hear what he knew I was about to say. Because he was so religious, I had assumed he would give me his blessing to go into a convent. I had supposed he would be saddened by the idea that his favorite daughter would be lost to him in the future, but I never anticipated a negative response from him. Nevertheless, my mother's reaction was so negative and his wavering will so dependent on hers that he didn't know what to do. So, he cried. Except for tears when his mother died, he had never cried in front of me.

My parents were very consistent at keeping their adult lives and problems away from the children. They never fought in front of us. In fact, I believed then that they never fought because I had never seen or heard them do so. In hindsight, I know they had to have had disagreements, and I am sure my mother had seen Papi cry multiple times.

Caught between my father's tears and my mother's fury, I was paralyzed. Embarrassed, I called Madre Berta the following week and told her I would not be entering the convent in September after all. "I am sorry," she said, "but God has His ways. Let's pray that His plan will be fulfilled in your life. I will pray for you."

Strangely, when I hung up the phone after my conversation with Madre Berta, I felt as if a weight had lifted from my shoulders. To my surprise, I felt relief that I did not have to become a nun after all. It was puzzling to feel so liberated by not getting what I had thought for years was what I wanted most. I didn't understand this quick transformation in my feelings. Why had I seen life as a nun as the only alternative to being trapped in an unwanted marriage? I knew I did not want my mother's life, but I knew other professional women who were not nuns, including some of my lay teachers. Was I just hoping to escape a life of dedication to a needy man like my father? Or to any man, for that matter? The convent had seemed like the only avenue to freedom from a fate I did not want. But apparently, somehow, I sensed that convent life was not what I wanted either. As doubtful as I was about marriage and motherhood, I was absolutely sure I did not want to be a devout *cucaracha de sacristía* or a *solterona* —an old maid, like my aunts, with little purpose in life. Becoming a nun had looked like the best alternative, but apparently, this was not what I really wanted.

I am glad that I did not enter a convent. I now agree with my mother that life had a lot to offer me beyond the convent walls. And besides, practically everyone I knew who entered a convent in the 1950s, left a decade later in the middle of the religious earthquake the Vatican Council of the 1960s created in the Catholic Church. I strongly suspect I would have done the same.

Delivering the Valedictorian graduation speech

Bread Winner

After my failed attempt at becoming a nun, I was disoriented. I knew I wanted to study at the University of Havana. But that was not going to be easy because I needed to work and earn money to help my family. I was not sure how to go about paying the fees to attend the University. I had already been told that whatever income I would earn after I finished high school would help support my family; there would be nothing left to pay college tuition.

One afternoon, shortly before my high school graduation, Tío and I were riding together on a bus, returning from a visit to a bookstore in downtown Havana. The sweltering humidity produced condensation on the crowded bus's windows. Fanning myself with the foldable Spanish *abanico* I always carried in my purse, I kept chatting with Tío as the bus rode toward El Vedado. At some point he said something like, "When you go to university…"

I responded flatly, "Oh, I am not going. Papi says we cannot afford it."

Tío snorted, "Well, we'll see about that."

His vexed expression signaled he would have a conversation with my father about this matter. The next thing I knew, I learned I could attend university after all. Tío would pay my tuition.

Not that this opportunity lasted long. In November 1956, barely a month after I had eagerly started, all public universities were closed by the Batista government. Fidel Castro and a few followers had disembarked in Oriente province. They had come from Mexico, where Castro had been in exile for the last three years, to start the rebellion that would eventually topple the Batista government. The government wanted to prevent subversive gatherings. Daily class meetings involving students and professors could facilitate support of Fidel's rebels or other plotting against the government.

Disappointed as I was that my lifelong dream of studying at the University of Havana was interrupted, I was, nevertheless, glad I had more free hours to earn money. I had begun tutoring children a few months before, in June, right after I had finished high school.

My father had closed his school while I was in my senior year. It had never been a profitable business, but the losses had accumulated, and it had become clear that the school was a total failure. He closed the school and sold the furniture, keeping only the glass fronted bookcases with his books. After negotiating with the owner of another school and referring all his students to this institution, he did not receive the fee the director had promised him for the referral.

He tried once again to work as a lawyer in a firm where a close friend was the main partner. His office was located at the Manzana de Gómez in Old Havana, across from Parque Central. Its location in the center of Habana Vieja, a block from the Capitolio, seemed like an encouraging place to start anew. The massive colonial style building of Manzana de Gómez had been built as a combination of office building and European-style shopping arcade in 1917. After decades of decay and deterioration the building was transformed into a luxurious hotel in 2017. The Manzana is currently being touted as the biggest and most expensive of all hotels in Cuba. But when my father rented his small office in the Manzana de Gómez, the building was already beginning to deteriorate.

The hope of a fresh start never materialized. After seven or eight months in 1956 and early 1957 without substantial clients, my father went back to teaching. He resigned himself to working as a teacher in schools owned by others. He taught fifth grade during morning and early afternoon in an elementary school for boys run by the Christian Brothers of La Salle and history to seniors in the late afternoon in a private non-denominational high school. In the early evening, after he was finished with his teaching jobs, he tutored children. And yet his ten- or twelve-hour work day did not produce enough income to keep us afloat.

At each step of the way Mami kept cheering him up. When he closed the school, she kept saying, "You'll see. It will be good to not have to worry about running a school." Months later, despite evidence to the contrary, she repeated, "I am sure you will be able to find law clients very soon." Finally, "Having a steady job doing what you do best without having to deal with the school overhead will be great." Papi looked at her, gave her one of his sweet smiles, and kept plodding along, hoping that, as she believed, this time it would be better.

It later became clear to me in adulthood, that she was not simply the grouchy mother I disliked but was essentially the reason my father could continue to stand up each day. She shored up his self-esteem. Despite all evidence to the contrary she continued to have confidence that good luck was around the corner and great achievements would be possible for him. She was lively and energetic where he was depressed and self-doubting. And this was not only because she loved my father, but because she never stopped believing that life offered great promises, was full of surprises, and one should never declare defeat without doing everything possible to conquer all odds. I knew that she never gave up. Her inexhaustible energy, her belief in the value of life, and her efforts to live it became even clearer after my father died several decades later. She was not always pleasant when I was growing up, but she certainly was always hopeful.

Mami discovered early that I was the goose that laid the golden eggs. In her exhaustion and frustration, after years of tight budgets and outright poverty, she set out to make me ease the family's financial situation as soon as I was able to. It was clear to her that, even at this young age, I knew how to earn a living. Had she had my marketable skills, she would have done the same. But she didn't, so she had to depend on my father and me. And considering his consistent "lack of luck" and my increasing productivity, she set out to extract as much from me as possible. For many years to follow, it was easy to disparage my mother and feel anger at her demands while revering my father. But my father was not innocent; she was his mouthpiece.

A year after I began tutoring children, I was earning as much money as my father. Had it not been for the money I contributed there would not have been enough to cover household expenses. Nery had a half-time job as receptionist in an architect's office; she gave my parents a portion of her salary, as I did. But, because I earned more money, my financial contribution was the largest.

Mami always said Papi had bad luck and I, on the contrary, had good luck. It took me some years and some therapy to realize that luck was not the issue. Eventually, I grasped the nature of my "luck" and my father's lack of it. The outcomes that my mother called "luck" had more to do with my resolve not to be a helpless or ineffective person. Something, I might add, I had learned from her.

For example, on the first day of each month, when I arrived for the tutoring session, I brought an invoice for the cost of the lessons to be given during that month. Usually, I received a check or payment in cash from the child's parents on the same day. If a few days went by and no money had crossed hands, I said something like, "Perhaps we should postpone Pepito's or Anita's lessons for a few weeks or wait until next month…" Almost immediately, a check or cash appeared, and the tutoring continued undisturbed. But my father, I discovered, would continue going to the house of his Pepito or Anita, even if money was not forthcoming, and he would continue teaching without saying a word about payment. Sometimes the parents of the children he tutored were a month to six weeks in arrears. Sometimes, they simply terminated the tutoring lessons without ever having paid him for the previous month or two. I may have learned to be effective about collecting my wages as a result of seeing my father get cheated. I was learning from his mistakes without even knowing it.

Each one of those lessons he did not charge for, out of shyness or embarrassment or the insecurity that bedeviled him, meant I had to tutor one more child and spend another hour of my day making money to support the family.

My family, late 1950s - my father and I standing

Despite any distress I may have felt, my life had a purpose; my dedication to my family's wellbeing made me feel proud and important. We could not survive on my father's income. My financial contribution was sorely needed. At seventeen I felt that I was a responsible adult. The internal "pull" to fulfill my father's expectations and compensate for his deficiencies was powerful. It was next to impossible to see the difference between my internalized sense of obligation to respond to needs and what could be reasonably expected of a teenage daughter. In the process, I was set up to be a surrogate parental figure, bread winner or protective figure. But elevating me to this role distanced me further from my siblings. Whatever they felt toward my parents, rubbed on me. It tainted my position as one of the children. It also distanced me further from my peers who did not have these obligations.

I obviously had less time for play. My heart felt the void even though my conscious mind did not register it.

And then, something happened that gave me a glimpse of the burden I was carrying.

One day, I bought a small record player for my scant collection of 78 and 45 rpm records, with the money I had saved during my first year of work after contributing to the household and paying for all my personal expenses, including my clothes and transportation. What I bought was one of those record players that looked like a square attaché case, carried by a plastic handle, and closed with a metal clasp. That evening, I brought the square green case home, carrying it by its beige handle. I was smiling, anticipating the pleasure of listening to my favorite songs on the half-dozen records I owned.

As I was coming into the apartment with my precious new possession, my father gave me a startled look.

"How much money did you pay for that?" he abruptly asked without any preamble.

"Not quite a hundred dollars," I answered, delighted with the bargain, looking forward to setting it down and using it. I was excited to have my own record player rather than having to borrow one every time we had a small party or to rely on the radio to hear my favorite music.

"How can you be so selfish?" he said, looking at me, tears welling in his eyes.

It was now my turn to be startled. *"Selfish?*

"There was not enough money to pay rent this month. I had to ask my friend Emilio to lend me the money. How could you go buy a useless object like that when there was no money to pay rent?"

I hesitated. *Perhaps I was selfish. How could I waste this money when I knew how hard he worked to make ends meet?"*

By now he had taken off his glasses and was weeping, his face in his hands.

Taken aback, I left him by the front door and retreated to my bedroom. I felt guilty witnessing his distress, but I knew in a confused way that this was too much to ask of me. I had already contributed a substantial amount to the household. As I did every month, I had given my parents more than half of my earnings. I had not been aware that he had borrowed money to pay the rent, but did that mean I needed to contribute even more?

After a sleepless night, the next day, I returned the record player to the store. But I put the money back in my savings account. If I could not keep the offensive record player, at least I would keep my money hidden out of sight. Shocked by my father's reaction, all I could manage was this small act of rebellion.

Despite my increased awareness of my father's limitations, I do not remember ever being seriously upset with him. My love and loyalty remained unflinching. It was not his fault; he just had bad luck, as my mother kept repeating.

Later, in therapy, I started to tease out the difference between his needs and my duties. But it takes only a string to prevent a bird from flying away. I knew in some unconscious way, that if I tried to live a separate life, my father would be wounded, incapacitated by my selfishness. My destructive desires for independence would produce tears, a heart attack, or some other damaging effect on my vulnerable father. Only a heartless daughter would want to build her own life at such cost to her loving and loved father. So, for years, I didn't.

A few months after I finished high school and started tutoring children, we moved from the house on calle C to another rented place in El Vedado. The old house was deteriorating rapidly, and the landlady refused to do any repairs. The new place was a flat in a three-story building on Twelfth Street—*calle Doce*, the street that started at the entrance to Colón Cemetery. Our apartment was about seven blocks north of the gates of the cemetery. At the other end, down a slow sloping hill, calle Doce ended at the waves of El Malecón. From our balcony, we could see a patch of blue ocean glinting in the sun.

The balcony of our flat on Calle 12 (1984)

The building where we lived on Calle 12 (2011)

Nery and I on the balcony, Calle 12

Twelfth Street was wider and less quiet than C Street. Buses went by the door of our new apartment on their way to the beach clubs in the Western suburbs of Havana. The accessibility of buses at the corner of where we lived made it easier to reach the homes of children I tutored.

The flat we now rented occupied a whole floor above the street level—*primer piso*, above the *planta baja*—of a building painted hunter green with black tile designs and trim on the edges of balconies. We had the same number of rooms as in calle C, but they were a bit larger. We had lost the narrow cement yard that separated our home from Belén's house. Instead, we had gained a hallway into which all bedrooms opened. This meant we did not have to walk through each other's rooms when it rained as we had to do in calle C. Windows stayed wide open day and night; the breeze coming from El Malecón gently moved the leaves and branches of the trees in the garden of the house next door. There was no building as high as ours on the side of the open windows. A little garden with roses, tended by the neighbors in the street level apartment, provided some color and greenery in front of the building.

Downstairs, at the entrance to our building, stood two wide square columns. On one of them, a bronze plaque with my father's name was now affixed. *Oscar Espín. Abogado*—Lawyer—announced the dark edged letters. My father never let go of the fact that he had a law degree, even though he practically never used it.

On my first morning back in Havana in 1984, I went to the house on calle C, where we had lived when we first moved to El Vedado. Despite the years that had gone by, I knew exactly which buses would take me where I wanted to go. Without hesitation, I boarded a crowded bus close to my hotel, at the familiar corner of 23ʳᵈ and L streets, where *los caballitos* had been and the Habana Libre stood now. For a short moment, I hesitated about which coins to deposit in the fare box and the driver prompted me impatiently, *"¡Vamos señora, que no tenemos todo el día!"*— "Come on, lady, we don't have the entire day!" Rather than being upset at his rudeness, I took it as a compliment. It meant I still belonged.

I arrived at the house in fifteen minutes after walking the few blocks from the bus stop. An official yellow note pasted on the door announced that this house was uninhabitable and it should be vacated immediately. The house was already old and dilapidated in the early 1950s when we rented it; I was not surprised to read the announcemnt. What was surprising was that a woman opened the door when she saw me standing on the porch reading the announcement.

"Good morning," she said, "Are you looking for someone?"

"Not really... I just... I lived in this house when I was an adolescent... I came back to Cuba last night after many years and wanted to see the house again."

"Oh," she said in a very friendly tone, "you are welcome to come in and look. It's in bad shape, as you can see."

I accepted her invitation and looked around quickly, trying not to disturb her or the children still sleeping in what had been my bedroom. An older woman sat on a rocking chair in what had been my brothers' bedroom. I did not want to be intrusive. Back in the living room, I told her, "In that corner, we had a Christmas tree one year and a Nativity scene below it. The tree was really a dry branch painted white, decorated with red balls. One day we woke up to a lot of commotion in the middle of the night and discovered that a stray cat had jumped in through that window," I pointed, enthralled by a flood of memories, not noticing that she was not following my story. "The cat was apparently terrified perhaps feeling trapped on the wobbly Nativity scene..."

Her facial expression told me that Christmas trees and Nativity scenes were as foreign to her as if what I was describing had happened in another planet and not in a corner of that living room. There had been no Christmas celebrations in Cuba for more than twenty years. She was young and could not picture what I was referring to. I stayed a few more minutes and thanked her for her kindness. And then, as I was leaving, I glanced at the house next door, where Nino and Chicha had lived. It was in much worse condition. The porch was shored up by big wooden beams; windows were barred with pieces of wood to cover the holes left by broken glass. Following my gaze, the woman said, "That one is really uninhabitable. Besides, they are all dead." I imagined the ghost of Nino smiling at me from the porch of his empty house as he had done so many times. I smiled back at my memories of Nino and my adolescent self.

It was still early on that Sunday morning, but I wanted to go to Colón Cemetery before the heat of the day. Another bus took me to the corner of Twelfth and Twenty-third streets. I walked the short distance to the massive gates of the Cemetery. It took me some time to find the family grave I had visited with my parents every Sunday when I was a child. The beauty of the monuments that surrounded me became more obvious after I had seen so many other plain graveyards in other countries, including the one where my father was now buried in Miami. I put flowers on the grave in Colón Cemetery where Abuela Boqui and Tío were buried, remembering those weekly visits from long ago. And then, I went back to my hotel to rest after my sleepless night and a morning of feverish walking.

Despite the previous experiences of odd familiarity with places in Havana, nothing had prepared me for what I encountered in the apartment on *calle 12* where we lived right before leaving Cuba. I went there on the evening of my second day in Havana. As I walked to the door of the building, something affixed to one of the columns at the entrance of the building grabbed my attention. It was too dark to see, but I knew what it was. I touched it and my fingers confirmed what I had realized in a fraction of a second: my father's nameplate was still affixed to that column. I returned the next day. And there, in the daylight, was my father's name etched on the familiar bronze plate. After twenty-three years, it had not been removed!

My father's name plate at the entrance of the building on Calle 12 (1984)

This time a young man opened the door. I told him more or less the same thing I said to the woman at the house on calle C, "I lived here before leaving Cuba. I am back for a visit and would like your permission to see the apartment for a few minutes, if you don't mind."

If the sight of my father's name on that bronze plaque had sent chills through my spine, the inside of that apartment provided me with an even stranger experience. The furniture was what we had left behind, the same furniture that had been part of my life. In fact, the man who opened the door had been taking a nap on my parents' bed, the bed on which I was conceived! Nothing had been moved in the quarter of a century since I had last been there. The experience was unsettling and disturbing.

The woman who had shared a cab with me from the Havana airport to the hotel had experienced a similar mix of emotions. She was the daughter of poet Carl Sandburg. When she heard this was my first visit to Cuba in more than two decades, she had told me that the house of her childhood, now a museum of her father's life, was both a familiar and strange place for her. At that moment, I had not fully understood her. Two days later, standing in the middle of the apartment that had been my home, I knew what she had meant.

IV

1958

...talk to our souls about a time long past

Even though six decades have passed, I still believe that 1958 was
one of the most significant years of my life, just as it was also an
important year in Cuban history: The last year before Fidel Castro's rise to power and the beginning of a Revolution that forever
changed the country. After 1958, the Cold War moved from Europe to
Cuba, ninety miles from U.S. shores. And Latin America became increasingly convulsed by guerrilla warfare. We have not lived in the
same world since 1958.

At the beginning of that year, I was immersed in my routine of tutoring children for eight to ten hours, five days a week. Day in and day
out, as 1958 unfolded, shrouded in political uncertainty, I continued
waiting for buses in the corners of Old Havana, El Vedado, and
Miramar, sweating under the bright sun that turned the humid air into
steam, or getting wet under umbrellas that did not offer effective pro-
tection from the sudden furious tropical showers. I used the long bus
rides to read. And when I got home in the evening, I read some more.

The public universities had remained closed since 1956. I missed
being in the classroom and among peers. To compensate for my forced
lack of a university education, I read books from Tío's glass-doored
wooden bookcases that covered the length of the main hallway of the
Almendares house. Discussing those books with him continued the informal educational process that had started when I was still in high
school. I read works of Cuban nineteenth century literature—*El Negro
Francisco*, a novel by Antonio Zambrana focused on the evils of slavery;
Cecilia Valdés, the masterpiece which novelist Cirilo Villaverde wrote
in the United States after forty years of exile from the Spanish colonial
government of Cuba; the poetry of Gertrudis Gómez de Avellaneda,
who also wrote a novel against slavery in addition to stage plays and
lyrical poetry. It was one of her poems that went incessantly through
my mind when I left Cuba in 1961.

Tío and I discussed all these works plus far-ranging topics of history. Notably, we did not pay much attention to the U.S. It was enough

to acknowledge that the Platt Amendment had been an imperialistic imposition, and Teddy Roosevelt had used his brief participation in Cuba's War of Independence as a steppingstone for his political ambitions. American intervention was now in the past; no need to give more time to humiliations when there were so many historical events and works of literature to focus on. The reading Tío encouraged as well as the reading I did on my own guaranteed that when the universities opened again, I would not have missed a beat in my education.

While reading and working, I continued to enjoy dancing at home parties and at the new hotels in El Vedado. Years later, after I left Cuba, I learned that two of the hotels where we went to dance, the Capri and the Riviera, had been built by the U.S. Mafia to house their casinos. The power of the Mafia and its casinos during the Batista years was frequently touted by Fidel Castro in his denunciation of bad U.S. influences and by those sectors of the American press favorable to the Revolution. But for us, dancing at those hotels was like dancing anywhere else. Cubans dance wherever there is music. And music was plentiful in Havana. Two hotels and their casinos were a minimal part of the total music and dance scene.

American tourists were the casinos' principal customers. Only a tiny number of rich Cubans gambled there. A relatively small number of Cubans earned their living working in casinos and hotels. Overall, the economic impact of gambling and tourism was greatly exaggerated both in the U.S. and by Fidel. Income from tourism amounted to about ten percent of the revenue provided by the sugar industry, which was the real motor of the Cuban economy. Most Cubans saw casinos, if they saw them at all, as just another expression of the oppressive corruption of Batista that would disappear as soon as he fell, which would probably happen sooner than later. The casino world was not a presence in our daily lives. Most Cubans were not aware of the existence of casinos, gambling, and the Mafia; but we were very aware of Batista's cruelty and corruption. The music and the dancing helped us forget his ominous presence for a few hours.

When we went to dance at the Capri or the Riviera, as when we went to the Habana Hilton or any of the nightclubs, we entered the vibrant music scene of the 1950s. Aside from traditional Cuban music, such as *danzón* and the emerging *cha-cha-chá*, we danced *boleros*. Bolero was one of the first Cuban musical expressions to gain international exposure. Its popularity increased in the 1940s and 1950s during the golden years of Mexican cinema because boleros were regularly played in those films. Boleros do not require big bands but rather lend themselves to small groups of musicians. The guitar playing and the romantic way of singing characteristic of boleros, focus on the ever-popular topic of love. Women divas were leading interpreters of boleros and sang them with the same dramatic passion of my poetry recitals.

Music was performed in nightclubs, hotel ballrooms, and theaters, where a film was frequently followed by a live musical show. Radio stations played a variety of Cuban rhythms, including compositions by internationally known Ernesto Lecuona. Recordings of boleros, Benny Moré, Pérez Prado, and la Sonora Matancera with Celia Cruz, its foremost interpreter, were constantly on the air.

The music I danced to in the 1950s is still alive today in every corner of Havana, in every small or large Cuban town, all over the world, and on YouTube and in CD collections.

My love of books and music notwithstanding, in early 1958, I was as uncertain about my future as anyone was about the future of Cuba. I kept hoping that the situation would change, and Batista would be gone once and for all. We were increasingly afraid to go to movie theaters or to go dancing because the rebels were planting bombs in public places and the police were making indiscriminate arrests. More and more we avoided being out at night.

I was bored with my tutoring routine. In typical adolescent fashion, I thought that a boyfriend would make everything better. I was absolutely sure that I had been truly in love several times. But I had not had a boyfriend for a while and I was not interested in any of my dance partners.

*In the early
months of 1958*

I needed something more and was not sure what.

In an effort to have more friendships and find other sources of enjoyment, I joined Congregación Rosa Mystica, an association of Catholic university women. Rosa Mystica—a name adopted from the litany in honor of the Virgin Mary—encouraged our theological knowledge and spiritual practice as we developed intellectually beyond high school and grew into adulthood. Nery also joined Rosa Mystica. By the time we joined, the group had been in existence for about ten years and had several hundred members who ranged from recent high school graduates in their late teens like Nery and me to women in their early thirties. Some were single, some married, but all were deeply involved in professional endeavors as well as in spiritual growth. Every day of the week women milled around the big house the organization rented a few blocks away from the University of Havana. Some members came almost daily either for a specific activity or just to relax and be with friends at the end of the day. Nery and I frequently rode the bus together to get there for services or meetings or just to pass the time.

The house rented by Rosa Mystica

The funds to pay for the house and run the organization were raised through membership dues and income from room and board for resident students. Belonging to the group required a daily discipline of Mass, prayer, and meditation. We attended Mass together every Sunday. Reading the Bible and other spiritual texts was also part of group members' daily lives. Religious convictions were taken as a given. However, this was nothing like the fundamentalism associated with the Christian right today. Far from being a call to subservience, I and other members of the group found it liberating to discuss Jesus's affirmative treatment of women in our study circles and to observe the encouraging examples of productive women's lives modeled around us.

At Rosa Mystica I found a spiritual home. My participation in the organization had a powerful impact on my life's path. These women helped me understand that my spiritual hunger could be satisfied without becoming a nun, as I had half-assumed and half-dreaded earlier. Initially, as always, I had trouble making new friends, but eventually, I developed friendships at Rosa Mystica that have lasted my whole life. Another transformative factor from 1958.

El Túnel

Like Machado before him and, like right-wing dictators anywhere in the world, Batista wanted to produce grand building projects to show how beneficial his power was for the country. In May 1958, he officially opened a tunnel under the waters of the narrow entrance to Havana Bay.

There were already two other tunnels in Havana under the Almendares River, but this one was unique because of its greater depth and length. It was meant as a feather in Batista's cap. The tunnel under Havana Bay was his crowning achievement in public works.

Fidel Castro and his rebels were in the mountains near Santiago and dead bodies were found with increasing frequency in the streets of Cuban cities; Batista needed something to distract the public and boost the prestige of his government. The novelty of the tunnel under Havana Bay turned some eyes away from the mounting violence and political unrest—at least temporarily.

My friends and I sang and danced to a popular *cha-cha-chá* about the tunnel. *"Vamos al túnel, mi vida. Vamos al túnel, mi amor."* — "Let's go to the tunnel, my love." The words suggested this tunnel was a dark and secret spot where couples could kiss unseen.

El túnel

Curious about the tunnel, about eight of us, boys and girls in our late teens, climbed into Guillermo's two-toned 1957 Chevrolet Bel Air, a gift from his father when he turned eighteen. Guillermo was a rich kid, always willing to give rides to his friends and acquaintances, partly wanting to be helpful, partly because it gave him an opportunity to boast about his car.

I sat squeezed on top of Rubén, a young man from Cienfuegos who was intent on being my boyfriend. Probably hoping to surprise me with a kiss as we drove through the tunnel, Rubén was lively, repeating his favorite joke. "Although nothing has ever been written about cowards—*de los cobardes no se ha escrito nada,* he declared, quoting a well-known saying—the only thing ever written about the brave is 'so and so died here.' So, I'd rather not be brave!" he finished with a big laugh. Instead of making me think he was funny, his apparent insensitivity to what was going on in Cuba disgusted me. Rumors abounded about people, particularly young men, being caught by police and killed. Perhaps he was trying to manage his own anxiety about the constant danger, but his words hit me wrong. I wanted a boyfriend. I felt lonely, but not so lonely that I would settle for Rubén. I said nothing and kept my attention on the adventure of riding in the tunnel for the first time.

Guillermo drove the packed Bel Air to the entrance to the tunnel, a descending spiral around the statue of Máximo Gómez, one of the generals of the Cuban War of Independence, at the edge of the Malecón. Once on the straightaway inside the tunnel, it took us less than a minute to reach its end in Habana del Este. Although the brightly illuminated stretch did not resemble the imaginary romantic darkness described in the song, we laughed, shouted our admiration and surprise, commented about this marvel of engineering, and took in the magnificent view of Havana across the bay from where we stood. And then, Guillermo turned his car around and we drove back to Old Havana. Again, the ride took us about one minute before we were circling Maximo Gómez's monument once more on our way to street level at the Malecón.

Havana Bay is a *bahía de bolsa*—a "bag bay" or "bottle bay." Like San Francisco, it has a narrow entrance that gives way to a vast expanse of water beyond it. The Golden Gate Bridge was San Francisco's solution to close the gap at the entrance to the Bay. But a bridge was not an alternative in Havana. The Old City with all its historical buildings and monuments could not be destroyed to create the needed structure at that end of a bridge.

The narrow entrance had made Havana Bay a protected environment for the fleets of the Spanish Empire centuries earlier. And the narrow entrance of Santiago Bay—another *bahía de bolsa*—had prevented the rapid exit and escape into the open Caribbean of Admiral Cervera's Spanish Navy Squadron in 1898, contributing to its defeat by the U.S. Navy. But as beautiful and useful as the geological formations of these bays are, Havana's was a problem. Until the tunnel was built, the municipalities on the other side of the Bay had been reachable only by small boats that braved the waves of the narrow entrance or by long bus or car rides over winding busy roads. The tunnel reduced the distance to almost nothing. A creative solution, the tunnel closed the gap at the mouth of Havana Bay without demolishing the Old City. Moreover, the modern project, designed by a French company, preserved intact the view of the Morro Castle from El Malecón, the view that is Havana's "signature."

But as delighted as the people of Havana were with the new tunnel, no one was fooled into thinking that nothing else was going on. Nervousness and apprehension pervaded everyday life. As the Batista regime grew more desperate, it became more murderous. The police picked up people in what seemed like random patterns, just to keep citizens in fear. Tortured bodies were found with growing frequency in ditches along country roads or in the streets of Havana, Santiago, and other cities. One young man with whom I had gone out had been found dead recently together with a few other of his friends. It was no secret that that they had been killed and dumped by Batista's *"esbirros,"* henchmen charged with pursuing suspected government opponents. Gory photographs of tortured bodies published in the weekly magazine *Bohemia*, increased the level of fear.

The rebels were also responsible for deaths. They placed bombs in theaters, hotels and government buildings and assassinated Batista's henchmen and official government functionaries or others they deemed their enemies. People of all ages were killed accidentally, caught in the crossfire of assassination attempts. Violence had become the political method of choice, used by both factions. We lived under constant fear of the unpredictable danger.

Underground activities against Batista's government intensified all over the island in 1958, particularly around Santiago, where the rebels were hiding in the nearby Sierra Maestra. Batista had done all he could to convince the Cuban people and the world that there was no organized rebellion going on, that there was no Fidel in those mountains. He allowed Herbert Matthews, a journalist who wrote for the *New York Times*, to come see for himself. But his public relations stunt backfired. Matthews published photos of Fidel in the Sierra Maestra and wrote about his interview with him, singing Castro's praises. He reported to everyone in the world who read the *New York Times* that Fidel Castro was a liberator and a patriot, not a Communist; that he intended to oust Batista to restore the Cuban Constitution, not to seek power. After Matthews' story ran, there was no denying that Castro and his followers were alive and fighting the regime. Matthews persuaded those who read his report that what was going on in Cuba was not a sporadic outburst of crazy exuberant students or insidious communist sympathizers, but a fight for freedom that deserved endorsement.

Inside Cuba the rebels were gaining territory with the support of many people, including powerful industrialists like the Bacardí family or professionals like the architects in the firm where Nery worked as part-time receptionist. The rebels signed off at the closing of their clandestine radio transmission every evening, stating they were firmly planted in *territorio libre de America*—the free territory of the Americas they were creating. Fidel's guerrillas were widening their operations from the Sierra Maestra, slowly advancing west toward Havana.

Knowing about the dangers of the repressive government and living under the tension of an open rebellion—or perhaps precisely because of that—did not prevent us from being excited about riding under the waters of Havana Bay. Most people felt that there had to be light at the end of this political tunnel as well. The government was losing its grip. People were scared, but also angry. Discontent was increasing at the same pace as fear. Something had to happen.

I was also hoping to find the light at the end of my own personal tunnel.

I could not anticipate what the rest of that year would bring.

TV Star
Gane Mil y Llegue Hasta Cuatro Mil

On four consecutive Mondays in June 1958, I wore big headphones and sat for an hour inside a sound-proof glass enclosure in front of TV cameras. Next to me was another glass cubicle occupied by someone also in headphones, usually a man many years older than I.

When the TV station called me the last Friday in May, I was sweaty and tired after hours of bus rides in the oppressive humidity of the Havana summer. The man from the station said that after reviewing my application, I had been selected to compete the following Monday evening in *"Gane Mil y Llegue Hasta Cuatro Mil"* ("Win $1000 and Get to $4000"). He explained what I knew: The program had been established to select participants for the "$64,000 Question" program on Cuban television. But with enough participants for the "Question" lined up, this segment of the program now stood alone.

"Are you willing to participate even though you won't get a chance to compete for $64,000," he asked.

"Yes," I said. "I do not mind being on a sideshow."

His call had taken me by surprise. The chance to win this money was a thrilling prospect, considering that I had never in my life seen $1000 in one place. In the 1950s, U.S. dollars circulated in Cuba at parity with Cuban pesos. A thousand dollars was a small fortune then; $4000 was an average year's salary in the U.S. at that time. In Cuba, it was outright wealth.

About a year earlier when the "$64,000 Question" had started, I had sent letters of application for the topics of History and Religion. In the intervening months, other people had been selected for both topics. All the selected participants had been middle-aged adults who obviously had more knowledge and experience than me.

I never knew how or why I had been selected this time. Perhaps they just drew out one of the letters of possible contestants on the topic of Religion, letting chance decide who would be the next contender. Or it may have been because my letter was convincing. Perhaps they selected me not knowing how young I was. Or, perhaps, precisely because of that. Whatever the reason, I was excited. I was glad that the questions would be on Religion. Several years earlier, while in high school, I had participated in a modest TV show answering religion questions. I won $32 with my answers but lost when the $64 question asked the language Jesus spoke. Since then, I have never forgotten that he spoke Aramaic. Perhaps this time I would have better luck.

During the two years since I had finished high school I had been earning a reasonable income. That Friday, I had spent the day crisscrossing the city, going to the homes of children I tutored, waiting in interminable lines for bus rides in the heat. If nothing else, appearing on TV would be more exciting than drilling some child on the multiplication tables or English vocabulary or the conjugation of a Spanish verb.

The "$64,000 Question" and the smaller "Win $1000 and Get to $4000" were part of the multitude of programs produced and hosted by Gaspar Pumarejo, who was quite a personality on Cuban television. His shows included Cuban versions of "The Price Is Right" and "Queen for a Day," as well as talent shows similar to "American Idol." Pumarejo discovered early the appeal and popularity of what is now called "reality TV," and he made it available live in black-and-white on Cuban prime time. The idea of winning $1000 or more in one of Pumarejo's shows was an exciting prospect.

Pumarejo also ran a membership lottery in which people participated from home. My aunt Marina had won a big item—a refrigerator she did not need—in one of these raffles. It wasn't difficult for Nery and me to convince her to exchange it for a console stereo system in fake teak that played 78 and 45 rpm records and long-playing 33 rpm albums. It looked elegant in our living room and became a focal point for our parties.

A year or so after the arrival of the stereo, the Revolution came, and Pumarejo's familiar face disappeared from TV, as did all programs remotely connected with the desire to possess anything material, considered evil remnants of imperialist capitalism. But in June 1958 we were not aware of what was coming in just a few months. Pumarejo's programs were watched all over Cuba every night.

I spent the weekend between the phone call on Friday and the scheduled program on Monday frantically reading anything I could think of about religion. I read the Gospels, a few things on Church history, and more. The topic was vague enough as to be endless. What religion? *What* about religion?

My father was excited. He was already making plans for how to use the money he had no doubt I would win. Once again, I would make him proud with my intellectual achievements and help him solve the family's financial problems. But I already knew that, if I won, I was going to Europe. First to Spain, a romantic place like no other, according to Abuela Fefita's stories, and then to other areas of Europe if I won more.

As I read and studied during the weekend, I worried about how my father could spoil my dream trip. By Monday afternoon, I could not contain myself. I made a decision. When he came home from the school where he taught, he started helping me study and quizzing me about different possible topics. We were sitting in the dining room poring over a pile of religion books.

He was asking me "How many epistles did St. Paul write?"

Rather than answer his question, I said, "I want to know right now if you are letting me go to Europe if I win. Because if you are not going to let me go, I am stopping right now and calling the station to tell them I am not participating in the program."

Papi's expression changed. He looked baffled and disconcerted as he considered the possibility that I would carry out my threat. He must have seen the resolution on my face and was taken aback by it. Even though I knew I was afraid at the thought that I was about to lose the chance of a lifetime, I was not entering this contest so that he could buy a needed appliance or furniture or pay his debts to Abuelo Cándido and the friends who had lent him money when he could not make ends meet. It had to be for me. He recovered his composure and said rather nonchalantly, "Just keep studying. We'll talk about that later." I took that as a yes.

That evening, right before the competition started, I was introduced to my opponent—a tall, lanky, prematurely balding man, wearing a dark suit and fashionable dark-rimmed glasses. "I work with your father. I teach religion to the high school boys," he said with a smirk as he shook my hand.

For a second I wondered if my father had known about this. But before I could fully form the question in my mind, he told me, "He knows I am here. Didn't he tell you?"

I didn't have time to fully digest this information as we were marched into our respective glass enclosures. I understood then why my father had opted not to accompany me to the TV station and why my mother had come instead.

We entered our soundproof glass cabins, were set up with headphones and a microphone. The studio audience numbered about 200 people. The huge TV cameras that would beam our images all over the country were lit up, pointing at us. I was wearing my best dress; it had tiny multicolored flowers printed on a white cotton background and was gathered at the waist. My wide, layered, crinoline petticoat of the 1950s—*la falda de paradera*—barely fit inside the tight enclosure where I sat. I had to squeeze it down with both hands to go through the narrow glass door and smooth it further as I sat on the bench where my feet barely touched the floor. My aunt Marina had put lipstick, blush, and eye shadow on my face and had combed my hair. She was skillful at making my hair look good; no doubt her work was now ruined by the headphones.

I could not see the studio audience, but I knew they were delighted to be there. Getting seats to a Pumarejo show took long-term planning. You had to request an invitation several months in advance and, if you succeeded in getting one, you had to stand in line outside the studio for quite a while on the specific night. My mother was out there in the audience, I did not know if she felt as anxious as I did. But I knew that my father and siblings, aunts, and Tío in Havana and my grandparents, aunts, and other relatives in Santiago at the other end of the island, were watching me. I was sure the relatives of my opponent were also expectant, as were TV fans throughout Cuba who didn't know either of us. For years, I had watched other contestants in Pumarejo's shows go through the same rituals. Now, I was the one inside the glass booth being watched.

The cabins' orientation made it impossible for contestants to look at anyone but Pumarejo, who was standing across from me on the other side of the glass door. I stared at his familiar figure, a daily guest in our home. He was wearing a brown suit, white shirt, and matching tie. Had he been told that brown looked good on black-and-white TV? Perhaps so, but it did not look good right there. The browns made him look more tacky than elegant. His hair was graying at the temples. His big dark-rimmed glasses shone under the bright lights. He was holding index cards in his right hand, which rested on his protruding abdomen, a perfect ledge.

Pumarejo smiled broadly at me. Under other circumstances it might have been exciting to have him so close, in full color, not mediated by a TV screen. But at that moment the music started, someone shouted an announcement; lights glared even brighter, and a green bulb lit up on top of the huge camera pointing at my face. I could barely hear applause from the other side of the glass. I was on!

Dramatically reading from his first card, Pumarejo directed a question at me. "What are the names of the four evangelists?"

I answered without even having to think: "Mathew, Mark, Luke, and John." A bell sounded; I had won ten points. The points showed on a device I could not see, but I knew was there, on top of the glass enclosure.

Pumarejo turned to the other contestant and asked him his ten-point question. He also answered his question correctly—an easy question about the bible. The bell rang; ten points for him, too.

Then, the twenty-point question. From the stack of cards, Pumarejo asked me, "Who composed the part of the Hail Mary that says: 'Blessed are you among women and blessed is the fruit of your womb'?"

"Elizabeth, the mother of John the Baptist," I answered. Correct again.

He asked my opponent something about one of Jesus's miracles. More bell ringing, more points above our heads on top of our respective cabins. A third question for each of us; thirty points more.

Only the fourth question—which I would learn was always the most difficult—remained. If both of us answered it correctly, there would not be a winner that night, and the two of us would return next Monday to compete again. I could feel my anxiety mounting, but a commercial break at this point gave me some relief. No one talked to us during the commercial break. Silence filled the four glass walls. We just looked straight ahead.

Pumarejo's makeup lady fluffed his face with powder. Then, abruptly, lights again, music again, Pumarejo again, beaming his smile at me. Question four was a three-part, complex question. "What is the name of the sacrament administered to dying people? What is the purpose of this sacrament? What secondary effect does this sacrament have?"

"Extreme Unction, The Last Rites, for the purpose of..." I answered the first two parts but hesitated too long on the third part about secondary effects of the sacrament, and my thirty seconds finished with a buzzer sound. Crushed, I realized I had not earned all the points for this question. I had won only twenty or thirty points out of the possible forty.

For the first time, I had fallen behind, and probably lost! Good-bye, dreams of traveling to Spain! I later learned that, at home, friends and relatives felt deflated by my misstep. Some turned their TVs off: why keep watching to see me defeated?

Pumarejo asked my opponent his final question. I was dismayed and disappointed. *If only I had been asked this easier question! I could have answered it without hesitation.*

But no sound was coming from the other cabin. Why hadn't he answered? The clock seemed to have gone on beyond the ritual thirty-second pause. The buzzer rang. My opponent had not answered. He had lost all points allotted to this question. Therefore, I was ahead by a few points. In disbelief, I realized, *I am the winner!*

The glass door opened, and as I stepped outside, I heard the full sound of the audience's thunderous applause. My opponent, who had stopped smirking, was being escorted out while I was ushered to center stage, facing the cheering audience. I could not understand how this cocky professor of religion could not answer such an easy question!

Pumarejo stepped in front of me, shaking my hand, handing me an envelope that contained a crisp, new, one-thousand-dollar bill, asking me what was I going to do with this money, inviting me to come again next Monday to compete against another contestant. In answer to his question about what I would do with my $1000, I proclaimed to the national TV audience, "I am going to Spain."

"But this isn't enough money to do that!" Pumarejo argued, still smiling at me. Rather than getting into an explanation of how I had learned in my short life to do lots of things with little money, I told him I wanted to go to Madrid to meet Manolo, a young man I had been corresponding with for about a year but had never met. In the weeks to come, Pumarejo made a big deal about this guy, who in reality had little to do with my motivation.

The ending credits and commercials rolled on TV screens. The audience, still applauding sporadically and commenting loudly about the program, started leaving the studio. My mother and I were escorted through a different back door, away from the crowd. We walked silently into the warm Havana night, stunned.

The tree branches on the wide Paseo del Prado, outside the TV studio doors, seemed to be applauding softly as they moved in the breeze. We had come by bus to Old Havana. But we went home via taxi; this was definitely a taxi night!

As we rode to the apartment where we now lived in El Vedado, the taxi veered from Paseo del Prado and moved along the Malecón, following Havana's coastline, with its beautiful view of the Morro Castle on the other side of the bay—the view of Havana everyone across the world could recognized. The ocean waves, high and white with foam, seemed to be jumping for joy, celebrating my triumph. I wondered what the driver would think if he knew there was a one-thousand-dollar bill riding in his cab. He had been driving around the city transporting passengers, not watching TV; he had no idea.

It was my father's suggestion to place the $1000 bill inside one of the books in the several glass-fronted bookshelves in the hallway. As I slipped the bill into a book, a thick collection of Spanish poetry, I discovered he had learned that morning in the teachers' lounge that my first opponent was to be one of his colleagues. Everyone at the school, from principal to students, had been strutting about all day because one of their own had been chosen to show his expertise in front of the whole country.

I can imagine Papi saying sheepishly to a few teachers in the lounge, "My daughter is the other competitor tonight." And I imagine those teachers would have expressed sympathy for him, anticipating the defeat of his young daughter, barely out of high school. I was thankful to him for trying to save me from fretting all afternoon about my opponent. But his silence did not save me from the feeling of intimidation that overcame me when I realized this man with whom I was about to compete had so much more knowledge and experience. I also understood that my father had yielded to my ultimatum that afternoon because he could not risk losing face in front of his colleagues. I am sure he was secretly hoping and praying that my triumph would raise his status among them. As always, my role was to give him reasons to be proud—reasons he could not find in himself.

The next morning, he took me to the bank to deposit the $1000 bill. Before we left home, he ruefully said, "We are also going to the Ministry to apply for your passport. Get ready for the photograph."

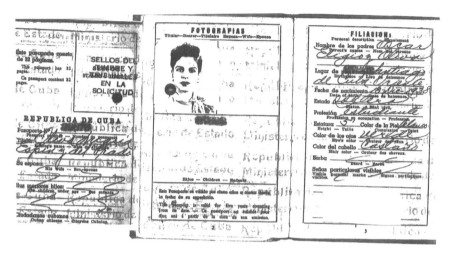

My first passport

I looked away, careful not to let him see my smile. I had won something more than a thousand dollars.

That is what I remember of the morning after the competition. Nery, however, remembers a different scene. According to her, that Tuesday morning I stood in the hallway, brandishing the $1000 bill in front of me shouting to my father, "If I am not going to Spain, I am tearing this bill into little pieces right now!" while my mother whispered, "Lower your voices; the neighbors are hearing you!"

Whatever the real events of that morning, by that afternoon, I had submitted my application for a passport to the Ministry.

The following three Mondays became progressively easier. The questions and answers blur in my memory. There was something about the first Vatican Council and its declaration of Papal infallibility in 1870, something about the Lateran Treaty that created Vatican City as an independent state in 1929, the name of the process of saint-making in the Catholic Church. The degree of difficulty of the questions varied but as the competition progressed, I knew every answer to every question I was asked. I knew the answers to the other contestants' questions, too. Unfortunately for them, they did not. One by one, the other three contestants in their 30s, 40s, and 50s failed, even though each was older, and better educated than I—and clearly convinced at the beginning of the program that they could easily beat this nineteen-year-old girl.

While still tutoring children, I spent those weeks studying hard, preparing for the Monday nights and for my trip to Europe. My itinerary kept expanding as I kept winning more crisp $1000 bills. On the first Monday, I knew my dream of visiting Spain, the country of my ancestors, would become a reality. The second Monday I added Italy to my itinerary, and on the last two Mondays also Paris, the French Riviera, and the Brussels International Exhibition.

On Monday June twenty-third, my last day of competition, my father came home from work ready to quiz me as he did every day. His questions strengthened my confidence. So far, I had been able to answer all of them, and, almost unaware of what was happening, had become knowledgeable on topics I had known little about just a month before: The Bible, Church history, the essential tenets of many religions. All questions so far had been about Christianity, particularly Roman Catholicism. This was not surprising, considering it was the official religious affiliation of the vast majority of Cubans. But, just in case, I had studied other faiths. I felt like a walking mini-encyclopedia of religion. Inside the now familiar glass cabin, I answered each question correctly, each time amazed I knew all those answers.

But that afternoon, I could not fully answer my father's question. "What Catholic dogmas center on Mary?" he asked. "And what are they about?"

I knew some of these, so I answered, "The Immaculate Conception. In 1854, Pope Pius IX declared that Mary had been conceived and born without original sin. The Assumption. Pius XII declared in 1950 that Mary had ascended to heaven in body and soul, like Jesus. But I cannot think of others." I asked, "Do you know?"

"No, I don't," he said, "but I know there are others, older ones. Let's find out." He dove into books, as he had done daily to help me. But this time, there was nothing on this topic in the books either of us was perusing. I called every knowledgeable friend and every nun and priest I could think of. It was about 5:00 p.m., and I was due in the studio by seven o'clock. Hardly anyone I called seemed to be home, and the few people who answered their phone knew nothing about these dogmas. Finally, I got through to a Jesuit priest who was a friend of a friend.

"Yes," he said, "those two recent dogmas about Mary, plus two ancient ones. One is the Virgin Birth of Jesus, meaning that Mary was always a virgin even though she was a mother; a different issue from her Immaculate Conception, which refers to her own conception and birth, not to the birth of Jesus. Mary's virginity has been a tradition since the times of early Christianity. Even some of the apocryphal Gospels that never made it into the Bible are explicit about this; they take it as a given." He told me that the other dogma from antiquity was defined in 431 by the Council of Ephesus that condemned the teachings of a heretic named Nestorius who taught that Jesus was two different persons, one human and one divine. The Council declared that Jesus was one person even though he had two different natures and, therefore, that Mary could be considered the Mother of God. *Theotokos*, in Greek. The Council of Chalcedon, twenty years later in 451, had ratified this dogma. I had another bit of information to tuck away in my brain.

I wrote it all down, thanked him for his help, and went to take a quick shower and grab a bite of food. Black beans with white rice and *tostones*, fried green plantains. I was running late already, but the Cuban June was too hot and humid for me to dress in clean clothes without showering. Also, I did not want to be preoccupied by a hungry stomach in the middle of the last competition. I put on a baby blue sleeveless blouse with thin vertical ridges of white lace and a black skirt, trying to look my best for the final event. This time, both my parents came with me. We took a taxi into Old Havana, rather than wait for a slow bus.

If I won again that evening, I would reach the $4000 maximum. If neither my competitor nor I won that night, we would come back the following week for a final match. But, even if I lost, I now had enough money to enjoy my trip to Europe.

More relaxed than I had been in earlier programs, I followed the routine of the previous three Mondays. My opponent and I were even after the first three questions. In his last question, the other contestant, an older professor in his fifties, gave the wrong answer and received no points. It was up to me. If I answered my last question correctly, I'd win my fourth $1000 bill and the whole competition. As in all the previous Mondays, it was hard to tell what would happen at the last minute. And then, of all possible topics, I could hardly believe what I was being asked. In his clear voice, reading from the last index card in his right hand that was, as usual, resting on his abdomen, Pumarejo asked, "What Council defined that Jesus was one person rather than two? Who was the man who had preached the heresy of Jesus's dual personhood? What other dogma was defined at that council?"

He was about to punch the clock that would tick for thirty seconds, giving me time to compose my answer. I smiled at him and said calmly, "I don't need the time."

His left hand stopped in mid-air. He looked at me with a worried expression. I could see he was thinking I was foolish to forego this precious time. "Are you sure?" he said. I nodded, smiled again and without hesitation said, "The Council of Ephesus, in 431. Against Nestorius' heresy. The other dogma defined was that Mary is the Mother of God, not just the mother of Jesus." Pumarejo had an expression of astonishment, followed by a big smile. "That is correct!" he exclaimed. As the door of the cabin opened for the last time, I could hardly hear the sound of applause, though it was stronger than ever before. In my mind, I was thanking my father for asking me about dogmas related to Mary that afternoon.

Party before leaving for Europe, after the TV competition. I am in black, Nery standing at my right

During the month of the competition, I was a minor celebrity in Cuba. People who recognized me from the TV show hugged me in shops, on buses, and on the streets of Havana. They wished me good luck in the next Monday program or in my trip to Europe. Sales clerks, bus drivers, bank tellers, waitresses, made a point of being helpful while wishing me well. The week after the final program, the embraces and cheers multiplied. Wherever I went, people congratulated me and wished me the best.

On one occasion, one elderly woman hugged and kissed me with great excitement as I was stepping down from a bus in Old Havana, a few days after the last program. "Enjoy that trip! You really deserve it!" she cried effusively. My father, who was accompanying me on one of my last-minute errands to prepare for the trip, asked me, "Who is this person?"

"I have no idea," I answered. Then I realized that while my mother, Nery, and Marina had become familiar with this frequent reaction from strangers, it was the first time he had witnessed my temporary fans' behavior.

Wherever I went in Havana during that month, people acted as if they were all proud of this nineteen-year-old girl who had won a competition against four adults. No matter how many times it had happened, although I was happy and pleased with the attention, I also felt embarrassed at this show of recognition and celebration from unknown people. I was as surprised about my success as everyone else. I did not know how to react. So, I just smiled and thanked them, flustered with all that attention at the most unexpected times.

I suppose people identified with a young woman who had proven herself against all her seemingly stronger opponents. My skinny body must have looked bizarre sitting inside that cabin. I have never been taller than five feet. I weighed less than 100 pounds: my mother used to call me *lagartijita*, little lizard. With big, anxious eyes, and those huge headphones around my short dark curls I must have looked strangely frail and tiny, especially compared to each of the other contestants. In the midst of the ironclad repression of the Batista government, terrified citizens all over the island who listened to daily whispered reports of mysterious executions and bodies found by the road, were delighted to see a scrawny girl demonstrate the power of the weak. At the beginning of that hot summer, when fear and death were on everyone's mind, I think my success became a symbol of the near-impossible: the powerful could yet be defeated.

No one could guess what was coming. None of us would have believed then that the champion of the oppressed would come down from the hills in less than six months and turn himself in a few short years into a more powerful and effective oppressor than anyone we had known before. But Cuban politics were not in my mind during those weeks in June.

The summer of 1958 changed me in ways that I realized only vaguely then. Those four Mondays in June marked the end of my childhood and adolescence and the beginnings of my declaration of independence. My internal universe would never be the same after I won that contest and spent three months in Europe. My success in the TV competition taught me that I could trust my mind, that I could make money from my thoughts, and that I could fulfill my dreams through my own efforts. For four weeks, I had challenged my opponents. I had also successfully challenged my father, though the full force of that lesson came to me only later.

A Whisper of Freedom

The competition over, Europe was waiting for me. Still glowing in the glory of my success, on June twenty-seventh I boarded a clunky Cubana de Aviación propeller plane for the twenty-hour flight from Havana to Madrid. I had no inkling then that in exactly three years I would be boarding the same flight to leave Cuba for good.

I walked on the tarmac, up the metal stairs to the plane, and sat in an aisle seat for what seemed an interminable number of hours in an uncomfortable outfit that I had bought for the flight. Everyone dressed up for airplane travel, particularly international flights. My new outfit was a two-piece, short-sleeved black linen suit with white trim around the collarless neck and the front of the straight, hip-length jacket. The skirt was also straight, below the knee down to my mid-calf. And, of course, I wore stockings with a garter belt and high heels. A bowl-shaped white straw hat trimmed with a black ribbon around its circumference and a thin black veil in front of my eyes completed the ensemble. I looked like a middle-aged matron.

Because flights across the Atlantic took so long, planes had to stop twice for fuel before landing in Madrid—once in Bermuda and once in the Azores. These were short stops. We waited in our seats while the plane was refueled. What did I do during the long hours of the flight? I must have slept some because the plane left Havana in the early evening. It was night over the Atlantic when we took off and night again by the time we landed in Europe. We arrived in Madrid past midnight their time. I know I took off my hat during the flight but not my heels; I had dollar bills on the soles of my feet inside my stockings. In addition to travelers' checks, I carried dollars in various hidden places of my clothes to keep them safe.

Just before landing I combed my hair, refreshed my make-up, and put on my hat.

Little did I know then that I was stepping into a new world of possibilities. That I, a nineteen-year-old Cuban girl in the 1950s got to Europe alone that summer still amazes me, but Papi had been so surprised by my determination to go and so proud of my success that he could not bring himself to say no.

Manolo, my Spanish pen pal who had so intrigued Pumarejo, was waiting for me at the airport with other people. While I hugged and kissed the ten or so young Cubans who had come to welcome me, he kept repeating, "¡Qué maja! ¡Qué maja!" the equivalent of something like "How beautiful and charming!" Clara Elena, my father's goddaughter, had gone to the same school as me in Havana and she was now studying medicine in Spain. She was at the airport with the fiancé she was to marry in a few days. Other young people studying in Spain while Cuban universities were closed were also at the airport, a fairly large reception party.

Only Manolo, Clara Elena, and her fiancé got in the taxi with me for the ride into the city. Manolo kept repeating "¡Qué maja! ¡Qué maja!" while Clara Elena inquired about her parents' feelings because they would not be able to attend her wedding. Half dozing because of sheer tiredness, I tried to answer questions and comments. And then, I sat up with a start at the sight of La Cibeles, the illuminated fountain that is to Madrid what the Eiffel tower is to Paris. I still think that this stone depiction of Cybele, the Phrygian goddess of fertility, is one of the most beautiful fountains in Europe. The imposing Cibeles, in her carriage pulled by lions with spouting jets of water all around was my first taste of Madrid's beauty.

After circling La Cibeles, the taxi entered La Gran Vía, Madrid's main thoroughfare—Avenida José Antonio, as it was called during the decades Franco was in power. Sidewalks were bursting with people sitting in cafés talking, drinking, and smoking even though it was the middle of the night. The *pensión* where I had a reservation was on La Gran Vía. I had a small room in Pensión Buenos Aires on José Antonio 61. I fell asleep immediately.

The next morning, I woke early to spend my first day in Europe walking up and down La Gran Vía and enjoying the sights of Madrid.

I bought postcards to send to my parents and others, I ate *"arroz cubano"*—a Spanish invention of "Cuban" white rice, fried eggs, and fried bananas at Cafetería California on La Gran Vía.

It was not until that night that I suddenly felt homesick and scared. My long dreamt about adventure in Europe did not seem so attractive on that night in Madrid, alone in my room at the pensión. Why had I so wanted to visit Europe? I had gone ahead with my plans for this trip even though neither Nery nor my mother—both of whom I had invited—had wanted to come with me. Nery did not want to come because she did not want to leave her boyfriend behind. Mami didn't come because my father did not want to let go of her presence and company. A few years later, when my mother and I were living in Madrid after leaving Cuba, I realized that it was practically impossible for my parents to be away from each other. When Mami and Nery turned down my invitation to accompany me, it was crystal clear that I wanted so badly to go to Europe I was willing to do it alone.

Why had Europe become the symbol of all I wanted in the world? Spain, of course, was my first priority. I had grown up with Abuela Fefita's stories and my mother's and my aunts' memories of the wonderful time they had in Spain three decades earlier. Spain, no doubt, was a dreamland. Plus, of course, I was curious about Manolo, even though I was not terribly interested in him.

My initial homesickness faded in just a few days. A small incident made me recognize for the first time the daily subliminal terror of life in Cuba. While watching "La Violetera," a new film starring actress Sarita Montiel in a theater in Madrid, I was suddenly overcome by the realization that I could enjoy the movie without worrying about the possibility that a bomb might go off, that the police might raid the theater, or that something similarly dangerous might occur. In Cuba, I was never near a bomb, nor was I ever arrested. But bombs had killed and maimed young people. Some people I knew had been executed or imprisoned, and I knew it could happen to me, too. I had learned to always be hypervigilant without even knowing it.

In Madrid, riding on the back of Manolo's Vespa, I went to El Escorial, to a bullfight, to a *zarzuela* in La Corrala—a street theater in old Madrid—to El Retiro Park, and plush Barrio Salamanca, and went past La Cibeles many times. In the late 1950s in Spain as in Cuba, women did not wear pants except for some excursion to the country, so I learned to ride in a very ladylike fashion sitting sideways on Manolo's Vespa, holding onto him. I wore a black skirt with its obligatory wide crinolines underneath and long-sleeved cotton blouses in blue, white or beige, bought specially for the trip, and black ballerina flat shoes.

Those first two weeks riding with Manolo around Madrid were more than enough of his company. His repetitive comments about *fútbol* became tedious, his scarce remarks about the interesting sights we were seeing were mostly dull…and his head and shoulders were covered with dandruff! Did he ever wash his hair? Or use deodorant? It was unpleasant to ride so close to his body when he did not smell very nice and some of his airborne dandruff was landing on my face. I did not see him again when I came back to Madrid after my traveling in other European countries during the next few months.

In those months, I crisscrossed Spain and lived my European adventure to the fullest. I relished every detail, every encounter, every moment. My memories of those months still feel as if they were my unique, personal travel brochure—a catalogue of the best sites in Europe, mixed with the specific details of adventures lived in those places.

I went to Asturias in Northern Spain to visit Abuelo Cándido's nieces and nephews. My relatives were thrilled to see me. They fed me constantly: strong Asturian *queso Cabrales, chorizo, morcilla,* roasted chicken—*pitín* as Asturians call it. They asked me questions about the family and about former neighbors who had moved to Cuba, people whom, undoubtedly, I must know. Having lived in their tiny village all their lives, they could not imagine the size of Havana and the impossibility of knowing everyone there.

I went to Andalucía to admire Moorish architecture in Granada, Córdoba, and Seville and to drink sweet *jerez* wine. The Alhambra was beautiful beyond my expectations, and even beyond the Washington Irving's stories I had read. Seville was as romantic as it appeared in the Spanish films I had watched since I was a child. From the tip of Gibraltar, I glimpsed the tantalizingly close outline of North Africa on the horizon. I was sure I would never see Morocco. In the summer of 1958, when this trip felt so extraordinary and beyond my expectations, I could not imagine any other international travel ever.

I joined a tour bus to Italy driving over the Pyrenees and along the French Riviera. I knew I wanted to visit Italy. The Pope was in Rome. Plus, I had just seen "Three Coins in the Fountain." After seeing the film's portrayal of the magical powers of the Fontana di Trevi, I had to go there and throw my coins in so I could return to Rome. It obviously worked! I have been back to Rome many times, although I could not have imagined it then.

The first day on the bus I met Tory, an impetuous *madrileña* already in her fifties who was intrigued by my travelling alone and by the story of how the trip came about. We sat next to each other on the bus the first day of the three-week tour and talked incessantly from the time we left Madrid in the morning until we arrived in the Basque beach town of San Sebastián that evening. Despite the difference in our ages we hit it off. I loved her energy and enthusiasm and spontaneity. I had no idea how important Tory was to become for me. It was Tory who housed us in Madrid when my mother and I left Cuba three years later.

I also spent time during the tour weeks with José Luis and Chelín, who were on their honeymoon, and with Merche and Mariano, siblings who were about my age. I had a crush on Mariano, fed by gondola rides in Venice and the romantic atmosphere of the French Riviera. He was cute, tall and thin, with very dark shiny hair and a sensuous mouth. I was young enough to fall for a cute boy. Mariano teased me gently every time he had a chance. Once, on a sidewalk outside a café in Nice, when I was uneasy about a dog sniffing me, Mariano said feigning seriousness betrayed by his smiling eyes, "Don't worry, he would bite you in French, so you would not understand!"

One evening on the French Riviera, the five of us, all dressed up for the occasion, went to Monte Carlo, excited about visiting the famous Casino. Merche and I wore elegant little black dresses. Mariano wore a dark blue suit and silk tie. But the guards were not impressed. José Luis and Chelín were allowed in but Mariano, Merche, and I were turned away after the guards took a quick look at our passports; neither of us was twenty-one yet. One of the guards almost threw my passport back at me saying disdainfully, *"Bah, dix-neuf!"* — "Augh! Only nineteen!" Thwarted in our desire to visit the famed Casino, Mariano, Merche and I made the best of our time in Monaco by going down the hill and walking by the water singing together some hit songs from the San Remo music festival, which were all the rage.

We also went to Capri together. I had just read Axel Munthe's "The Story of St. Michele." I could not miss Capri. There, we entered the Blue Grotto in a small boat, through a tiny hole that was almost underwater, propelled by the physical strength of the boatman. Inside, a concave "cathedral" of intense cobalt blue stone dazzled me. No painting or photograph could reproduce the stunning beauty and color of that space.

After the three weeks in Italy and the French Riviera, I switched to another tour before re-entering Spain. I had decided to wait in Lourdes for the arrival of my second tour. That year was the centennial of the apparitions of the Virgin Mary in Lourdes. The celebrations were not to be missed. I hoped to join the crowds who were looking for miraculous cures or finding ways to celebrate the centennial while praying devoutly to the Virgin Mary.

Unbeknownst to me, I was arriving when hordes were coming to Lourdes, guided by conservative Assumptionist priests who had made Lourdes their bailiwick since the late nineteenth century. Four or five people were packed in each hotel room to accommodate the crowds.

I had a voucher that showed I had reserved and paid for a single room at the Hotel Sainte Catherine. But it was obviously impractical for the hotel to give me a single room, when they could make four times the amount from people coming in groups. Besides, here was a young woman who did not speak French and could be easily turned away without further consequences by simply denying any knowledge of the voucher.

The guy at the hotel desk said very gently in Spanish that this voucher I was holding was not valid, "Most sorry, but we do not have a room for you."

"Well, then," I said, "help me find a room in another hotel."

"Oh, you do not understand, mademoiselle, every hotel room in Lourdes is taken for this national pilgrimage. Every year, the largest pilgrimage is on this week in August, but this year it is much more so because of the centennial. I am sorry, mademoiselle, there is nothing I can do."

Panicked, but also outraged, I said the first thing that came to mind.

"Ok, then, I will sleep in that chair right here in the lobby next to my suitcase until the tour group I am expecting picks me up in three days."

"Oh, no, you cannot do that, mademoiselle! The police will fine us for having guests sleeping in the lobby! I am terribly sorry but you will have to leave."

"I am not leaving!" I retorted, my sense of panic increasing. "I have a paid reservation and this voucher to prove it!"

As he was about to say no again, I had a flash thought. "Perhaps you can call the police and have them help you find me a place to stay," I blurted.

A look of astonishment in his face, the clerk got on the phone and started conferring in French with someone while I stood there in front of the desk. When he hung up, he said, "I can offer you a room in the servants' quarters in the basement for those three nights."

"Fine," I said, relieved that I did not have to sleep on the street. "I need to take a shower before I settle in the basement and go out for dinner."

"A shower! Mademoiselle, even the bathrooms have beds in them, we are so short of space!"

"I won't mind taking a shower in a bathroom that has a bed in it." I said firmly, "It is the least you can do, since you are not honoring my reservation for a room with a shower."

He shook his head and with an air of resignation handed me a key for a very tiny room in the basement and another key for a large bathroom on the second floor that in fact had two single beds in it against each of the walls at the corner farthest from the bathtub.

Perhaps because of this incident and also because of the distressing spectacle of so many sick people in the streets all over the town, I did not feel at ease in Lourdes. Having heard lovely pious stories about the sacredness and specialness of Lourdes while I was growing up, I was terribly disappointed with the reality I found. Supposedly miracles happened there every day; non-believers converted at the sight of newly healed bodies that had been previously ravaged with illness. But the place did not inspire devotion in me.

All over town, small stores sold gaudy statues, rosaries, candles, holy cards, snow globes with the Virgin or the sanctuary inside them, and other religious trinkets. Plastic bottles to collect miraculous Lourdes water were popular—some in the shape of the Virgin Mary with a blue crown that could be unscrewed to pour water in through her head. In the streets of Lourdes, in the sanctuary, and near the grotto of the apparitions, people pushed and shoved each other. I got pushed into one of the slippery fountains supposedly full of holy water when I was trying to fill one of the plastic Virgin Mary bottles and almost lost the blue crown that screwed over her head.

Near the Sanctuary, the sick cried and screamed, jerking and contorting convulsively in despair and disappointment when an immersion in the pool or a blessing with the Eucharistic host did not produce the miraculous cure they had hoped for. I could not blame them; this visit to Lourdes was probably their last hope. But the spectacle was ugly, and it did not contribute to any remote sense of prayerfulness for me. When my three days in Lourdes were up, I was very glad to be out of there.

Off to Paris I went with a new group of people. Paradoxically, I was not terribly interested in Paris. A friend of my father's, who had recommended the pension I was staying in in Madrid, had said emphatically that Paris was not to be missed. So, without much enthusiasm, I agreed to include Paris in my itinerary.

When I arrived in Paris, a letter from Nery was waiting for me at the hotel. She was telling me that my aunt Marina, who was hospitalized with diverticulitis, would probably be dead by the time I returned. The doctors thought she could not survive much longer. The thought of Marina dying while I was away, was heartrending. Marina did not die until decades later, after I had left Cuba, but the news tainted my first experience of Paris.

With a heavy heart, I visited the usual tourist sites. Despite my worry about Marina and my initial lack of interest, I discovered that Paris was a feast for the eyes. Notre Dame's exterior was then dirty and dark. But regardless of the dirt accumulated on its walls, I was astonished at the beauty of the building. On the inside, the celebrated stained glass provided an extraordinary experience of light. I marveled at the fact that I was really looking at these places and having these experiences. I would probably never have another chance to see important places like these. Nothing of importance ever took place in Cuba; I was convinced of that.

Our guide in Paris was Monsieur Girard, a very old history professor who kept confusing left with right. He kept stumbling over his directions, inviting us to turn our heads the wrong way. In a heavily French-accented Spanish, he repeatedly said, *"A mi derecha...digo, a mi izquierda..."*— "On my right...I mean, my left..." His translation and pronunciation of Spanish words caused great hilarity among the tour participants. Saint Geneviève became Santa "Ginivova." Napoleon's grave became some strange color of marble rather than red in his peculiar translation of the word *rojo*.

But he clearly was knowledgeable about French history, art, and architecture and I found myself learning a lot from his narratives. In that first visit to Paris, following Monsieur Girard, this very ancient man with his watery eyes, his rumpled suit, his even older hat and cane, inspired in me an unwavering love for Paris. He was clearly stirred by monuments, buildings, paintings, sculptures, and the French history that thread them together. His voice—despite the thick accent, grammatical mistakes in Spanish, and confused directions—replays every time I revisit the places I saw for the first time under his guidance.

The entrance to the Louvre was then on what has become a locked side door after the construction of I. M. Pei's glass Pyramide, the current entrance. As I entered the famous museum through that door, a marble staircase opened wide to show at its top the sculpture of the Victory of Samothrace. Its unanticipated beauty startled me. I stood paralyzed at the bottom of the staircase. I did not know this sculpture existed. I had never seen a picture of it.

The Victory of Samothrace – Louvre, Paris

The placement of the Victory is still the same. But now visitors to the Louvre see it later, not at the very moment of entering the museum. I don't know if her beauty continues to affect others as it affected me. It still amazes me that the sculptor could create in stone the appearance of a thin veil ruffled by the wind over the ribs, navel, and curves of a woman's body. The wings of that sculpture became the unconscious symbol of my freedom and independence, so much so that when I decided to get a tattoo a few years ago, several decades after I saw the Victory for the first time, I chose a facsimile of her wing. Her wings symbolized that summer and my life.

I learned to fly in the summer of 1958, although I did not recognize it then. In fact, it took me decades to understand the full significance of that summer and its impact on my life.

After Paris, nothing was too interesting, but nonetheless, I went to Brussels for the World's International Exposition where I rode the escalators inside the Atomium and gawked at Dalí's haunting painting of the Christ of St. John of the Cross in the Spanish Pavillion. I was pleasantly surprised in Brussels when I bought stamps to send postcards to Cuba and no one asked me where Cuba was, as in France and Italy. The Belgian royal family had gone to Cuba the previous winter; every Belgian knew where Cuba was; Cuban music played in restaurants and hotels. Now, practically everyone in the world knows at least the name of Cuba. But Cuba was an unknown little island then. Its fame would come later, after 1958.

While in Brussels, I took a one-day tour of the Netherlands. After that, it was time to return to Spain. Back in Madrid, I spent time with Tory, I visited more museums, went to the theater, ate plenty of *tapas*, walked around the city. And started realizing that I did not want to go back to Cuba.

My new freedom had crystallized during this trip. I did not want to lose it.

Those three months in foreign countries—changing trains, booking hotels, eating unfamiliar foods, figuring out how to say something in unknown languages, fending for myself in small and big ways—had taught me that traveling brought delicious adventures worth the unavoidable inconveniences. Also, I knew now that I could rise to unanticipated challenges.

I thought I could register at a university in Madrid and continue studying, something I could not do in Cuba. It was impossible to know how much longer the University of Havana would be closed. I had enough money left from my TV winnings to do it. That was a concrete reason to want to stay. But there was something more, something difficult to define. Being by myself in Europe, walking alone in Madrid for long hours, gave me a sense of something undefined, but clear enough. I wanted to stay. In Madrid I was living for myself.

During that summer and early fall, Cuba and its political situation were miles away, both literally and in my awareness. I had many interesting things to attend to and didn't think much about evil forces lurking on the other side of the Atlantic. No one knew that Batista had less than three months left in power and our world was about to be turned upside down.

Some friends of my mother's family in Madrid kept telling me that Fidel Castro was a Communist. His advisors in Mexico had been Communist Spanish exiles. But I didn't believe them. I was sure these comments were coming from their conservative *franquista* politics. Batista was a criminal dictator. Fidel Castro was a hero. I didn't know when he would win over Batista's forces. But I was sure he would never be a Communist.

In early October, gathering my courage, I wrote to Nery asking her to help me tell my parents that I did not want to go back and I was staying in Spain to study like Clara Elena and other young Cubans. Nery read the letter aloud to my parents as soon as she opened the envelope. My half-formed plans were out in the open. In a week, I had a letter from my father with one peremptory message, "Come back immediately!" And then, a letter from Nery apologizing for exposing me unwittingly and explaining what I had not known before: all my letters had been public family documents rather than my private communication with her.

The importance of accepting my parents' authority was still ingrained in me. I had always been a dutiful girl. And so, after being temporarily rich and free for three months in Europe, I returned to the reality of my quotidian constraints in Cuba in mid-October with a sense of inevitability and regret. I knew I was going back to tutoring children in a country convulsed by political strife and violence. I knew this was not what I wanted. But I persuaded myself that I had no other alternative. This was my country. I belonged there with my family and friends. After all, I was not yet twenty. And besides, coming back had the enticement of being able to tell everyone all the details of my adventures and describing for them what I had experienced.

My European adventure was over. Nevertheless, ever so subtly, I was aware that this summer had changed me and eventually would contribute to shape my life.

V

Revolución

... jirones de amor y de dolor/
...shreds of love and pain

¡Abajo Batista! ¡Arriba Fidel!

Barely two months after my return from Europe, in January 1959, the world watched in fascination as bearded men wearing olive green uniforms and rosaries around their necks descended on Cuban cities from the surrounding hills. Cheering crowds welcomed them. At that exhilarating moment, Cuba and the world witnessed something remarkable.

I was one of the little heads in the crowd filmed and photographed and circulated internationally welcoming Fidel Castro on the chilly January day when he arrived in Havana. I was among those sharing the hopeful feelings that Fidel's presence and promises generated.

Batista had slipped out of the country in the middle of the night on December 31st, under the cover of New Year's celebrations, after six years of dictatorship. This time he never returned. He died in Madeira several years later.

In mid-December 1958, when I turned twenty, insistent rumors had circulated in Havana. Che Guevara, one of Fidel's lieutenants, was pressing forward relentlessly toward the capital. He was already in Santa Clara, in the middle of the island. The *casquitos*—as Batista's government troops had been nicknamed—were changing sides as Che advanced. And then, on the last night of the year, the rumors became news. Batista had fled with his family and closest associates to the Dominican Republic on a Cuban military plane.

On New Year's Day, 1959 Fidel began his descent from the Sierra Maestra. He stopped in Santiago where he spoke from the City Hall balcony to jubilant crowds standing across the street in Parque Céspedes, where I had played so many summers during my childhood. After his first public speech in Santiago, he continued moving

West to Havana. Along the length of Cuba, he was received with a hero's welcome by crowds cheering, dancing, and singing. When he finally arrived in Havana a week later, I was there applauding and shouting my approval. The waiting throng booed the policemen still wearing the dark blue uniforms of the old regime, even though these were only rank and file traffic police who had never arrested anyone. The officers ignored the taunts and continued trying to impose order. They joined in the cheering when they saw Fidel.

It is hard to explain the joy, the hope, the extraordinary sense of jubilant expectation that pervaded the crowd. The moment I saw Fidel on top of an open truck is engraved in my mind's eye. He looked handsome and tall in his olive-green garb and his black beard, surrounded by other prominent figures of the Revolutionary movement.

The persecuted hero was now triumphant. Batista was gone. We were free. Justice would prevail now, just as Fidel had promised in his historic defense when he was tried and condemned to prison by Batista after the failed 1953 attack on the Moncada Barracks in Santiago. After his release from prison, Fidel had gone into exile in Mexico, and from there he had come back to Cuba in 1956. Now, three years later, he had succeeded in toppling Batista. But he was not to be called "General" like Batista. He was only "Comandante." He was not the President, just maybe "Prime Minister." This was proof that he did not intend to dominate and elevate himself. Others referred to him as *"el máximo líder,"* which was a well-deserved title.

Before Fidel's triumph, shortly after my return from Europe at the end of 1958, I had resumed my routine of tutoring children and reading a lot to compensate for my lack of formal study. I also continued my long intellectual conversations with Tío and my active participation in Rosa Mystica. The memories of my months in Europe were still very much alive. Telling stories about my trip to family and friends in Rosa Mystica, sharing photographs and souvenirs, wearing my stylish new European clothes seemed to be enough. What else was there to expect? This was my life.

Just a few weeks after the triumph of the Revolution, Rosa Mystica created a school for the semi-illiterate *guerrilleras* who had come into Havana with the *Ejército Rebelde*—Fidel's Rebel Army. We donated several hours a week to teaching them to read and write and providing health and childcare. We offered everything from concrete skills—basic literacy, arithmetic, typing, shorthand, knitting, sewing—to discussion of ideas. The presence of young peasant women in uniform gave our group a new twist. But within a few months, it became evident that the new government was not happy that a group of Catholic women was offering services that might "contaminate" the budding revolutionary ideology of the *guerrilleras*. Eventually, the *guerrilleras* stopped coming. Two years later, in April 1961, a few days after the Bay of Pigs invasion, government-sponsored militia men occupied the house Rosa Mystica rented near the University of Havana and disbanded our association.

But in 1959 there was no way to anticipate this turn of events. Fidel had promised a new era, and we believed him. He was full of fire, and so were most Cubans. In those first months of the Revolution, I said to a friend in a casual conversation, "I am so glad we can freely say *'¡Abajo Batista!'* – 'Down with Batista!'"

Dryly, she responded, "That means nothing if we cannot also say, *'Abajo Fidel'* without being punished."

I dismissed her comment. Why would anyone want to say, *'Abajo Fidel'*?

However, in a few months, after my initial enthusiasm as a fellow traveler of the Revolution, I started seeing trickles of injustice perpetrated in the name of justice. My excitement was invaded every so often by a filament of doubt. Hints of cruelty were presented as just expressions of revolutionary justice. They were subtle, difficult to pinpoint. But the trickles increased to a flow, and then became a torrent. Suspected Batista sympathizers, policemen, and soldiers were put on public trial in front of TV cameras without real proof of the individuals' participation in human rights abuses or crimes. They were automatically believed to be guilty of wrongdoing, including murder and torture, before they were tried. Most of those convicted in revolutionary tribunals were executed by firing squad near the walls of the centuries old La Cabaña fortress—where Che Guevara was the commander—the *Paredón* that so excited the crowds. I had no doubt that many of them were indeed murderers and torturers. But it was hard to believe that all of them were, particularly because, in many cases, only hearsay was presented as proof of their involvement.

Fidel's three- or four-hour long speeches mixed soothing promises with threatening warnings. Despite the intensity of revolutionary fervor, while most people continued to be enthralled by Fidel's words, many of us began feeling some vague sense of discomfort and puzzlement. I heard occasional negative comments from friends, and a trickle of people started leaving the country.

The expropriation and nationalization of land and industries that started with the Agrarian Reform in 1959, progressively expanded to all businesses. Everything now belonged to the people. First, owner-ship of big sugar mills was transferred to the government in the name of economic justice. Then, in October 1960, small businesses such as family-owned corner grocery stores, dry cleaning shops, seamstresses' home workshops, and anything else that implied private enterprise, no matter how small, were confiscated and "nationalized." The shop-keepers were thrown out of their businesses by soldiers carrying heavy guns. Small merchants who had been just trying to survive were viewed as enemies of the people, holding on to their properties out of capitalistic greed. The father of a friend who had owned a small dry-cleaning shop operated only by him and his wife had it expropriated. It was hard to understand how he could be a "capitalist enemy of the people."

Occasionally, Che Guevara himself presided over the expropria-tions. Those who watched him in action from across the street, kicking and shoving people who resisted the loss of their lives' work, hesitated in their belief that he was a hero. Their hesitation was only whispered. It was clear that saying any variation of "abajo Fidel" was as danger-ous now as saying "abajo Batista" had been before 1959.

The government forcefully denied these measures had any connec-tion with communist ideas. Anyone who mentioned Marxist influ-ences in the government was deemed a traitor to the Revolution and the country. Fidel had come to the United States in 1959, right after he took power and publicly declared that even if "the world thinks we are Communists, we are not." That was the official story. Saying oth-erwise was counterrevolutionary. Active denial of the doctrinal affili-ations that eventually became synonymous with the Cuban Revolu-tion was part of Fidel's political ploy.

Manuel Urrutia, the judge who had refused to condemn Fidel when he was a prisoner of Batista, had been appointed acting President in January 1959 at the triumph of the Revolution. When Urrutia ex-pressed concerns about the Marxist leanings of some government offi-cials, Fidel made a show of resigning his post as Prime Minister, claim-ing that Urrutia's "fevered anti-Communism" was having a detri-mental effect on the country. Urrutia was forced to resign in July after people marched in the streets in support of an aggrieved Fidel, hurt by the temporary President's bad-mouthing the Revolution by accusing it of communism. In 1959, Hubert Matos, one of Fidel's lieutenants who fought alongside him against Batista in the Sierra Maestra, was also condemned to twenty years in prison as a traitor for commenting publicly that Marxist ideologues were taking over the ideals of the

Revolution. His true crime was that he alerted people to what was coming before the government had a firm grip on the country.

Anastas Mikoyan, the Chairman of the Presidium of the Supreme Soviet under Khrushchev, visited Cuba in early 1960. Mikoyan's position in the Supreme Soviet made him the second most powerful figure in the Soviet Union at the time. In the middle of the Cold War, no visit by a high-ranking Soviet leader to any country in the world was an innocuous event. But the Cuban government insisted that this was just a "cultural" visit.

Mikoyan was the first Soviet official to go to Cuba after the beginning of the Revolution. He travelled with Fidel around the island in a Russian helicopter. He left Cuba after ten days with a trade treaty and a promise of resumed diplomatic relations.

There were plenty of signs that many Cubans found the new warmth between Havana and Moscow distasteful and dangerous. In the streets, groups of students shouted, "Out with the Reds!" despite the risk this implied. On Mikoyan's first day in Havana the armed forces attacked the students who protested his visit. The opposition Havana newspaper, *Diario de la Marina,* commented, "Señor Mikoyan, your visit has clarified many things and defined the camps: on one side, the Communists and their knowing and unknowing accomplices; on the other side Cubans who want to continue being free men in a free world."

Yet, others thrived in the new revolutionary enthusiasm and did not hesitate to express their support publicly and furiously. The pro-Castro Federation of University Students of the University Havana voted to censure anti-Mikoyan demonstrators. People fought venomously among themselves about the meaning of Mikoyan's visit. Acquaintances accused me of being a counterrevolutionary because I had said I did not believe the purpose of Mikoyan's trip was just "cultural," as the government claimed.

"What proof do you have that there are ulterior motives to his visit?"

"Don't you think it is about time we show the Americans that Cuba is an independent country making its own diplomatic connections regardless of what the U.S. wants us to do?"

"Why is it bad that the Russians want to help Cuba and the Revolution? It's good that we get support from other countries!"

I heard a barrage of comments in a similar vein. If I responded that they were being naïve, they retorted that I should be ashamed of doubting Fidel's honesty and I must not love my country well enough.

Emotions were high. To express displeasure or disagreement was an indication of a lack of social consciousness, a demonstration of selfishness, a betrayal of the revolutionary ideals. Skepticism of any kind made you suspect of possible counterrevolutionary activities.

I did not know then that it is in the nature of revolutions to create twists and turns to confuse the people immersed in them and to turn them against each other. Having believed in Fidel's promises, I could not understand why blatant injustices were perpetrated every day in the name of justice. I still wanted to believe that it was possible to work for social justice in this context while avoiding the tilt to Soviet communism that was becoming more evident each day.

The world in which we lived, combined with my work schedule, absorbed all my energies. There wasn't much time and energy left to think about my personal life. Whatever I had dreamed about and imagined during my trip to Europe the previous summer was now swallowed by the turmoil of Cuba's new reality.

One long awaited development also increased demands on my energy and time. Public universities were re-opened in May 1959. And so, after more than two years of waiting, I was finally enrolled at the University of Havana. Professors and students worked hard to make up for the hiatus years. I took Latin, Greek, Spanish Medieval Literature, Ancient History, World Geography and Latin American Political History. This was a heavy load to carry together with my usual tutoring schedule, but it meant new learning and a stimulating set of readings. Eventually, to have a more manageable schedule while keeping a reasonable income, I found a job in a girls' school teaching English as a second language. I still did some tutoring but did not spend as much time running from one child's house to another's.

The University was full of political effervescence. In particular, the Latin American Political History course burst with heated discussions about the similarities and differences of the current Cuban revolutionary process with previous movements in Latin America and Cuba itself. The struggles against U.S. intromission in Latin American affairs were paramount in these discussions.

The professor who taught Greek was a very strict woman. The students mockingly used Greek grammar terminology to characterize her. They had nicknamed her *Espíritu Aspero*, which literally translates as "rough spirit"—*spiritus asper*—the rough breathing pronunciation of some Greek letters. She knew of her nickname and informed us about it on the first day of class, to warn us that neither Greek nor she were to be taken lightly. Both she and her subject matter were indeed rough, but to this day, thanks to her good teaching and my enthusiasm, I still can read words written in the Greek alphabet, even though I don't know modern Greek.

And so, time rushed by like a tropical hurricane during most of 1959, transforming or obliterating the old and creating new realities. I was absorbed by my studies, still hoping that the Revolution would live up to its promises.

Then, in September 1959, months after the beginning of the Revolution and my return to University, Tío died of a cerebral hemorrhage. He was fifty-three. His wake was held in the same house where Abuela Boqui had died and Tío had lived.

Barely twenty years old then, I did not cry in public during the wake. I had learned to repress my grief at the time of my grandmother's death when I was nine years old, as something shameful or unnecessary. Now, I was unable to grieve openly for Tío. During the hot, tiring hours of the wake, I felt stunned and numb, not aware of any feeling, except anger when one of my cousins started crying loudly. *What right did he have to weep so openly? I had lost so much more than he and was not making any public displays of grief!*

Unbeknownst to me, at that moment, my own personal revolution was about to pick up where it left off after my return from Europe the previous year.

Panic

A week or two after Tío's death, without warning, I began having panic attacks.

The first of these paralyzing, terrifying incidents struck on a Sunday morning, in the middle of Mass, at Rosa Mystica. Suddenly, I started feeling as if I were choking. I tried to breathe deeply and slowly, wondering if I had been abruptly afflicted with asthma or something similar. I tried to calm down and waited for the awful physical sensation to go away. But the difficult breathing did not abate. It was as if the air I needed was being consumed by the other women in the room. Bursts of heart palpitations began, and they seemed to intensify with each attempted breath. I thought I was having a heart attack and would die on the spot, in front of everyone. Although I was surrounded by women who knew me, rather than thinking that they might be able to help prevent my impending death, I felt embarrassed and self-conscious that they were going to witness my fainting or demise.

Nery was sitting nearby. We were both dressed in black and white, the conventional expression of mourning in 1950s Cuba, because of Tío's recent death. We stood out among the hundred or so women attending Mass dressed in colorful clothes. I gestured to Nery. The next thing I recall is the two of us quietly and quickly exiting down the big stone staircase at the front of the Rosa Mystica house.

Shortly after that, we arrived at the emergency room of the health cooperative my family belonged to. The young doctor on duty was Freddy, one of our circle of partying and dancing friends. It upset me further that Freddy was on call that Sunday morning rather than some unknown doctor. Regardless of how humiliated I felt, I was too alarmed. I told him what was happening. Unsure why I felt embarrassed by these symptoms, I described them to Freddy. He examined me, listened to my heart and lungs with his stethoscope, and then said with a nice smile, "Nothing wrong with your heart or your lungs, no need to worry." *But how could I not worry when I had these alarming symptoms? How could nothing be wrong if I felt this horrible?*

He gave me a prescription for some pills to take in case of a recurrence. *What were these pills for? What was this medication?* And then he said in the same even tone, "You may need to talk to a psychiatrist."

"I am not a nervous person. Why do I need a psychiatrist?" I protested aloud while thinking, *I am brave and self-assured, I have gone to Europe alone, I can take control in a crisis, I am steadfast and dependable. I am a pillar in my family… just what are you talking about?*

Trying to reassure me, Freddy said something like, "Sometimes emotional distress is not consciously evident, but that does not mean it is not there."

I smiled back at him, took the prescription, thanked him, and left with Nery.

The symptoms had subsided by then. I believed that this strange spell of whatever it was had been an aberration. I was sure the bizarre experience would never be repeated.

But as the days passed, not only did the perplexing and harrowing episodes occur repeatedly, but each one got worse. On multiple occasions, I relived the experience of the first incident. I was certain I was about to suffocate because my lungs were not contracting properly. I knew that deep breathing would be useless; no air seemed to reach my lungs no matter how deeply I inhaled. My terror intensified the breathlessness and sent my heart racing. Other times I was certain that some strange and deadly disease was creeping into my bones and destroying me from within. Once, riding on a city bus on my way to tutor a child, my lower jaw went rigid. Feeling unable to open my mouth, I became convinced I might die of tetanus. I had a small cut on a finger that I was sure had given me the disease. I was certain that, unable to open my mouth to cry for help, I would fall on the crowded, filthy bus floor, only to be trampled by astonished passengers.

It is hard to describe the panic that engulfed me with each one of these episodes. The whole ordeal was characterized by perpetual, pervasive confusion. I was never at peace. From the moment I opened my eyes each morning, until the moment I went to sleep at night, I experienced nearly uninterrupted terror, whether I was going about my daily life, watching my students perform some school assignment, or sitting at the dining room table with my family. Despite the repetitive nature of the attacks, each new occurrence evoked a unique panic, a terror that never abated despite the episodes' frequency or familiarity. The effect was worse each time: whatever the mysterious cause, I was absolutely convinced that, this time, I would die; this time, annihilation was certain. As the episodes succeeded one another, they were compounded by my constant fear of the fear. Under the weight of whatever was happening, I was either experiencing a panic attack or terrified that I would begin experiencing one shortly. Mercifully, sleep came every night to save me from the torment of my waking hours.

I lived in a fog of psychic torment while the Revolution gained momentum and swirled around us. On a day when attendance at a *concentración*—a "concentration" of citizens—at the Plaza de la Revolución was demanded by the government, as had become common in recent months, the streets of Havana were empty. People were at Revolution Square, cheering Fidel as he spoke or in their homes with windows and doors closed, pretending that they were not there, fretting while listening on their television to Fidel's several-hours-long speech.

My mother warned me not to go out unnecessarily because of soldiers, volunteer *milicianos,* or overexcited government supporters who might be on the streets. But the anticipation of the panic that would overcome me when I was at home, sitting in an enclosed space in the company of my thoughts and my family, was more frightening than walking alone in the empty streets and running the risk of encountering patrolling soldiers who could question why I was not in Revolution Square or listening to Fidel's speech as expected.

She kept insisting, "There is no need for you to be out. What is the matter with you? Why can't you just sit here and do something like everyone else? Read, knit, listen to music or whatever!"

I ignored her and left. I could not tell her why. She would not have understood. And, I could not explain to her any better than I could explain to myself what my problem was. In the middle of the afternoon, while Fidel's speech blared from all TVs as I passed by windows or porches, I walked to the nearby home of an acquaintance seeking anything to distract me from my racing thoughts. Everyone else was mesmerized by Fidel's long speeches, which seemed progressively more menacing. But to me, he felt less dangerous than my constant panic.

The long months when I was gripped by panic were the first time in my life when I could not enjoy studying. I couldn't think about anything beyond my terrors for more than a few minutes. Eventually, I had to drop out of the university. There was no point in continuing to go to class when I could not concentrate enough to complete any assignments. I constantly left with some excuse in the middle of lectures afraid that I would make a spectacle of myself.

Yet I continued teaching and tutoring. My income was vital to my family, so off I went to teach children how to do math, read and write Spanish, or learn English as a second language. Despite my constant state of anxiety, I sat at my desk at the school where I taught part-time or at a table in my students' homes, and continued teaching, talking, smiling, and performing my duties.

My terror continued to escalate even though I was taking the pills—probably tranquilizers—Freddy had prescribed. I shared very little about my panic at home. There was no point in telling my family that I was going insane, struggling to stay alive each day. The few times I tried to explain, my parents, Nery and my aunt Marina gave me puzzled looks. After all, I was still functioning. I was successfully disguising my anxiety. Despite the fog in my mind, I learned a skill during that horrible period: to continue functioning despite any emotional pain I might be experiencing; to not let personal issues or emotions interfere with daily responsibilities.

Several weeks after the initial episode, on a quiet Sunday afternoon, one quasi-hallucinatory image shook me more than all the panic attacks. I was trying to take a nap to keep the panic at bay; sleep was my best escape. Then, without warning, I felt as if it was real the clear-cut sensation that my father was right there trying to strangle me. That was the proverbial last straw. I realized at that ever more frightening moment that I could not deal with this terror alone. I decided I needed therapy as Freddy had suggested and called Rosalba, the director of Rosa Mystica, who was a psychologist. I pleaded for her help.

I saw Rosalba for one hour of therapy every Wednesday morning from that day on. After a few sessions, Rosalba said something that seemed preposterous: "Indeed your father *has been* strangling you with unspoken demands that you support the family financially and take care of his emotional needs." Rosalba's interpretation was that Tío had been the true protective paternal figure in my life, and his death had left me without any safeguard against the unreasonable demands placed on me since childhood in the name of love. It took me some time to consider this plausible. Her evidently accurate interpretation of what had precipitated my panic did not automatically make the attacks disappear, however.

Each Wednesday, I would arrive at her office by bus, coming from wherever in Havana I had been tutoring. I sat for a few minutes in the small waiting area of the office suite, until Olga, another member of Rosa Mystica who was about ten years older than I, came out of Rosalba's office. Olga—with her perfect black hair and full lips carefully painted with bright red lipstick—impressed me as the image of beauty and poise, but, like me, she was there every week. We said hello self-consciously. At that time, no one talked about being in therapy, but there was no hiding why we were there. I barely knew Olga and had no idea what brought her to Rosalba's office every Wednesday at ten, but I felt an unspoken bond with her.

Luckily, lunch time came immediately after my session, so no one was sitting in the waiting room when I came out. I left my therapy sessions feeling shaky, but hopeful that I was going to be fine, despite my near constant anxiety.

In my therapy with Rosalba I explored my life history and the causes of my painful emotional state from different angles. Slowly, I started seeing new perspectives on my obligations to my family and my desires. Therapy made me aware I needed to free myself from expectations that I would be the family's breadwinner forever and from my own dutiful response to those expectations. I knew I needed distance, but also felt I could not abandon them. My father's vulnerability and ineffectiveness and my mother's demands pulled at my heart incessantly.

After months of weekly therapy sessions, I started feeling a reprieve. The frequency, intensity and duration of the panic episodes subsided. Eventually, I noticed that several hours would go by in which I'd had no panic, and then longer periods, days, and weeks passed without an episode. Even when I stopped taking the pills that Freddy had prescribed, the panic attacks did not return. There was more I still needed to work through in therapy, but the daily terror, the immediate symptom of my psychic struggles, had completely disappeared by the end of 1960. Something was shifting internally.

Thanks to therapy, I was able to start studying again, this time at the private Catholic University, where, in the fall of 1960, I received a scholarship to study Psychology. I began to feel normal again amid the drama of political upheaval. Several months later, I was strong enough to make decisions about leaving Cuba.

While I was living inside the terrors of my mind, events of enormous consequence were swirling around us. During long those months of therapy, while I was putting together the fragments of my inner life with Rosalba's help, the outside world was becoming more fractured. As my internal world was calming down, life in the streets was increasingly full of turmoil. The palpable tension mounted each day, affecting everyday life and personal relationships. Friends and family members turned against each other, berating those who dared express doubts or opinions critical of the Revolution or those who still believed in its promise.

Batista had punished those who acted against his government. But now, not only actions were punishable; thoughts also were. Anyone on the street felt entitled to challenge your loyalty to the Revolution. To keep quiet, let alone contradict the vociferous revolutionary rhetoric, could become dangerous because it could make me a target of rage or worse.

I remember vividly one such incident during a bus ride. The passengers were reaffirming one another in their unflinching conviction that the devastating, May 1960 earthquake in Chile had been caused by an American subterranean nuclear attack. Comments like, "This earthquake is the best proof of U.S. ill-will and aggression against Latin America," went back and forth among them for a while. I kept quiet looking out the window. But the other passengers were not about to let me avoid the issue. When it became clear that I had not expressed my enthusiastic agreement, a thin woman in her forties, yelled at me across the aisle, "Well, why are not saying anything? Do you like the *yankis*?"

Within seconds, others started questioning me with the same tone and the driver turned an angry look on me from the rearview mirror. I mumbled something about needing to get off at the next stop. Even though waiting for the next bus to continue my trip made me late for my tutoring session, it was better than confronting the increasingly threatening anger of passengers and driver.

Progressively, the Revolutionary government was taking hold of

Cuba, still pretending that communist ideology was not involved in the country's transformation. Vigilant secret police became a constant threat; they monitored conversations in bus stops, shops, and among neighbors.

Yet, the crumbling of my emotional life after Tío's death had terrified me in ways the dangers of draconian measures and persecution by the government never could. Although real events were frightening, they were less so for me than the elusive panic in my mind. As long as I felt in one piece psychologically, I could deal with anything else. It was almost a relief to contend with tangible events that warranted fear, rather than deal with internal monsters that, in their very unreasonableness, were ever more frightening. The fact that my panic attacks vanished despite the political events surrounding me, confirmed that their cause was thoroughly within my personal story.

Rosalba

When I met her, Rosalba was a petite woman in her early forties. She had a thin voice, big green-gray eyes and frizzy, sandy-colored hair. She always dressed carelessly, even shabbily, demonstrating that appearances should not be the most important concern of any woman. She managed to make commands sound as if they were only suggestions. But behind her subdued tone and frequent smile was a powerful will.

I didn't know then that she was going to change the trajectory of my life.

Rosalba had yearned to be a mother, but after ten years of marriage and all the fertility treatments available at the time, she could not conceive. While trying to get pregnant, struggling to compensate for the lack of what she wanted most—children—she had accumulated higher education degrees in chemistry, physics, pharmacy, and, finally, psychology. After she turned thirty, she gave up the hope of motherhood and the hope that acquiring more university degrees would fill her void. A Jesuit priest suggested she should start Rosa Mystica. Possibly, she hoped that mentoring a group of young women might become more significant and satisfying for her than one or two adopted children. She made it explicit that we were a rewarding antidote to the emotional pains of her infertility—she now had three hundred daughters!

Rosalba earned a living as a university professor and was married to a successful physician. I knew that her part-time psychology practice consisted mostly of free psychotherapy, a service she provided to those who needed it. She kept her eyes open for members of Rosa Mystica who could use her skills as a psychologist.

My first encounter with her was when I was nineteen and had been made fleetingly famous by Cuban television. When I won the TV contest, I was already a member of Rosa Mystica. Initially, Rosalba had no idea of who I was. I was just one among several hundred. But after I was catapulted into fame by the TV program, she took notice of me. It was obvious that I knew a lot about religion.

"Would you like to facilitate the Thursday study circle?" she asked me one of the many early evenings I was at the Rosa Mystica house not doing anything in particular. I said yes immediately.

Study circles met for one hour every week to discuss spirituality and theology in the context of our lives. I remember how much I enjoyed leading the group. That was my first experience teaching other young women by eliciting discussion. In my everyday working life, I felt mostly bored teaching English to elementary school children. But in the study circle I discussed ideas with my peers and facilitated collective learning, including my own. I had participated in study circles led by others for the previous two years, but now I could choose the topics, the questions to be addressed, the issues to be tackled in the discussion—I was in heaven!

A few months after I started leading the study circle, Rosalba approached me again. "How about taking charge of the training seminars for the *catequistas*?"

These were the members of Rosa Mystica who taught catechism to children and provided weekly services in poor neighborhoods throughout Havana. Apparently, she thought I had done a respectable job in leading the study circle; she was giving me more responsibilities. I was delighted. Sometime later, in the summer of 1960, when my panic attacks were clearly subsiding, she also put me in charge of giving introductory talks to the newcomers who were joining Rosa Mystica.

The assignment of organizing seminars for the *catequistas* coincided with my volunteering to teach basic reading, writing, and arithmetic to the *guerrilleras* who had arrived in Havana with Fidel's Rebel Army. I felt creative and appreciated and enjoyed these opportunities.

Earlier, Rosalba had also noticed that not all was well with me. She had detected a fragility I was not aware of or not ready to acknowledge.

She asked if I wanted to come see her at her office. I said I would but did not act on it. I did not want to be identified as a troubled soul. Psychotherapy seemed intimidating, even though several years before meeting Rosalba, when I had taken a psychology course taught by my favorite high school teacher, I had decided I wanted to become a psychologist. I still cherished that dream and didn't want to be perceived as someone in need of services rather than capable of providing them.

However, when I finally called Rosalba in tears on that Sunday afternoon in the middle of the terrifying, almost hallucinatory moment in which I felt as if my father was trying to choke me, it became clear to both of us that I needed her services.

Later, after we both had left Cuba, Rosalba also gave me a reason to move away from my family by asking me to jump-start a branch of Rosa Mystica in Panama and, later, Costa Rica. If God wanted me to go to other countries to do this work, leaving my family was not an abandonment. I could let go of my self-reproach.

The notion of making important life decisions based on a desire to follow the will of God may sound preposterous. But it was my guiding force. The idea that one plans life according to what one believes to be the will of God was a principle for me as it was for many others I knew, including my father. Papi could not compete with God; he knew it and didn't even try.

It helped that this was what Rosalba expected of me. Her approval had a strong pull. Her wishes were easily confused with the voice of God in my mind. I came to trust Rosalba with my life because I felt I owed her my survival. Thanks to Rosalba, I had not lost my sanity. It was Rosalba who had encouraged me to go to the Catholic University to study Psychology. She had helped me break free from my family's yoke. She was my savior.

But my relationship with Rosalba had many layers, some of them not conducive to my well-being. One day, during therapy, I was reiterating how those three months in Europe had given me a taste of freedom and subtly evoked the pleasures of my childhood summers in Santiago when being away from daily life in Havana was synonymous with happiness. Rosalba responded irritably, "If you could travel constantly, you would not mind never being a mother!" Even then, when neither she nor I knew how my life would turn out, I could intuit she had put her finger on a truth about me. But her assessment of my priorities touched a raw nerve in her. Having struggled with her infertility for more than a decade, she could not understand how any woman who was able to conceive could *choose* not to have children. Her comment was more than an observation; it expressed her intense disapproval regarding the choices neither she nor I could be certain I would make.

It was true that after my return from Europe, routines and expectations that had felt normal before became progressively more burdensome. This had been made even more evident by my emotional crisis. But it wasn't just the magic of travel that shaped my dislike of motherhood. I had spent long hours caring for my little brothers during my childhood and adolescence, and I had no illusions about the delights provided by babies. I knew what I enjoyed best, and child-rearing was not it. I was not sure if her disapproval of my distaste for motherhood was warranted, but I knew that motherhood was not a priority for me as it had been for her.

To my surprise, when I was still in therapy with her, on a quiet Sunday afternoon in early April 1961, Rosalba called me at home. She asked me to go early the next day to the girls' high school, where I was working part-time, to give a message to a member of Rosa Mystica, Rosalba's second in command. The coded message I was to deliver to this woman, also a teacher at the school, meant that she was now in charge. Rosalba and her husband had gone into hiding.

Her office had been vandalized the day before; the danger signals were too strong to be ignored. The government considered Rosalba—and her husband by association—dangerous, because of her influence on the members of Rosa Mystica. The government bosses were always leery of views that did not conform to their agenda. Hence, their earlier suspicion of the *guerrilleras'* contact with Rosa Mystica. Perhaps Rosalba was involved in some counterrevolutionary activities. I didn't know. But, in any case, the police had issued an arrest warrant for her and her husband.

As I rode the bus to Miramar on the next day to deliver her message, I wondered if the records of my personal pain were in the hands of the vandals—who were obviously government thugs. I didn't know if Rosalba had destroyed her records before the thugs arrived. If she had not, no one could guess what the government knew about her therapy clients, all of us members of the suspect Rosa Mystica. And although I did not have any politically dangerous issues to hide, I resented the possibility of anyone reading about my life and troubles, no matter how unimportant they may have seemed to the secret police looking for counterrevolutionary activities.

Rosalba called me again a week or two later. The failed April 17th Bay of Pigs invasion had taken place between her two phone calls.

"Hola, Oliva, this is Rosita. Could you accompany me downtown for some errands?" she said in a soft, calm tone. She was distorting her name, but I knew the sound of her voice too well. I was startled but acted as if there was nothing unusual in this call. We never knew who could be listening to phone conversations.

"Yes, of course," I responded. "Where shall we meet?"

"I'll wait for you at the corner of San Rafael and Galiano. Just under the porch, at the front door of *el tencén.*" *El tencén* was the Cubanized name of Woolworth's five-and-ten store located at a busy corner in the center of Havana.

I met Rosalba at ten the next morning at that corner, across from the charred remains of what until a few days earlier had been the luxury department store El Encanto. It was never clear whether the fire had been an act of sabotage against the government or a government action against a symbol of luxury and capitalism. Tall trees grow now on the site of the demolished store, sixty years after all these 1961 events.

Rosalba and I went first to La Filosofía, a nearby department store to buy some clothes. Then, we took several taxis to multiple destinations. We went to a pharmacy to refill a prescription; she made a few phone calls from a public booth while I stood guard outside; we chatted about everything and nothing during the taxi rides we took from one place to another.

Havana felt like a ghost city in the days after the abortive Bay of Pigs invasion. Few cars and fewer pedestrians were on the streets. The "enemies of the Revolution" were either under arrest or in hiding, trying to figure out what to do next. The government and its supporters were still astonished at the thought that they could have defeated the invaders and their American backers. Both supporters and enemies of the Revolution had believed in the inevitability of an overwhelming American-led invasion. Suspended at the edges of their opposing perspectives, they were equally rattled and amazed by the fact that the Cuban exiles at the head of the anticipated invasion had been abandoned by the Americans on a swampy beach, left to fend for themselves. Neither the jubilation of victory nor the certainty of defeat had yet settled in; everyone seemed stunned and withdrawn, trying to assimilate what had happened.

Whispering in the back seat of a taxi, Rosalba shared her view about the unsuccessful invasion. "This botched landing was only a sham concocted by the Americans," she assured me. "The Americans are so intelligent that they aborted this expected invasion on purpose so they could follow it up with the real one."

If this failed invasion was only a distraction and the prelude of a genuine attempt at overthrowing the regime, there was still hope. Desperate as I was to believe her, I had come to realize she did not always acknowledge reality. As I was to experience repeatedly in the years ahead, she distorted obvious truths when they did not fit her needs and desires. However, on that late April morning in 1961, her absolute certainty about her interpretation of the events and my naïve loyalty combined to make both of us think that she was right.

I didn't want to grasp how dangerous our little adventure was. All that mattered was that it gave me a chance to be useful to her. She had brought me back from what had felt like the depths of madness, and had done so generously, without asking for anything in return. This time, I was protecting and helping her.

I knew she could not risk being alone in the streets of Havana. Together, we'd look like any two women going about their business. A middle-age woman and a younger one, we might be taken for mother and daughter. The police knew Rosalba had no children and would have expected to see her out alone or with her husband. By asking me to accompany her, she was inviting me to help her evade the police; a task I undertook eagerly for her sake despite the possible consequences. Had I been found with her, in that feverish moment, I could have been sent to prison, or even executed. However, the awareness of danger did not make any difference to me on that day.

Rosalba may not have realized that she was risking my life by asking me to act as her cover. She was immersed in her own fears. It was just short of miraculous that we did not run into anyone who could recognize either of us; there were plenty of people from among the three hundred plus Rosa Mystica members who could have identified us or others who might recognize her. Considering that there were such scant numbers of passersby in the streets, we could have been spotted easily. But those who could recognize us were probably too afraid for themselves or too confused still to be out in the streets.

Several weeks after our perilous adventure, Rosalba and her husband found asylum in the Mexican Embassy. I visited her in the Embassy, where she was among other asylum seekers. I was included in a small group of her "closer ones" from Rosa Mystica. She chose the visitors to be admitted with the limited entry passes she was granted. We met in the embassy's central yard, and sat on the grass. Cuban guards checked the names of the people who had been granted passes, and Mexican officials stood by watching to make sure all proceeded smoothly. I was glad that Rosalba had chosen me as one of her few visitors, but the conversation that included six or seven other members of Rosa Mystica in the middle of a yard surrounded by several dozen similar small groups of visitors, proved unsatisfying. I preferred having risked my safety to have time alone with her. I especially wanted her attention because, for the first time, I was considering leaving

Cuba; I badly wanted Rosalba's opinion, but could not ask the dangerous question in such a public forum.

The immediate consequence of Rosalba's seeking asylum and leaving Cuba was that the course of therapy I'd begun was never finished. My panic attacks had ended, but my dependence on Rosalba had not. As a psychologist, I know that having the therapy process end so suddenly, without further notice, was a recipe for confusion and incompleteness. I was left with a partial understanding of my internal puzzles. Nonetheless, the therapy with Rosalba gave me some self-understanding, in addition to helping me recover from panic attacks. I felt something awakening in me, a sense of self I had not previously possessed; something stronger than the fragile awareness ignited by my trip to Europe. And thanks to that internal transformation, I felt strong enough to start contributing to the resistance.

Andrés

His name, of course, was not Andrés. It was a code name to protect his identity when he was part of the clandestine resistance movement against the government.

Before he came to hide in my home, I had had a crush on Andrés for as long as I could remember, since my high school years. But prior to his going underground, we had never talked. He probably had not even noticed me. I, on the other hand, had noticed him, and thought him handsome and intelligent. I could not believe my luck when a trusted friend approached me, asking if I was willing to hide Andrés. Despite the danger it involved, I felt excitement rather than hesitation or concern about the risky request. The only way to survive some dangerous situations is not to think too much about their possible consequences. That is exactly what I did.

I was now free of the panic attacks that had taken over my life the previous year. It was time to act on my concern about what was happening in Cuba. Those who opposed the government were involved in a variety of resistance activities. Their actions ranged from distributing leaflets with news that contradicted official versions of events or pointed out government flaws to actual acts of sabotage such as planting bombs in government facilities or burning public buildings. I knew nothing or very little about these subversive activities since I had not been involved in any of them. Precisely because these were clandestine actions, no one really knew who was engaged in what; no one knew what others were doing. The less you knew the safer it was. Too much knowledge could easily land you in jail.

The women of Rosa Mystica as well as the men in the parallel male association—to which Andrés belonged—relied on their connections to protect one another in these perilous times. The mutual aid processes that had been part of our life under normal circumstances intensified now and enjoined us more than ever to provide assistance.

I was connected to a network of people through Rosa Mystica. My parents had a very small circle of friends. Years of concealed financial hardship had isolated them from peers whose financial standing had remained unchanged. They were not in touch with anyone who could have participated in clandestine activities. I must have asked them if I could hide Andrés, but my decision was made before I asked. Their immediate answer was yes. We shared a commitment to help those who were endangering themselves at that crucial moment.

In fact, my mother, following a request that had also come through me, volunteered to act as phone contact between two men she never met. She transmitted messages from one to the other about activities the nature of which she was never fully aware. I guess this was her opportunity to do something outside of the ordinary, to feel that she too could help with some small actions in the middle of her daily routine, and to lay bare the courage she had silently exercised during all those years of cheering up my father against all odds and doing those housewifely tasks she so hated. Perhaps this was her chance to show herself what she could have done if her life had been different. Whatever the impetus for her saying yes to my request, she was "María Luisa" for several months without knowing anything about these two men who had daily conversations with her.

Andrés need not have been involved in some antigovernment activities to be in danger. He was president of the student body at a university. In Cuba, during times of turmoil, becoming the student president of a university was almost tantamount to signing your own death sentence. His role made him a public figure; he did not have to be involved in anti-government activities to attract attention and persecution. He had been forced into life-and-death decisions by political circumstances. Student leaders had influence over other students and students were usually the first to rebel against unjust regimes or autocratic dictates. Student leaders were considered dangerous enough by authoritarian governments to warrant being eliminated. During the Batista years, all the presidents of the student body of the University of Havana had been gunned down by government forces. The Castro regime seemed intent on continuing the same tradition.

I have clear images of Andrés, sitting in what had been the maid's room in our apartment, reading or praying. He spent most of his time there. He had his meals with us and every so often would watch a bit of TV, but otherwise, he remained unseen. Although we must have talked regularly during those days, I cannot remember his individual interactions with me. I do remember, however, that he appeared serene, although he must have been terrified.

While Andrés stayed with us, my fantasies about him were replaced by direct experience of his behavior. I was touched by his shyness, his kindness, the affectionate and gentle way in which he played with ten-year-old Mario, my youngest brother, who quickly became very fond of him. They talked earnestly about baseball, Andrés lying on his bed, looking at the ceiling with hands behind his head; Mario sitting on the floor next to the bed. Or they sat on the floor and enacted toy truck races in which Mario always won. They laughed together or were very serious while Andrés explained something to Mario related to his homework.

As a further disguise, Mami had bleached Andrés's hair blond in the bathroom sink. She used the same hair product in a darker color every three or four weeks to cover her developing gray strands. Its pungent chemical smell filled the hallway while she was working on his hair. One evening at dinner, Mario, who had been told Andrés was a cousin from some other part of Cuba, suddenly looked at him in disgust, exclaiming in a loud voice, "Hey, guy, you color your hair! Men don't do that!"

We all froze. Andrés smiled and quietly explained to my brother, "No, no, my hair is just odd, it is both blond and dark."

Quickly, my mother admonished my little brother in her habitual no-nonsense way, "Mario, what kind of a remark is that? Never make such a comment to a guest!"

Mario either accepted the explanation Andrés had just given him or heeded my mother's reprimand, because he never mentioned the hair color again.

Andrés did not stay with us for long; no one was left in the same safe house for more than a week or two, to assure the safety of fugitives and hosts. But while he stayed with us, I felt privileged to hide and protect him from the government forces. When he had to be transferred to another safe house, I missed his silent presence, his quiet strength.

How we received the message that he was to be moved someplace else, I don't remember. But I do recall standing on the balcony of our apartment, looking up the street, watching for the car that would pick him up, signaling to Andrés who was waiting with his hand on the bolt of the front door that the car was approaching. At my sign, he rushed down the stairs and, from the balcony, I saw the top of his fake-blond head as he ducked into the car that sped away in the direction of El Malecón. That was the last time I saw him in Cuba.

Andrés was the first of a silent trickle of people we sheltered. For several months, until I left Cuba in the summer of 1961, a dozen or so political fugitives whose lives were in danger found refuge with us. Some of them I remember clearly. Others are vague, blinking memories. The process became almost routine. Someone came, stayed perhaps a week or ten days, then left quietly; another fugitive came, and the process repeated. Once we hid a married couple whose children were staying with her mother until they could find a way to leave the country together; later, two brothers came at the same time. But for the most part the "guests" were individual men or women.

By hiding them, my family and I became accomplices in the anti-government conspiracy. Had we been caught, we would have landed in prison. But my parents and I felt that this was a small contribution to Cuba's freedom. We were foolish enough to expect that Castro would soon be overthrown, overestimating the impact of our actions. In any case, we did not talk much about the implications of those actions; we just acted.

Hiding political dissidents was made easier after the departure of my two younger brothers to the United States with the Peter Pan program. Our situation could have become extremely dangerous by an indiscretion from children who did not know that Andrés was no distant cousin at all, and neither were those who followed. If Mario's remark about Andrés's hair had been made outside our home, or if he'd mentioned anything about our "guests" at school, in the nearby playground, or in any place where he could be overheard, it would have put us at risk.

Andrés had stayed in the windowless, unoccupied maid's room in the back end of the flat, near the kitchen. Others stayed in my brothers' room after they had left for the States. All of them followed the same silent routine. They kept noises and voices to a minimum, with windows shaded and, obviously, never went out on the balcony.

Our apartment was an ideal hideout. No neighboring building was as high; no one could peer in our windows. Only one family of four adults who lived on the floor above us passed the door of our flat when climbing the stairs to their place. Although we never revealed to them anything about the presence of our "guests," we knew about their political opinions. If by some chance they detected an unusual presence, they would not betray us.

We were never caught. Except for Andrés, who was captured not long after he had stayed with us, all the others left the country safely and so did we, a few months later.

Nery had also left Cuba and gone to Miami around the time of my brothers' departure, so only my parents, my aunt Marina and I were in the apartment as the other fugitives arrived.

Our household routine appeared unchanged. My father, Marina and I continued to go to work, while my mother stayed at home performing her usual household tasks and answering the daily phone calls to "María Luisa" from the two unknown men. My aunt went to the hospital where she was an administrator. She kept silent about what was going on at home, even though she remained sympathetic to Castro's regime all her life. I have no idea how she reconciled this contradiction, but I suspect Andrés's thoughtful and quiet demeanor must have made her, like the rest of us, want to protect him. In any case, because she loved us, she would not have made the slightest move to risk our safety, even though by our decision to hide fugitive dissidents we were risking hers. Her love for us was more important that her political positions.

When Andrés was apprehended, the woman who was hiding him then was also imprisoned for sheltering a fugitive. Andrés was sentenced to twenty years in prison. His imprisonment made me feel as if our efforts to save him had been in vain. A few years before the end of his sentence, the government declared an amnesty for a small group of political prisoners; he was among those who were freed and allowed to leave the country. Through the grapevine, when I was no longer living in Cuba, I'd heard about his imprisonment, amnesty, and exile.

Death, Theater, and Revolution

On Saturday, April 1, 1961, shortly after Andrés had left our apartment, two weeks before the Bay of Pigs invasion, I performed the role of Blanche de la Force in a dramatic reading of Georges Bernanos' *Dialogues des Carmélites* at the Catholic University where I was studying Psychology. I enacted Blanche's fate of being guillotined in front of an expectant, surprised, and moved audience.

Blanche de la Force was a fictional character, born in the imaginations of German novelist Gertrude von Le Fort and French writer Georges Bernanos, who created the stage play based on von Le Fort's novel. In the play, Blanche de la Force, a young woman from the nobility, enters the Carmelite convent in Compiègne, near Paris, in the spring of 1789, to hide from her fear and anguish which preceded and were exacerbated by the approaching Revolution.

The old prioress, who received Blanche into the monastery, died shortly after Blanche became a novice. Her death was preceded by a horrible agony, during which her terrified screams shocked the other nuns. One of them ventures the opinion that the prioress seemed to have died someone else's death.

Outside the convent walls, the French Revolution had become a death machine. The French government declared all religious communities illegal; the Carmelites of Compiègne were ordered to leave their cloister.

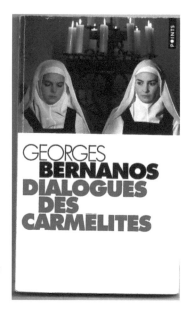

Dialogues des Carmélites

In Bernanos' play, before disbanding, the nuns vowed to offer their lives as a sacrificial prayer to end the terrifying wave of executions. As her own terror mounts, Blanche was shamed into making the same vow. But taking advantage of the disbanding of the cloister, she ran back to Paris and hid in the basement of her family's abandoned palace; she was willing to break her vow to avoid death. Soon, Blanche's worst fears materialized—the Carmelites were arrested in Compiègne, condemned to death, and taken to Paris for execution.

On July 17, 1794, as they descended from the cart that brought them from their prison in the Conciergerie and climbed the steps of the scaffold, the Carmelite nuns sang hymns. In the play, as the guillotine falls, one by one, their voices stop abruptly. And, suddenly, when there is only one voice left, another voice rises from the crowd assembled to watch the killing. Unexpectedly, Blanche, who has come to witness the executions, ascends the steps voluntarily to meet the death she has so feared until a few moments before. Bernanos and von Le Fort are telling us about the power of grace. After a lifetime dominated by fright and anxiety, Blanche finds the courage to die in the mysterious grace earned for her by the former prioress, her miserable death exchanged for Blanche's, her terrible agony mysteriously liberating Blanche from her visceral fear.

In our dramatic reading, the actors sat in different areas of the stage. A light shone over each actor's head as we read our parts; we sat in darkness when others read. The students reading the parts of the nuns, all dressed in black, sat at a long table on stage left. At a table on the right, wearing black pants and white shirts, sat several young men who alternately played the Marquis and Chevalier de La Force—Blanche's father and brother—the chaplain of the convent, the revolutionary leaders of the town, the jailers and executioners. At a small table in the center of the stage I sat by myself as Blanche de la Force, a bright light overhead throwing shadows on my face, hands, and body.

Only in the last scene of the play, the moment of the execution, was there movement on the stage. The women playing the roles of Carmelite nuns walked across the stage, singing the *Salve Regina*. As each one of them exited, a sharp wooden strike sounded, the fall of the guillotine; each woman's voice stopped in mid-word. When only one voice was left, as Blanche, I got up from my chair and crossed the stage—wearing the same black suit I had worn on the flight to Europe three years earlier—and joined that last voice, then sang alone for a few moments, until my voice was also silenced by the guillotine. Because there was no movement during the rest of our reading of the play, this last scene was dramatic and powerful.

The mixture of historical fact and fiction in Bernanos' play was particularly moving to our Havana audience. We, too, were in the first few years of a Revolution. We, too, did not know where it would take us. Bernanos' scenes gave flesh to our feelings of doubt, fear, and confusion. But the play and historical events suggested that courage and prayers would be rewarded. Watching this play, then and now, we are left with the conviction that these are heroic deaths.

In France, in 1794, shortly after the execution of the historically real Carmelites of Compiègne, the Terror ended. In Cuba, in early 1961, terror was still present. Like the Carmelites, many of us were considered "enemies of the revolution." People in our audience had friends or family members jailed for expressing misgivings or opposition. Anxiety and expectation hung over the country like a solid cloud. Two centuries after the historical events on which the play is based—and two weeks after our staging the dramatic reading—we would confront the meaning of death and life and what could happen to enemies of a revolution.

In Havana in 1961, warning signals had been in the air, literally. About a month before our first performance, while we were in the middle of a class at the university, we heard the noise of a low-flying plane and saw, through the classroom windows, a shower of little white leaflets fall to the ground. The noise of anti-aircraft guns followed very quickly as the plane disappeared. We knew this small aircraft had made the forty-five-minute flight from southern Florida to fly over Havana delivering the anti-revolutionary leaflets.

The professor stopped in mid-sentence. Some of the students laughed nervously.

Virgilio, a student who was sitting in the first row, turned around and yelled toward the laughter, "Stop it! People we know may be dying right now!"

Silence followed his words.

On the eve of the Bay of Pigs invasion, another unmarked, one-engine plane started shooting at us while we were rehearsing in a quiet garden area of the university for the planned additional performances of *Dialogues des Carmélites*. When the shooting started, we ran for cover. My hands cold and clammy, my heart beating rapidly, I crouched under a stone bench. Shots ricocheted on the stone benches and cement walkways for about two or three minutes. And then the plane flew away. No anti-aircraft fire followed it. We knew this was another attempt from the government at intimidating students and faculty at the Catholic University. The planes that flew from Florida did not shoot anything but pieces of paper. When the plane stopped shooting at us and disappeared in the direction of the nearby Columbia military camp, the Armed Forces headquarters, we looked at each other in silence, frozen in place. Luckily, besides knees bruised in the scramble to hide under the benches, no one was hurt. Quickly, we said goodbye to each other and went home.

Our play was never staged again. We were never again together at the University.

Both airplanes had signaled ominous, if different, messages about the impending destruction of our world.

In the turmoil of the Bay of Pigs Invasion, after his outburst in class, Virgilio was either executed by the government or killed in a gunfight, I never knew which. Virgilio was not the only one who disappeared, perished, or was jailed. Our young director and his brother went into hiding. In the days before the invasion, government raids took away every person suspected of anti-revolutionary activity or sentiment. When the invasion arrived, anyone who might have aided or collaborated with the invaders was unavailable to assist them.

In early May, riding the wave of revolutionary fervor created by the failed invasion, the government nationalized all private schools and closed the Catholic University. My classmates and I never finished that academic year. With the Bay of Pigs invasion, our lives came to a halt.

For many Cubans my age, this was a moment of self-definition. Everyone I knew had longed for Fidel's triumph and the defeat of Batista's corrupt and cruel regime during the six years he had been in power. For as long as I could remember, I had abhorred Batista because he had arbitrarily fired my father from his post and sentenced my family to poverty; he had enriched himself at the expense of the country, and he had killed and tortured innocent people. But this was different. To have placed hope in the transformations promised by the Revolution and then to feel betrayed by it was an embittering experience as well as a dangerous one. It had been easy to hate Batista and know that he was evil. But as I experienced the daily contradictions of the Revolution, I no longer knew how to think and feel. I went about my everyday life feeling as if I were living inside a washing machine.

In Cuba in 1961, there were no guillotines. But the cries celebrating the death sentences and executions of those considered enemies of the Revolution had been in the streets for more than two years. Crowds screaming "¡Paredón! ¡Paredón!"—referring to the stone wall in the old La Cabaña fortress where executions by firearms took place—were the equivalent of the "ça ira! ça ira!" that had been heard in Paris two centuries earlier during the French Revolution.

After performing the role of Blanche de la Force, I always felt an eerie curiosity about the Picpus Cemetery in Paris because Blanche was buried there. Or, to be exact, the sixteen real-life Carmelite nuns from Compiègne, who were guillotined in 1794, in the nearby Place de la Nation, were buried there. Their bodies were thrown into two hastily dug ditches, along with the more than 1,300 guillotined bodies of the preceding few days. When I visited Picpus Cemetery in 2006, long after playing Blanche, the place felt as somber and solemn as I had imagined it for fifty years. The tombs looked abandoned and decayed, ravaged by time. The names of those victims who could be identified, including the Carmelites, are inscribed on the wall that divides the two segments of the cemetery. I stared at the locked iron fence separating the ditches from the rest of the cemetery. And, for the first time, I realized that the fictional eighteenth-century Blanche de la Force had symbolized for me the powerful connection between History with a capital H and my personal history.

I had not known why I, among several young women who auditioned, was chosen to play Blanche. I assumed that years of reciting poems at patriotic and religious events during elementary and high school together with the recitation classes I took in early adolescence had taught me to project my voice and to express a range of feelings. Because this was a dramatic reading, rather than acting per se, the ability to convey meaning with one's voice was key.

After my visit to the Picpus Cemetery, however, I started to see how my role as Blanche de la Force and my panic attacks had fit together. I became conscious that by playing Blanche de la Force, I enacted multilayered lifelike truths. I realized that my fear and anxiety were not different from Blanche's. Playing Blanche had not been just a stage role for me. Like her, my personal fears dwarfed the real dangers of the outside world. My fears and Blanche's had played against the backdrop of Revolutions which altered our worlds. Perhaps I was chosen for the role because my fragility was evident regardless of what I thought about myself. The director had intuited that I could become Blanche just by delving into my personal experience. The role was me, and I could become the role without much effort. I could identify so closely with her character because, even though the Cuban Revolution did not extinguish my life, it changed its course.

In Paris, in 2006, I spent days recalling the pain, the losses, the fears of my last few months in Cuba, and writing about them. I became keenly aware of the mysterious ways in which memory, writing, and life intersect and recreate experiences.

Like the fictitious Blanche de la Force, I had been temporarily saved from real danger by the pain and humiliation of my debilitating and constant fear. For more than a year, I had been completely incapable of doing anything other than performing daily, almost mechanical routines. I had no strength to contend with the sweeping transformations our daily lives were undergoing. And then, paradoxically, while others were devastated because of the increasing overpowering force of the Revolution, I started to feel free from my own demons after a difficult struggle. As with Blanche just before her execution, I felt the unexpected grace of overcoming fear just when everyone around me was immersed in it. It seemed a miracle that despite the real danger, I had managed to free myself from panic attacks and was able to act and help others in the last few months I lived in Cuba. When, playing Blanche de la Force, I crossed that stage at the university theater to be symbolically guillotined, I had no inkling that in barely three months I would leave Cuba for good. By then, I had realized that to stay and fight would be useless and dangerous. I did not feel heroic at all. Escape was the only avenue left.

Blanche de la Force has stayed with me all my life. I continue to have a very personal attachment to Bernanos' play. I have been moved to tears seeing it staged in Latin American countries suffering from political violence.

Those of us who left Cuba after the events of 1961 and our production of *Dialogues des Carmélites* scattered in all directions and lost contact with one another. A couple of years after leaving Cuba, I received a letter from Tony, who had played the Chevalier de La Force, Blanche's brother. The play opens with him coming into a room and asking anxiously, *"¿Dónde está Blanca?"*— "Where is Blanche?" Tony's letter started with that same question. He had been searching for me for some time. I answered his letter immediately, delighted to reconnect with this "brother" I was so fond of. But we never met again; we were living in different countries and travel was not possible for either of us.

Blanche-like fears have not completely disappeared from my life. I still dread revolutions and political violence. Even as I write now, I am afraid of antagonizing someone who has views different from mine or perhaps endangering someone still in Cuba. A vague anxiety pervades my thoughts and interferes with my choice of words. Although I have never again had panic attacks, and even though more than half a century has passed, for me, the heightened emotion connected with all things Cuban persists.

Life has gone on. During these decades, my life has settled into new routines. Cuban contexts carry anxieties for me but, at times, they are a balm for my soul. Therefore, I accepted the invitation of dear, long-term friends who asked me to go with them to the celebration of the feast of St. Ignatius at the Jesuit prep school that my father, my brothers, and many of my male friends had attended. The school was transplanted from Havana to Miami in the early 1960s, as so many Cuban institutions were.

The gathering in mid-summer 2007 attracted a few hundred people—among them, some I had not seen for many years. There was music I seldom hear, including some of the old rhythms I had danced to with Alfonso and some romantic songs from those times. On a wall, a poster announcing a performance of *Dialogues de Carmélites* that had taken place at the school a few years before made me smile, evoking bittersweet memories of my days as Blanche.

And suddenly, in front of me, gray-haired, but otherwise exactly as my memory had preserved him, was Andrés!

A second later we were hugging. After the initial emotional response, Andrés turned to a thin, attractive, middle-aged woman walking beside him, and told her, "She was one of those who hid me." Turning to me, he said, "This is my wife."

She laughed softly and asked me, "So, what color was his hair then?"

One friend responded, also laughing, "The color Oliva's hair is now," referring to my blond-dyed hair.

As we continued down the school corridor, his wife engaged in conversation with others, Andrés said to me in his soft voice, "You know, I don't remember many things of that time, but I do remember your place, and I still remember the address…" He went on to recite it correctly.

I answered something like, "In moments of high emotional stress, memories get blurred or heightened," drawing on my psychology expertise to conceal the fact that I felt as if I'd just turned into my twenty-year-old self. I was as self-conscious and flustered as I had been in his presence back then. The gray at his temples made him look more mature and more self-possessed than ever. Even when his life had been in danger, he always managed to seem serene.

The memory of those long-ago events was vividly present to me as I continued to walk with Andrés for a few more minutes along the school hallway. We talked briefly about retirement, a new stage of life for both of us, and about what we had done in the intervening years. I was conscious of how absurdly emotional I felt. Finally, we were both swallowed by the crowd of milling guests. As the crowd swirled, I lost sight of Andrés.

I ate my share of Cuban delicacies and continued saying hello and being reintroduced to others, but I was stunned by the encounter. When I left the reception, Andrés was nowhere to be seen.

In the next few days, thoughts of the encounter unsettled me. It exacerbated my persistent preoccupation with "what could have been." Ruminations about what life might have been if I had remained in my homeland, or migrated to a different country, or at another stage of my life. Meeting Andrés threw me into a spin of endless reflections about what could have been had Cuban history and our own personal histories been different—an endless chain of "what could have beens," a spiraling of fantasized unknown possibilities. What could have been had I never left Cuba, had I married one of those boys who are now grandfathers... and what would I have missed from the life I have lived, so different from the one I probably would have had I stayed in Cuba. And I ruminated on the detours that have taken me to unexpected places, transformed my very self.

Obviously, I don't know the person I would have been; the only me I know is the one who has lived most of her life away from Cuba. These are not new or unusual considerations for me. But somehow the encounter with Andrés brought them back more intensely. For days, I could not stop thinking about so many things rendered either possible or impossible by the historical upheavals in Cuba that completely altered the course of our lives.

The pull of our shared history was strong in the surge of emotions that overcame me when I saw Andrés, in the conversations with other people I saw that night, in the background music that echoed through the festivities, even in the mini-*empanadas* and *pastelitos* served at the reception. The pain of all the losses, of all that could have been is activated in subtle forms when I become aware of the everyday absence of familiar smells, familiar foods, familiar music, familiar routines for doing the small tasks of daily life.

...perhaps you were that small so I could carry you within my heart...

When I entered *la pecera* in July 1961, I had no idea that this was a permanent departure and even less of an idea about how my life would change in the long decades since that hot and humid summer evening. How could I have known when I entered *la pecera* that this moment would produce repercussions that were to last a lifetime? How could I have known that this was a break from all I had known until then? How could I have known that from that moment on, my life would be transformed into something my twenty-two-year-old self would not recognize?

In 2011, exactly fifty years after I had left, I returned to Cuba again. I made a point of returning on that special anniversary of my departure. And, walking once again on the streets of Havana, looking once again at Parque Céspedes from the balcony of Hotel Casa Granda in Santiago, I could not stop thinking about those moments that changed my life forever.

The familiar streets and buildings were waiting for me, but other things were very different from the country I had left and even the one I visited in the 1980s. Cuba was now a tourist paradise of Hop-on Hop-off buses and luxury hotels built inside renovated, centuries-old colonial palaces that were tenement houses when I was growing up in Havana and are now beautifully restored buildings.

The topic of overheard conversations in 2011 was not the construction of socialism, as in the 1980s, but rather money—dollars—in a characteristic new Cuban way: "My family came to visit and brought me this much money." "My family came to visit and practically did not leave me any money." "So-and-so is going to lend me money to do this or that." "It's possible to make more money working for that hotel because the tourists there give larger tips." A most dramatic change in a place where owning dollars was once illegal and could land you in jail. Now family remittances, gifts from visitors, and tips in foreign currencies, particularly dollars, are exchanged legally in government established bureaus of exchange or banks for Cuban Convertible Pesos—CUCs. One of these CUCs is roughly equivalent to one U.S. dollar and to twenty-five of the regular pesos in which Cuban salaries are paid.

In every hotel lobby, in street corners and along the Havana seashore on the Malecón, prostitution is rampant because it is a quick way of getting dollars. Scantily dressed young women parade themselves in front of hotel reception desks or sit on terraces with crossed legs and pasted-on smiles, offering themselves to foreign tourists. Beggars sit on sidewalks in areas where there is tourist traffic, hoping to attract dollars by shaking little metal containers or pointing to small baskets with cards of saints' images glued on them. So much for a Revolution that promised to uproot prostitution and poverty forever from Cuban soil.

People seemed to feel freer to criticize, if not the authorities directly, at least the inefficiency of public services such as transportation, water and electricity shortages, and the slowness of personnel in government offices. Any of those people mumbling their displeasure in public would have landed in jail in the 1970s and 1980s when the fear of Soviet style state policing was palpable. Not that spying on dissidents or on anything remotely resembling political dissidence has diminished. Carrying out and fostering domestic espionage against its own citizens is still a priority for the government. In fact, it has been said that if the

Cuban leadership ran the economy as efficiently as they run state security, Cuba would be the richest country in the world.

My day-to-day experience during this trip was very different from my previous visit. In 1984 people were not sure how to place me. Most foreigners then were Eastern Europeans, so I did not fit expectations. I still had my dark curls; my cheeks did not get shrimp red after a few days in the Cuban sun like those of pale Eastern Europeans. Back then, at a store reserved for foreign travelers a sales clerk told me I couldn't buy some T-shirts because these were only for tourists and looked at me askance when I showed her my U.S. passport. Now, Cubans are used to foreigners who do not look Russian. They have seen thousands of expatriates who have returned to visit family. This time it was easy to spot me as one of those returning Cubans who do not fully belong there any longer, or perhaps as a European or Canadian among a population who is now mostly non-white. After all, my gray hair is now colored blond; the dark curls of my youth are no more. I don't "look Cuban," even to people used to seeing all skin shades.

Lion sculpture, Paseo del Prado, Havana

Still, it was startling that people approached me, trying to identify where I might be from, when I least expected it. As I walked slowly down the wide Paseo del Prado, along its soaring, hulking trees and dark bronze lion sculptures, a man asked me, "Are you from Spain?" I shook my head no and kept walking, having learned from childhood in this same city that one does not respond to strange men's comments on the street. "French?" an older disheveled woman asked me, smiling broadly. *"No chica, cubana como tú"*— "…as Cuban as you"— I responded in my best Cuban accent. Startled, she excused herself and scurried away.

Ironically, I am conscious that *"hablar cubano"*—speaking in this Cuban accent—is almost an imitation for me because this isn't truly my accent. Cubans' way of talking has changed considerably with the passing of time. Intonation and pacing are different, emphasis is placed on different words, some words and phrases are new, common expressions used when I was a child are not heard any longer. Perhaps I have not spoken with the "right" Cuban accent for years. Once, in Madrid in the 1990s I was told by some Cuban dancers that I spoke *"como la gente de antes"* – "like people used to speak before." This is not unique to Cuba; the sounds of spoken language are different everywhere after half a century. One only needs to watch any U.S. film or hear a U.S. radio broadcast from the 1940s or 50s to notice that the rhythm of words and phrases is different than what we hear now in films or TV.

And yet, my Cuban accent generated several curious incidents during this visit. The woman at the admissions booth in the Museo de Bellas Artes—where a collection of Cuban art from the eighteenth to the twenty-first century is housed—needed to decide how much to charge me, but she was not sure where I was from. When I answered her question about my nationality saying, "I am Cuban," she pointedly looked at me for a few seconds and with only a slight hesitation, said, "But you don't live here," and proceeded to charge me the five dollar-equivalent CUCs that foreign tourists are required to pay. However, in another museum, as I was taking a five CUC bill out of my wallet, the young woman at the booth said that I could pay with regular Cuban pesos and at the retiree rate. I guess my Cuban accent made her believe I was not a foreigner. In my modest hotel in Havana, where guests were mostly Latin American Spanish speakers, the woman who cooked the breakfast omelets, could tell immediately that I was born in Cuba and started telling me about all her financial woes, asking if I could leave some toothpaste and soap for her before I left. But in the *Cayo* in Santiago Bay—where I had regularly visited for summer vacations as a child and played with dolphins that jumped out of the water around the small boat I steered teasingly around them—several people followed me, calling out "Yuma! Yuma!" the Cuban new slang for tourist, alerting everyone that a possible source of dollars was passing by.

Experiences like these alternated, making me unable to anticipate reactions in ordinary encounters. And making me aware that I no longer have the skills of daily living in Cuba. The familiar streets, the familiar buildings were not enough. I did not know the new bus routes as I used to and had to rely for transportation on tourist taxis or the collective cars that provide service for ten Cuban pesos a ride. Now I am a foreigner in a country where foreigner is equivalent to source of dollars.

The government itself finds ways of extracting dollars from every visitor through the cost of visas and hotel rooms, the foreign currency exchange at a fixed priced that favors the CUC over dollars and Euros, the invented ceremonies and rituals created to amuse tourists such as the cannon shot every evening at 9:00 p.m. in La Cabaña fortress and other similar strategies that reek of capitalism, despite constant proclamations of socialism.

The woman who wanted to know if I was French had been ready to start begging for some dollars or Euros; my being Cuban disrupted her plan... and I was left with a heavy heart for her and every Cuban reduced to begging. A few days later, sitting on the terrace of Hotel Casa Granda in Santiago, I was approached by a tall brown woman who wanted to know if I felt "*solita*"—a little lonely. She and another woman had been trying to pick up two European men sitting at another table. The men told them bluntly that they were gay and had no interest, so she looked around, saw me, and decided I was her next target. Clearly, their goal sitting in the hotel terrace was to hustle anyone who in any way could produce some dollars using whatever tactics might work—sex with men, chatting with an older woman who might be an easy target to pay for a good meal. When I said curtly that I was not lonely and, in fact, wanted to be left alone, she made a disgusted face and left promptly followed by the other woman, probably looking for another hotel where guests would be more willing to accept their "help." The musicians who had been playing in Parque Céspedes across the street were more persistent. They approached the hotel terrace and kept playing the same two or three songs over and over; even though I was not looking at them they could tell I liked their music. Finally, they succeeded in getting a tip from me. I felt they deserved it; at least I had enjoyed their songs and not simply been conned into buying drinks or just giving money.

Jesuit Church of the Sacred Heart (La Iglesia de Reina), Havana

Another jolting experience happened at the Jesuit church—*la iglesia de Reina*—near the location of my father's school in the area of Havana where I grew up. I entered this church, so full of my childhood memories, on a clear morning, and was startled to see several women dress-

248

ed in the distinctive white garb of *santeras* sitting on the front pews. *Santería* is a distinctive Afro-Cuban religion dating back several centuries, developed by African slaves during Spanish colonial times. It mixes Yoruba beliefs with Catholicism. Its unique rituals and music have permeated Cuban culture. *Santería* practitioners dress in white and wear necklaces in different color beads based on their connections to specific deities or *"orishas."* While the male *santeros* wear just white pants and shirts and perhaps a white cap, the female *santeras* wear scarves tied around their head in a sort of "Aunt Jemima" style, below the knee dresses and elbow length capes, all in white. Despite its undeniable popularity, when I was a child, *santería* was considered a religion of non-white lower-class Cubans and its practitioners were not usually seen in regular churches.

Eventually, I saw so many *santeras* and *santeros* in other churches that I was no longer surprised. Not only are churches now full of *santeros*, but they also walk freely on the streets of Cuban cities dressed in their religious garb.

A few years ago, espousing any religious belief would guarantee that you would never be promoted in your place of employment and your children would not be admitted to University. But after the economic and social crisis created by the fall of the Soviet Union, in the 1990s, during what was called "the Special Period," the government started to allow church participation without penalizing those who attended religious services. It helped that churches provided material assistance to the needy population. Food and clothing opened the door. And slowly, attending church and practicing whatever religion became acceptable. Churches of all denominations benefited from the new opening. *Santería* also did. But the proliferation of *santeros* isn't just a return to religion; I did not see so many *santeros* walking around in their white clothing wearing bead necklaces when I was a child. Aside from the newly acquired lack of restrictions, they seem to have become a picturesque tourist attraction. Some of them charge to have their pictures taken with foreign visitors.

Countries change. Half a century is a long time and transformation is inevitable. The U.S. has changed, too, since the time of Eisenhower or Kennedy. Cuba has, indeed, changed in this long half century. And yet, even with the recent dramatic twists and turns in Cuban society, some things remain very much the same.

The *"choteo"* –the irreverent commentary about politicians and all things difficult to bear with which Cubans have made light and managed to endure the most difficult political and economic circumstances, the pride of challenging history and surviving oppressive

249

forces against all odds, the shrewdness displayed to *"resolver"* daily difficulties, relate strongly to material and cultural forms that have existed for centuries.

The same is true for the dilapidated buildings.

An example of 20 century architecture in Havana*

Havana's architecture is magnificent, no matter how broken, as the careful restoration of a few historical places makes obvious. The massive colonial buildings of Old Havana compete with the 1930s and 40s luxury homes and apartment buildings in El Vedado. The disrepair and decrepitude of so many buildings cannot fully hide their elegance and beauty. The gracefulness of the wrought iron on windows, of *medio punto* stained glass and curved columns on balconies and porches, the intricate designs on tile floors, the traces of the now faded bright colors on the façades are still there, no matter how deteriorated. Many architectural treasures form an endless display in every street of the city. The craggy local limestone characteristic of Havana construction through the centuries contributes to its beauty.

The city has made an effort to maintain and restore some of the colonial buildings I saw with my father on our Saturday morning strolls. The imposing eighteenth century Palacio de los Capitanes Generales, where the Spanish governors ruled the island for several centuries, or the restored buildings in Plaza Vieja contrast with the shabbiness of most of the Art Nouveau and Art Deco constructions that populate the city. But those rundown buildings in various states of disrepair would not be there today were it not for the lack of new constructions that has characterized Cuba in the last half century. They would have been replaced by tall glass towers that characterize cities in the Western hemisphere. What makes Havana unique is precisely that it has *not* kept pace with the rest of the world. The building fever that signified progress in other Latin American, European, and U.S. cities has not obliterated Havana's past.

A Colombian woman who rode with me on the Hop-on Hop-off bus I took one afternoon to ride around the city, told me in amazement, "I didn't know Havana was so beautiful! So many old, incredibly beautiful buildings! I had no idea it was so full of architectural treasures." I felt proud and yet sad. All that beauty is crumbling, despite the effort of some international bodies and institutions to repair and restore some architectural gems.

Now that much of my life is behind me, these recent visits to Cuba have made me recognize that I am truly not of my country anymore, even though I carry scraps of Cuba inside my deepest self. I am made of conflicting intersections, memories, people and places where I have learned to be who I am. Who I am is influenced by absence, the absence of people and places that shaped my childhood and adolescence, many of which do not exist anymore. But I am also made of all the encounters, places, and experiences that would have never happened had I not lived in so many other places. Distance from my place of birth necessitates understanding myself in a different geographical and cultural setting than the one in which my early memories were formed. My need to recover the past remains, though, intensified by the distance and the memories of what was. But despite that, I have lived a good life. And I dare say that perhaps, if given the choice, I would not have wanted any other.

The sum of accumulated absences and unexpected encounters that characterize my life create the need to organize my memories to make them intelligible to others in my everyday environment, but also to people in my country of birth who only know the space of an island. Sometimes I feel as if I must explain myself constantly. I am forever foreign in memories and language; I cannot express myself fully using only one of the languages I speak. Major events of my life have occurred in other places, away from Cuba, yet Cuba still colors all my life experiences because of its absence. Lost geographical locations and places feel like wounds; the quiet but unabated sense of grief creates a constant urge to search for and find the lost love object, the lost place of birth. But that place, as lost time, can never be recovered. Now, after more than fifty years away from Cuba and after several return visits to the places of my childhood and adolescence, I not only *know* that leaving Cuba changed the course of my life, I cannot avoid wondering what my life would have been had I stayed in Cuba, even if there had never been a Revolution.

In the intervening decades I have encountered many people who still believe Cuba is the incarnation of the utopic ideals they hold dear. In a society where educated ideologues are not shot in the head or interned in labor camps, but rather sit in comfortable armchairs lecturing those of us who have abandoned what they imagine as paradise, it is difficult to convey the price some of us have paid for refusing to be told what to think. It is difficult to explain the emotional cost of my decision without seeming to over-dramatize. Even more so, because my loss is no more self-evident than the self-delusion of the utopians who never had to confront the realities of the utopian places they preach about. The risk of sounding melodramatic and, furthermore, the uninvited assumptions about what my life was like in pre-Revolutionary Cuba are forever present.

But despite those risks, I have to acknowledge that Cuba is my own lost paradise; it is an open wound that I know will never heal. It is the place where the life I never lived will remain forever hidden.

For those of us who have left our countries for whatever reason, "going home" is more than travelling to the place where we were born. It becomes an emotionally charged project. Our fragmented lives and psyches are split between here-and-now and there-and-then. We are set apart from others who have not shared this experience—because this experience is deeper and denser that the trite "you can't go home again."

All the challenges of my young life in Cuba pale when contrasted with the uprootedness that has been the legacy of my life. But I know that I have learned invaluable lessons from that uprootedness. I would not be me if I had lived any other life. The only me I know is the one that incorporates the consequences of my uprootedness.

I am who I am because I was born in Cuba *and* because Cuba is no longer my home.

Epilogue
The Moon from another World

On the last evening of my 1984 visit to Cuba, as I walked on the tarmac at the Havana airport to board my plane back to the United States, I looked up and saw a bright full moon in the cloudless night sky. It soothed me to see its liquid silver surface in the darkness. Somehow, its presence was reassuring even though I was leaving Cuba again.

Cuba had been like a forbidden paradise for half of my life. For the two weeks I had just spent there, the paradise was present, and clear, and the sky was blue, and everything was as it always was and as it was always supposed to be. And everyone spoke with a Cuban accent! This deep sense of familiarity, of everything being right, of all things being as they are supposed to be was something I had not experienced since 1961. I would not experience it again, even when I returned to Cuba after a few more decades.

On that November evening, after the quick return flight from Havana, I descended from the charter plane in Miami International Airport feeling both sadness and relief. The intense experience of my first trip back to Cuba after two decades of absence reverberated inside me. As I walked to the airport building, I looked up again at the full moon shining in the clear night sky. I was jolted by the realization that the moon I was looking at in that moment in Miami was the same I had just seen in Cuba less than one hour earlier. And then, in a confused and yet distinct way, I thought, "No, this is not the same moon. That one, the one I just saw in Cuba, is a moon from another world."

After another quarter century, I saw the world of that other moon again.

As the plane carrying me away after my last visit to Cuba pierced the clouds, I could see the skyline of Havana, the greens of the luscious vegetation, the royal palms that lingered in the distance becoming smaller by the minute. Many things have changed, but that curving coastline and those royal palms are a constant.

I don't know if I will ever see Cuba again. But, in my imagination, I want to stand indefinitely at the spot where the Malecón starts, forever looking at the Havana coast while I stand by the low wall of the seafront promenade. I want to look at the Morro Castle on the other side of the water, at the sun or the moon reflected on the water.

And I know that one day, my ashes will wash on that shore, carried through the distance by the foamy blue waves.

FOTOGRAFIAS
Titular—Bearer—Titulaire   Esposa—Wife—Epouse

Hijos — Children — Enfants

Este Pasaporte es válido por cinco años a contar desde la fecha de su expedición.

This Passport is valid for five years counting from its date. — Ce passeport est valable pour cinq ans à partir de la date de son emission.

2

About the Author

Oliva M. Espín is Professor Emerita in the Department of Women's Studies at San Diego State University and the California School of Professional Psychology of Alliant International University. Dr. Espín was a pioneer in the practice and theory of feminist psychology and therapy with women from different cultural backgrounds, for which she has received multiple awards from the American Psychological Association, the Association for Women in Psychology and other professional organizations. A native of Cuba, she received her BA in Psychology from the University of Costa Rica and her PhD from the University of Florida. She did post-doctoral work at Harvard University with a fellowship from NIMH, studying Latina healers. Dr. Espín held the Fulbright Distinguished Chair in Gender Studies at the University of Klagenfurt, Austria. Throughout her career, she has taught psychology of women, the psychology of immigrants and refugees, women saints, and other topics. She has presented at national and international conferences and published many articles and books on psychology and psychotherapy of Latinas, women immigrant and refugees, women's sexuality, language in therapy with fluent bilinguals, historical mem-ory and memoir, feminist and psychological understandings of the lives and writings of women saints. She recently published *Gendered Journeys: Women, Migration, and Feminist Psychology*. Her most recent book is *Women, Sainthood, and Power: A Feminist Psychology of Cultural Constructions*.